A University's Challenge

Cambridge's Primary School for the

Edited by **Peter Gronn** and **James Biddulph**

CAMBRIDGE
UNIVERSITY PRESS

CAMBRIDGE
UNIVERSITY PRESS

University Printing House, Cambridge CB2 8BS, United Kingdom

One Liberty Plaza, 20th Floor, New York, NY 10006, USA

477 Williamstown Road, Port Melbourne, VIC 3207, Australia

4843/24, 2nd Floor, Ansari Road, Daryaganj, Delhi – 110002, India

79 Anson Road, #06–04/06, Singapore 079906

Cambridge University Press is part of the University of Cambridge.

It furthers the University's mission by disseminating knowledge in the pursuit of
education, learning and research at the highest international levels of excellence.

www.cambridge.org
Information on this title: www.cambridge.org/9781316612170

First published 2016

20 19 18 17 16 15 14 13 12 11 10 9 8 7 6 5 4 3 2 1

Printed and bound in Great Britain by CPI Group (UK) Ltd, Croydon CR0 4YY

A catalogue record for this publication is available from the British Library

ISBN 978-1-316-61217-0 Paperback

CONTENTS

NOTES ON CONTRIBUTORS

Julia Barfield

Julia Barfield, MBE, RIBA, FRSA, is a founding director of Marks Barfield Architects (MBA) with David Marks. MBA has won more than 70 awards for design, innovation and sustainability, including Architectural Practice of the Year, 2001; Sports and Leisure Architects of the Year, 2009; the Stirling Prize shortlist, 2000; Best Design for a new School, 2008; National Arts Prize, 2008, and Best Public Space Award, 2015. Julia is involved in projects across sectors, from culture and education to bridges, sports, leisure and master planning. David and Julia are also originators, designers and creative entrepreneurs behind the London Eye and the Brighton i360. Julia is a member of the National Awards Panel for the Royal Institute of British Architects (RIBA) and the Quality Review Panel of the London Legacy Development Corporation, and is an advisor for the Design for the Built Environment Master's course at the University of Cambridge.

James Biddulph

James Biddulph started his career following a PGCE at the Faculty of Education, University of Cambridge. He has been a primary school teacher since 2001 and is now the first Headteacher of the University of Cambridge Primary School. In 2002 his creative approach to teaching gained him Advanced Skills Teachers (AST) status in Music and in 2003 he was awarded Outstanding New Teacher of the Year for London. Having transformed two failing schools in East London, UK, as Deputy Headteacher, he opened a new primary school. He is currently completing his PhD, which is focused on creative learning in ethnic minority home contexts.

Sir Leszek Borysiewicz

Since October 2010, Leszek Borysiewicz has been Vice Chancellor of the University of Cambridge. He was previously Chief Executive of the UK's Medical Research Council, and before that was Principal of the Faculty of Medicine and Deputy Rector at Imperial College, London. In 1988 Leszek lectured in Medicine at Cambridge, from where he went on to be Professor of Medicine at the University of Wales. It was in Cardiff that he led a research team that carried out pioneering work on vaccines and conducted clinical trials for a therapeutic vaccine for human papillomavirus (a cause of cervical cancer).

Catherine Burke

Dr Catherine Burke is a Reader in the history of education and childhood in the Faculty of Education, University of Cambridge. She is currently researching cultural and material histories of education and childhood in the nineteenth, twentieth and twenty-first centuries. Her research includes an examination of the relationship between innovation in teaching, and the design of formal and informal learning spaces; the view of the child and young person in the design of education; and the history of twentieth-century school architecture. A major focus of the research is bringing an historical awareness to current initiatives to transform education via school building renewal. Recent funded research has enabled her to lead an international network exploring the phenomenon of the decorated school and particularly the history of the school mural. She has published on the history of school architecture, the participation of children in the design of schools, and on contemporary school architecture. She edits the 'Sources and Interpretations' section of the journal *History of Education* and is president of the History of Education Society, UK.

Penny Coltman

Penny Coltman gained extensive experience teaching in both pre-school and Key Stage 1 settings in Essex. She now lectures in early education in the Faculty of Education, University of Cambridge, where she contributes to the Early Years and Primary PGCE course. Penny has worked with several major publishers on an extensive range of curriculum materials. She shares the role of co-ordinator of the East Anglian Regional Cambridge Primary Review Trust Network. She is also co-editor with David Whitebread of *Teaching and Learning in the Early Years* (fourth edition, 2015, Routledge), and is a governor and trustee of the University of Cambridge Primary School.

Peter Gronn

Peter Gronn is Emeritus Professor, University of Cambridge. Between 2011 and 2014 he was Head of the Faculty of Education. For part of that period, he was Deputy Chairman of the trust and governing body of the University of Cambridge Primary School. He has researched and published extensively in the areas of leadership, policy and history. He is a Fellow of the Academy of Social Sciences.

Riikka Hofmann

Riikka Hofmann, PhD, is a University Lecturer in Education at the University of Cambridge. Her research in the UK, Finland and the Global South focuses on the development and effectiveness of teaching, learning and leadership in schools and hospitals. She also advises the Cabinet Office and various UK government ministries on policy evaluations.

Sonia Ilie

Sonia Ilie is a Research Fellow at the Faculty of Education, University of Cambridge. She works on projects related to inequalities in the access to, learning during, and outcomes of, education. Her research focuses on both England and developing countries, and she uses quantitative methods applied to large-scale survey data from a variety of sources.

Mary James

Mary James, PhD, FAcSS, taught in schools for ten years before moving into higher education. She then taught and researched at Cambridge University for a total of 25 years, and also at the Institute of Education, London and the Open University. She retired as Professor in 2013. From 2011 to 2013 she was President of the British Educational Research Association. She was Deputy Director of the ESRC's Teaching and Learning Research Programme (TLRP) from 2002 to 2008, and she directed a major development and research project within TLRP: *Learning How to Learn in Classrooms, Schools and Networks*. She has authored ten books and over 100 articles or chapters on curriculum, assessment, pedagogy, teachers' professional development, organisational leadership and education policy.

Jonathan Nicholls

Dr Jonathan Nicholls has been the Registrary of the University of Cambridge since October 2007. He previously held similar roles at the Universities of Warwick and Birmingham. He studied English at the Universities of Bristol, Cambridge, and Harvard, and has published in the field of medi-eval literature.

Hannele Niemi

Hannele Niemi, PhD, is Professor of Education at the University of Helsinki. She has published a number of books and articles about the Finnish educa-tion system and teacher education, and has been invited as an educational expert to more than 35 countries.

Dame Alison Peacock

Dame Alison Peacock leads a Hertfordshire primary school that was des-ignated as a Teaching School in 2011. She is also an elected member of the Teaching School Council and a co-opted member of the North West London and South Central Headteacher Board for the Regional Schools Commissioner. Her involvement as one of the newly emerging strata of system leaders places her in a unique position to comment on the potential impact of the University of Cambridge Primary School.

Andrew Pollard

Andrew Pollard supports research development at the Institute of Edu-cation, University College, London. Formerly he was Professor of Primary Education at the University of Cambridge. He was Director of the ESRC Teaching and Learning Research Programme from 2002–9, and of the UK Strategic Forum for Research in Education from 2008–11. As a former school teacher, Andrew's research interests include teaching–learning pro-cesses and learner perspectives, as well as the development of evidence-based classroom practice. He is responsible for a popular series of textbooks and support materials on reflective teaching within early, school, further and higher education.

John Rallison

Emeritus Professor John Rallison was Pro-Vice Chancellor (Education) at the University of Cambridge until September 2014. Currently, he is Chairman of the trust and governing body of the University of Cambridge Primary School.

Mike Roden

Mike is a geography graduate from the University of Manchester. He has held senior leadership roles since 1995 and was appointed to his first headship in 2003 at King Edward VI Camp Hill School for Boys in Birmingham. Mike took up his position in April 2014 as Principal of the University of Birmingham School – the first secondary University Training School in the country. The School was already one of the most popular secondary institutions in Birmingham when it opened in September 2015.

Jonathan Rose

Jonathan Rose, BArch (Hons), DipArch RIBA, is an architect and Principal at AECOM Design & Planning and a Masterplanning Practice Leader. Notable long-term projects include the masterplans for the University of Cambridge at both North West and West Cambridge. Both of these major development initiatives will help the university maintain its leading role into the future, while addressing sensitively the need to create contemporary new urban environments within the much-loved context of Cambridge. This combination of integrating major development drivers including wider social and environmental objectives, together with a careful approach to local context, underpins Jonathan's approach.

Kenneth Ruthven

Professor Kenneth Ruthven joined the Faculty of Education, University of Cambridge, after teaching in schools in Scotland and England. His research focuses on curriculum, pedagogy and assessment, especially in school mathematics. He is former Editor-in-Chief of *Educational Studies in Mathematics*, recent Chair of the British Society for Research into Learning Mathematics, current Chair of Trustees of the School Mathematics Project, and a Fellow of the Academy of Social Sciences.

Jeremy Sanders

Professor Jeremy Sanders, CBE, FRS, studied Chemistry at Imperial College and the University of Cambridge, and has been an academic in Cambridge since 1973. He led the 800th anniversary celebrations in 2009, and from 2011 to 2015 he was Pro-Vice-Chancellor for Institutional Affairs, responsible for human resources, environmental policy, local and civic engagement, and North West Cambridge.

Jan Vermunt

Jan Vermunt is a Professor of Education in the Faculty of Education, University of Cambridge. He is an educational psychologist interested in students' learning, teachers' professional learning, and the interplay between learning and teaching. Jan is a Fellow of Wolfson College, Chair of the Faculty's Psychology and Education Academic Group, and Editor-in-Chief of *Learning and Instruction*, a world-leading scientific journal in the domain of educational psychology.

Anna Vignoles

Anna Vignoles is a Professor of Education in the Faculty of Education, University of Cambridge, and an economist who specialises in the evaluation of education policy and practice. She has published widely on the determinants of pupil achievement, and inequalities in access to, and achievement in, education. Anna is a Research Fellow at the Institute for Fiscal Studies and a Visiting Professor at the Institute of Education.

David Whitebread

David Whitebread is a Principal Research Associate in the Faculty of Education, University of Cambridge, and the Director of the Centre for Research on Play in Education, Development and Learning. He is a developmental psychologist and an early-years education specialist (having previously taught children in the 4–8 age range for 12 years). He is currently directing research projects investigating the role of play in children's development of metacognition and self-regulation, and their impact upon children's learning. His publications include *Developmental Psychology and Early Childhood Education* (2012, Sage), and *Teaching and Learning in the Early Years* (fourth edition, 2015, Routledge).

SERIES EDITORS' PREFACE

The manifold dimensions of the field of teacher education are increasingly attracting the attention of researchers, educators, classroom practitioners and policymakers, while awareness has also emerged of the blurred boundaries between these categories of stakeholders in the discipline. One notable feature of contemporary theory, research and practice in this field is consensus on the value of exploring the diversity of international experience for understanding the dynamics of educational development and the desired outcomes of teaching and learning. A second salient feature has been the view that theory and policy development in this field need to be evidence-driven and attentive to diversity of experience. Our aim in this series is to give space to in-depth examination and critical discussion of educational development in context with a particular focus on the role of the teacher and of teacher education. While significant, disparate studies have appeared in relation to specific areas of enquiry and activity, the *Cambridge Education Research Series* provides a platform for contributing to international debate by publishing within one overarching series monographs and edited collections by leading and emerging authors tackling innovative thinking, practice and research in education.

The series consists of three strands of publication representing three fundamental perspectives. The *Teacher Education* strand focuses on a range of issues and contexts and provides a re-examination of aspects of national and international teacher education systems or analysis of contextual examples of innovative practice in initial and continuing teacher education programmes in different national settings. The *International Education Reform* strand examines the global and country-specific moves to reform education and particularly teacher development, which is now widely acknowledged as central to educational systems development. Books published in the *Language Education* strand address the multilingual context of education in different national and international settings, critically examining among other phenomena the first, second and foreign language ambitions of different national settings and innovative classroom pedagogies and language teacher education approaches that take account of linguistic diversity.

We are delighted to include *A University's Challenge: Cambridge's Primary School for the Nation* within our series. The book represents a unique collection of different perspectives of what is involved in the creation of a university training school in England. This is the story of the physical and institutional genesis of the first university primary training school in England, but it is also the story of how policy, theory and pedagogical imperatives can combine in the formation of a new educational environment. How does a central policy-initiated and theory-inspired idea materialise into an innovative primary school which addresses the learning needs of its pupils while incorporating broader research and teacher training functions? The challenges and successes chronicled in this book provide a valuable contribution to the growing international literature on university–school training institutions.

Colleen McLaughlin and Michael Evans

INTRODUCTION

John Rallison and Peter Gronn

Cambridge is a small city on the edge of the Fens in the East of England. It is home to an ancient university which has established an international reputation for excellence; the university has recently celebrated its 800th anniversary. The past 40 years of its history have seen an astonishing flowering of ideas in Cambridge, many generated in university departments and often in areas of information technology that have given rise to growth and economic prosperity in the city and the surrounding area. This 'Cambridge Phenomenon', called by some the development of the 'Silicon Fen', has in turn given rise to a significant challenge for the university itself: the historic centre of the city is congested, housing for the key workers on whom the university relies has become increasingly expensive and the need for research space constantly grows. Several areas of the city have been earmarked for growth, one such being the site previously occupied by the university farm to the north-west of the city centre. This area is now to be called Eddington, and it will provide housing, accommodation for postgraduates, academic space and social facilities for about 8500 people when the site is complete.

It was recognised at an early stage that a primary school would be an essential building block of the new community and this book tells the story of the creation of that school, the ideas and vision that inspired it, and the (sometimes tortuous) route by which those ideas crystallised. The chapters record strands of the thinking that underpins the foundation of the school, but they do not provide instructions for a self-assembly kit; pragmatic compromise was inevitable as the plans for the school developed. But what about the book's title and subtitle? Viewers of BBC television are likely to be aware of the longstanding and popular programme 'University Challenge', in which student teams from English universities, including Cambridge (and Oxford) colleges, compete annually to win an intellectually demanding quiz contest. Over many years, a number of these contestants have gone on to become persons of note and public identities in the UK and beyond. This book documents a challenge of a different scale and order of magnitude for a university, but one that has proven to be equally if not more demanding intellectually and in other ways: the conception, design, construction and commencement of a primary school, a process that (as one of the authors of this introduction is fond of repeating *ad nauseum*) began life humbly in 2012–13 as a mere blank sheet of paper and concluded successfully in Michaelmas 2015. Not only was that A4 sheet of paper blank but, on a day of inclement weather in mid-November 2014, at the groundbreaking ceremony at Gravel Hill Farm, so too was the sopping wet and muddy building site on which everyone present huddled for photo shoots. Thirteen months later, however, a stunning new building had been completed and handed over to the trustees of the school by the builders, Willmott Dixon, and the first intake of 120 children was in attendance. To that point, it had been three years since December 2012 when the then Head of the Faculty of Education (the second author) had convened a meeting (chaired by the first author) of university and Faculty colleagues to kickstart a collaborative process, the outcome of which is the University of Cambridge Primary School (UCPS).[1]

As to the subtitle, 'Cambridge's Primary School for the Nation', this wording is deliberately intended to communicate two points. First, the words 'Cambridge's Primary School' signal not merely the school's physical location but also a sense of its membership: recognition that the UCPS takes its place as part of the sprawling conglomerate in the Fens that comprises Cambridge – the central university core, the various schools, faculties and departments, the 31 colleges, along with the range of affiliated arms-length bodies, and various associated enterprises and activities. Second, the words 'School for the Nation' have been chosen to convey a sense of the UCPS's intertwined identity and mission. Rather than attempting to capture any sense of inward-looking triumphalism or privileged status, this terminology accords due recognition to the fact that, through its designation as one of only two University Training Schools (UTSs) in England, the UCPS owes at least part of its identity to the UK (i.e., the national) government. As to the UCPS's sense of its mission, that is at least partly national as well, simply because of the expectations (again, of the government) about what

An aerial view of the University of Cambridge Primary School. (Photos: University of Cambridge)

this particular school, to be resourced as a UTS, might be able to accomplish by working both in company with, and on behalf of, other English primary schools. The longer story of how these various strands came together around the idea of a 'national educational dividend' – as it was referred to in the original documentation submitted to the government to approve the establishment of the school – along with their implications for the UCPS, is to be found in a number of the following chapters.

Institutions like the UCPS do not materialise with a click of the fingers and out of nothing, and this book captures how the new school has come to fruition, placing on record the contributions of numerous Cambridge and Cambridge-associated colleagues, without whom this exciting new venture would not have happened. In that sense the book tells a story that is very 'Cambridge'. But the UCPS is not the university's first and only venture into schooling. From the perspective of history, in fact, this school is simply the most recent of a number of initiatives in both the provision of school education and the preparation of teachers by teacher educators with which the university itself and parts of collegiate Cambridge have had some form of connection. One noteworthy early example of an educational link with the University of Cambridge originated as far back as the early eighteenth century. In this instance, the name 'Old Schools' – currently the building in the centre of the city that is adjacent to the Senate House and accommodates the senior level administration of the university – was the title given to a trust-funded network of primary schools founded in 1704 by William Whiston, a Cambridge professor of mathematics, and administered by the incumbents of Cambridge's (then) 14 Anglican parishes (Martin, 2011, p. 34).

Prior to considering other important educational precedents, however, two general observations are necessary. First, because historical developments in one or other of the domains of schooling and teacher education invariably intruded into the other, little point is served in trying to disentangle any discussion of them. Second, in parallel with developments in schooling and teacher education (particularly from the 1860s), an emerging movement of ideas was taking shape in England, Europe and North America. This phenomenon was known as the New Education. To cut short a very long story, there was a groundswell of opinion in England that reacted to late nineteenth-century (or high-Victorian) educational orthodoxy in which, to use a then-contemporary adjective, an 'instrumentary' view of schooling prevailed (Selleck, 1968, pp. 25–77). This latter perspective had taken root as a result of Parliament's adoption in 1862 of the Revised Code introduced by Robert Lowe (vice president of the committee of the Council on Education). While the Code underwent a series of revisions over the succeeding three decades, it required that the total government grant paid to a school depended on the number of children attending for a prescribed number of days. In addition to attendance, there was also a result grant: all children were tested by inspectors in respect of their age-based (rather than level-based) attainments in reading, writing and arithmetic. Test failure resulted in the docking of one-third of the grant per child per subject – with a child's failure in all three subjects ensuring, of course, that he or she earned no income for a school (Selleck, 1968, p. 34) – with additional per capita grant money also deducted for shortages of trained teachers and poor quality equipment (Heffer, 2013, pp. 424–5). The unintended consequences arising out of this measure (that was meant to incentivise the system in the pursuit of efficiency gains) were disastrous. A focus on the notorious Three Rs (as the key tested subjects became known) as the be-all and end-all of primary schooling severely narrowed the curriculum, catapulted rote learning, cramming and the inculcation of facts to the status of dominant pedagogical techniques, and entrenched a system of payment by results. To such a constricting mould there was bound to be a reaction and it was the self-proclaimed New Educationalists with their mission of New Education who set out to break that mould (Selleck, 1968, pp. 45, 69).

Like any movement of ideas, there were a number of strands to the New Education, and it was beset by its own internal contradictions and tensions. Prominent among the numerous thinkers who influenced the thinking of these reformers were the American philosopher and educator, John Dewey, and a key New Education activist, perhaps Dewey's 'most important interpreter' in England, J.J. Findlay, Professor of Education at the University of Manchester from 1903 (Selleck, 1968, p. 208). Both men were prominent in defining important new models of the relationship between schools and universities (see below). It was as the New Education began to build a head of steam that the University of Cambridge, when requested (by some headteachers and teachers) to provide secondary teacher training for men, established the Teachers' Training Syndicate in 1879 (Searby, 1982, p. 5). This initiative was followed in 1891 by the launch of the university's own programme (also for men) for training primary school teachers (with secondary trainees admitted from 1898): the Cambridge Day Training College (DTC) – except that, in what was a curious double-barrelled misnomer, there was no college as such and the course was residential. The DTC provided professional training with degree study (Martin, 2011, pp. 100-101). The Cambridge DTC was one of 13 such colleges established in English and

Welsh universities (Searby, 1982, p. 12). In the 1930s, Cambridge's DTC was recast into an academic unit – to which the first professor of education was appointed in 1938 (G.R. Owst) – that became the forerunner of the current Faculty of Education, dating in its most recent incarnation from 2001.

But sandwiched in between the birth of the Syndicate and the DTC was perhaps the most noteworthy venture with which personnel from the university community were associated, a pioneer initiative in the further education of women: the establishment in 1889 of the Cambridge Training College for Women Teachers (CTC). The impetus for the CTC had come from Miss Frances Buss, the famous headmistress of the North London Collegiate School and a pioneer of women's education. Miss Buss had failed to woo either Newnham or Girton Colleges as possible locations to realise her plan for a Cambridge-based teacher training programme for women and, after an uneasy start, the CTC transferred from Newnham Croft in 1895 to a building in Wollaston Road, leased from Gonville and Caius College, and now part of the present day Hughes Hall. Miss Buss approached Miss Elizabeth Phillips Hughes to be the founding principal of the CTC. In 1949, with the creation by the University of the Department of Education and the absorption into it of CTC staff, the CTC was renamed Hughes Hall in her honour. Since 2006–7, Hughes has been the thirtieth constituent college of the university (Martin, 2011, pp. 34, 40, 119). Essentially, then, the early-twentieth century teacher training situation in Cambridge comprised separate provision for men and women provided by the DTC and CTC respectively. From the outset, the CTC experienced an 'uneasy' relationship with the male Syndicate (Searby, 1982, p. 11), and then subsequently with the DTC. The failure of the CTC and the DTC – housed from 1904 in Warkworth House, 'just minutes away from Wollaston Road' (Martin, 2011, p. 126) – to cooperate (or even coalesce) is due largely to irreconcilable differences that arose between Miss Hughes and the Director of the DTC, Oscar Browning, that were exacerbated by prejudicial male attitudes towards women's education in Cambridge. Appointed by the university as secretary of the Syndicate and subsequently as Director of the DTC, Browning was an ex-Eton housemaster and fellow of King's College who, during three decades until his retirement, was 'one of the best-known characters of the university', thanks principally to his 'extravagant personality, corpulent physique and reputation for dilettantism and sensual indulgence' (Searby, 1982, p. 5).

Sad to say, in addition to sexism, the advocates of teacher preparation and closer links with the university also encountered a climate of negativity that, at times, manifested varying degrees of indifference, inertia, frostiness and even downright hostility (see Martin, passim). Thankfully, there were a few exceptions who championed the cause of teacher education – Sir Will Spens, Master of Corpus, 1927–52, being an important example. But the feature that sets apart the establishment of the new UCPS from these earlier sporadic and stuttering forays into schooling and teacher education, and the historical track record of mutual stand-offishness, is that the new school has been founded with the full blessing and encouragement of the university, as a deliberate act of official policy and resource commitment. And yet how does the UCPS compare with other contemporary and earlier examples of university-linked schools? In a 2007 report for the Gates Foundation, Streim & Pizzo (2007, p. 5) of the University of Pennsylvania – which itself has a university-linked school, known as the Penn Alexander School[2] – distinguished four forms of partnership between US universities and schools (albeit secondary schools): professional development schools, early college high schools, management partnership schools and university-created public schools. The authors' professional development category encompassed conventional teacher preparation programmes (through block classroom placements) and ongoing teacher professional learning. Early college schools included about 130 dual-credit model institutions in which students could earn up to two years' credit towards a four-year degree. Management partnership schools were those in which universities combined with schools to try to accelerate students' attainment of academic standards. Finally, university-created schools expressed an 'institutional commitment on the part of the higher education partner to establish substantial, long-term relationships with public schools in the communities' (Streim & Pizzo, 2007, p. 7). Universities cited in the report as examples of this category include such globally high-ranked institutions as Stanford, Chicago, Columbia and the aforementioned Pennsylvania. Clearly, the UCPS is an instance of this last category as are two older examples of note: the Laboratory School of the University of Chicago and the Fielden Demonstration School in Manchester.[3] The differences in approach and philosophy among these three, however, are sufficient for the UCPS to be distinctive. Whereas the Cambridge initiatives documented earlier in this introduction were concerned mostly with the training and preparation of school teachers, the uniqueness of the UCPS stems from its three-fold provision of nursery and primary school education (for children aged 4–11), its offering of teacher education classroom placements for trainee teachers and teacher professional learning, and its leadership in the conduct of research.

Unlike the UCPS, the University of Chicago's Laboratory School was not a training or practice school, and in respect of research it functioned primarily as a centre for the application of research, 'in which theory could be tried out in action', rather than the generation of it (Connell, 1980, p. 74). In the Chicago school's initial years (1896–1903), that research came to be associated almost exclusively with one individual: Professor John Dewey (1859–1952), the then head of Chicago's departments of philosophy, psychology and pedagogy – although, in practice, Dewey collaborated closely with his academic colleague, Ella Flagg Young, and Alice Dewey, the principal of the elementary school (and wife of Dewey). The 'main hypothesis' of the Chicago school – which became known subsequently as the Dewey School – was that 'life itself, especially those occupations and associations which serve man's chief needs, should furnish the ground experience for the education of children' (Mayhew & Edwards, 1936, p. vi). In so far as the relationship between the Chicago University and its school was concerned, Dewey himself was unequivocal about a number of its distinguishing features. The first was that the Laboratory School was an experimental enterprise, a conception that provides a marked contrast with Cambridge's school, because Dewey conceived of the Chicago school as bearing 'the same relation' to educational theory as laboratories of physics, chemistry and physiology bore to 'university instruction in those subjects'. In this respect, the purpose of Chicago's school was to test ideas derived from philosophy and psychology, in which the underlying theory of knowledge emphasised the role of problems in 'active situations' in the development of thought and the testing of thought by action (Dewey, 1936, p. 464).

Dewey's second feature, however, that the school was a form of community life, is consistent with the underpinning approach of the UCPS. Dewey, whose name and thinking are frequently invoked by proponents and critics of progressive schooling – and, of course, the period in which Chicago's school achieved its fame was known and referred to as the Progressive era – disavowed forms of education that were not built around cooperation and coordination. The overriding aim of schooling for Dewey was not the unleashing of personal liberty, but social development or 'the harmonizing of individual traits with social ends and values'. Education could only prepare young people for future social life 'when the school was itself a cooperative society on a small scale' (Dewey, 1936, pp. 465, 466). In progressive schools, which emphasised the instincts and aptitudes of individuals on the basis of psychological analyses, however, 'coordination with social purposes is largely ignored'. Moreover, by according 'complete liberty' to individuals, as part of their 'child-centred' approaches, Dewey claimed that progressive schools were culpable in ignoring not only social responsibilities, but also the idea of mental development as 'essentially a social process' and 'a process of participation' (Dewey, 1936, pp. 465, 467). In the teaching of curriculum subjects, then, Dewey's preferred view was that, rather than adopting 'the traditional arrangement of studies and lessons' (i.e., imposition) or the progressivists' 'free flow of experiences and acts which are immediately and sensationally appealing, but which lead to nothing in particular' (i.e., hands-off), the appropriate alternative was to facilitate personal discoveries by children which lead into the future as well as into a 'wider and more controlled range of interests and purposes' (Dewey, 1936, p. 469).

Chicago's school was small. It was not a practice school for trainee teachers. The Laboratory School began in January 1896 with a dozen pupils aged six to nine, a figure that rose to 60 by the following October and 95 by the Autumn of 1898, including, with the opening of a nursery, 20 children under six years of age. At this point there were 12 full-time and seven part-time teachers (of whom the latter were volunteer University of Chicago students). The Laboratory School charged tuition fees and shifted premises three times during Dewey's association with it (DePencier, 1967, pp. 26–7). After a falling out with the president of the university, William Rainey Harper, as a result of his 'indifference and hostility' to the school, Dewey left Chicago in 1904 for the Columbia University in New York. Shortly afterwards, 'School' became 'Schools', because in addition to the experimental elementary school and nursery school, there was a separate practice school, a manual training school and an academy, all linked to the university's School of Education. By the early 1930s, the Laboratory Schools 'were no longer a center for experimentation, for trying out new ideas' (DePencier, 1967, p. 145). Today, five fee-paying schools educating nearly 2 000 students comprise the Laboratory Schools, and they retain their affiliation with the University of Chicago.[4]

In England, it was after World War 1 that the groundwork prepared by the previously mentioned New Education found revitalised expression in the advocacy of a number of English educational progressives. Unlike the New Education movement, which largely seemed to have passed Cambridge by, some quite high-profile inter-war progressive influences were evident on the fringe of the university. One was the educational reformer Caldwell Cook, who was influenced by Dewey and taught at the Perse School until 1933. While at the Perse, Cook published a book for which he became well-known for a perhaps 'unfortunately named' method (Selleck, 1972, p. 40), known as the 'play way'. Another was the Malting House Garden School (1924–9), viewed by many people as 'the epitome of the progressive school' (Selleck, 1972, p. 38). Founded by the journalist and speculator G.N. Pyke, it opened in October 1924 (in a building that is now part of Darwin College) with Susan Isaacs – mentioned as a source of educational inspiration by a couple of the authors of chapters in this book – as its principal. Isaacs, a noted psychologist and psychoanalyst, remained in the post for four years and, after a falling out with Pyke, was then appointed head of the new department of child development at the Institute of Education in London (previously the London Day Training College) in 1933. Isaacs' experiences at the Malting House were formative in shaping her subsequently published views about children's development.

Apart from the CTC, the other main Cambridge-associated institution engaged in teacher education was Homerton College. Following its move from London in 1868 to occupy the former Cavendish College buildings next door to the current Faculty of Education in Hills Road, it continued (as part of the Congregational Union) to train women teachers for elementary (or primary) schools. Although the CTC did not have a practising school (see footnote 3) – so that for trainee teaching practice Miss Hughes relied on Professor Whiston's network of schools and the newly-established Perse School for Girls (Martin, 2011, pp. 32–4) – Homerton, which required 12 places weekly for teaching practice, had two such schools (Timms, 1979, pp. 40–1). These were the Morley Memorial School (from 1899 until 1904), now Morley Memorial Primary School in Blinco Grove, Cambridge,[5] and a former ragged school in New Street (from 1901 until 1912–15), part of which survives as the Brunswick Nursery School.[6] Meanwhile, up north in Manchester, a primary and a secondary school opened in 1906 as training schools for the Department of Education of the University of Manchester. They were private schools which, although not owned by the university, received financial grants from it. In 1908, following receipt of a benefaction from Sarah Fielden,[7] they were renamed the Fielden Demonstration Schools. It was the Fielden benefaction that also made possible the Sarah Fielden Chair, held by J.J. Findlay, who worked with Catherine Dodd, Mistress of Method (1892–1905) in the Manchester Women's Day Training College, to try to overcome with a demonstration school what he believed were the shortcomings of practising and model schools (Robertson, 1992, pp. 363–4). (Unfortunately, their partnership lasted only until 1905 when Dodd departed after the two fell out.) Demonstration schools were intended to provide 'structured opportunities for observation and experiment and for demonstrating to students the best methods of teaching', thereby bridging the theoretical work of universities and colleges, and the practical activities of schools (Robinson, 2004, pp. 73–4, 75).

By 1913, the Fielden Demonstration School – the early wording used by Findlay is plural, while in later writings it tends to be singular – was educating about 180 children aged four to 15. There was a primary department (Kindergarten to Class 3) and an upper department (Classes 4–8) (Findlay, 1913, p. 3). Unequivocally, Findlay regarded the school as a laboratory, and the approach taken to training teachers and the learning of children as experimental. Earlier, Findlay had proclaimed the schools as the only ones in Manchester in which research was being attempted:

> Just as the medical student requires his Anatomy and Physiology before he turns his attention directly to Medicine, so the student of Education should know something of the subject of Education, the child, before being sent to teach or train him. True, he already possesses popular knowledge of what school children are like, but his knowledge is of no greater value for scientific purposes than the popular knowledge of the laity about the human body compared with the more exact knowledge of the medical student. (Findlay, 1908, p. 6)

As was the case in the Dewey School, the instruction of the children was viewed as a 'social, co-operative affair', with the teacher acting as a guide and counsellor. Findlay (1913, p. xxx) portrayed the children as 'combining, giving and taking from each other, governing and being governed – displaying, in fact, all the phenomena of a social body, which the expert in social psychology is beginning to investigate on the teacher's behalf'. In addition to the Deweyian influence on the school, Findlay adopted Montessorian educational principles[8] which were especially evident in the kindergarten classes. There was regular discussion about, and adaptation of, the curriculum and methods at the Fielden Schools, and open-air teaching was undertaken whenever possible. The boys and girls were equipped for mercantile or industrial careers, and they were well accustomed to being observed and taught by a number of members of staff. There were regular investigations of teaching and aspects of children's lives, which were in turn discussed by university staff and students (Robinson, 2004, pp. 81–2). In 1926, the Fielden Demonstration Schools closed due to financial problems.[9]

Unlike the rather patchy historical record displayed by these few precedents for close university–school links, and the at times idiosyncratic role played by a small number of high profile individuals, Cambridge (in contrast with its own earlier uneven efforts in teacher education and schooling) has tried with the UCPS to approach and plan for it systematically. The first stirrings of need for the new school date at least as far back as 2010 when the university sought planning permission for the Eddington development. The opening chapter in this volume by Jonathan Nicholls, Jeremy Sanders and Jonathan Rose describes the planning process. It was soon recognised that many of the key workers and other residents of the area would have young children so that a local primary school was a social necessity. The obtaining of approval for the new school, which Nicholls and his co-authors describe as being at the heart of the development, is documented by Peter Gronn in chapter 2. As events transpired, the planning process for the development coincided with a proposal from the UK government to the university's Faculty of Education that a new UTS should be established and that it would be (required to be) a free school, free that is of local authority control. There was considerable discussion (political, philosophical and practical) in the Faculty regarding the form that such a UTS might take. There was additional similarly focused discussion in the Faculty – following the appointment of Marks Barfield as the architects – of what the new school building might look like. This was a lengthy and informed consultative process of achieving finality that drew extensively on historical and contemporary building design precedents, and that is ably recounted by Catherine Burke, Dame Alison Peacock and Julia Barfield in chapter 3. One of the significant points discussed here is the need to achieve an architectural design and construction that conduces to good pedagogy and quality learning for children.

If chapters 1–3 summarise what was entailed in giving tangible expression to the UCPS, chapter 4 is the first of three chapters that deal with the substance, in respect of children's learning, of what the school might accomplish. In chapter 4, Alison Peacock recounts her vision for primary schooling in England, and suggests that Cambridge's new school should have ambitions to become a beacon of excellence in spreading good teaching practice, appropriately informed by research, nationally and internationally. This vision would require the active involvement of the Faculty of Education, and offer the possibility of a relationship between the Faculty and the new school that might be analogous to that between the university's biological departments and nearby Addenbrooke's Hospital. Just as the hospital exploits research findings in the medical field and provides training for doctors, so the UCPS might provide a direct route by which both research ideas and teacher training methods could be explored in a class-room setting or translated into classroom practice. In chapter 5, the UCPS headteacher (and co-editor of this book), James Biddulph, who has worked closely professionally with Alison Peacock, considers the values framework that underpins the school's work and the ethos that he intends (in collab-oration with teachers, children and parents) to bring to the school. James' excitement and that of his colleagues about the possibilities that they might realise in the UCPS comes alive in his graphic account of some ini-tial professional development activities at the school. The final chapter in this bracket of three is authored by Penny Coltman and David Whitebread. In chapter 6, they consider education in the early years and the role in the school of the planned nursery. They show how, in a country (England) in which early years learning provision is often not well joined up, this im-portant innovation should be able to provide an educationally desirable level of pedagogical and curriculum integration.

In a final bracket of four chapters (7–10), the focus switches to the UTS element of the new school, and specifically to its potential research offer. Riikka Hofmann and her co-author Hannele Niemi review in chapter 7 the experiences and track record of the Finnish equivalent of (and the UK Secretary of State's source of inspiration for) England's two UTSs. With their detailed knowledge and experience of Finnish education – touted by many observers of international league tabling as setting the bar high in school performance measures – both authors played an important role in a familiarisation visit to Finland by Faculty of Education colleagues in 2010. In chapter 8, Kenneth Ruthven discusses a selection of groundbreaking and influential research projects that have emanated from the Faculty of Education, all of which focused on the use of research in teaching and teacher education. This chapter helps position the UCPS and its future role in these spheres as the heir to a tradition of research geared to building closer, almost clinical, links between universities and schools. Still with a focus on research, chapters 9 and 10 concentrate on different aspects of the current debate about what it means to adopt an evidence-based or evidence-informed approach to teaching. In chapter 9, Anna Vignoles, Jan Vermunt and Sonia Ilie review the problems and pitfalls of the use of evidence, including what counts as evidence, and the chaining of (in par-ticular) knowledge about teacher and child learning that is entailed be-tween its discovery and its implementation. They provide examples of both official and user-driven initiatives to harness knowledge of learning. Mary James, Andrew Pollard and Peter Gronn in chapter 10 traverse similar terrain, except that they shift the focus to a series of wider professional developments with which the UCPS, potentially, might engage, including the recently launched College of Teaching. Once again there is a history (documented by James and her co-authors) of national projects and initiatives, promoted both by the government and teachers themselves, in which success so far has been mixed. With the UCPS's national dividend in mind, the lessons documented in chapters 9 and 10 ought to provide invaluable background resources for professional learning activities emphasising the use of evidence that might emanate from the school. Following these two chapters, there is an interview by Peter Gronn with Mike Roden, Principal of the Birmingham University School, the second (secondary) UTS in England; a short conclusion by James Biddulph, and an afterword by the Vice Chancellor of the University of Cambridge, Sir Leszek Borysiewicz, who has been such a strong supporter of, and advocate for, the UCPS.

This quick sketch of what awaits readers brings us to the question of how the new school has worked out in practice so far. At the time of writing (April–May 2016), the UCPS has been open for about eight months. The builders did a remarkably good job in meeting the tight deadline for the opening of the first classrooms in September 2015, and three months later the remaining buildings were complete. Inevitably there have been teething problems, but the school is widely acknowledged as a handsome and generous space. In its first year the school has 120 pupils of the more than 700 ultimately intended. In line with the plans, for the time being the school is on the edge of a very large building site as the housing, shops and community facilities are constructed. The staff are doing an excellent job, though they are conscious that the school cannot aspire to become a beacon of excellence for others unless and until it has itself established a reputation for excellence. At times the scale of that ambition can be oppressive. The parents are happy and, most importantly, so are the children. Applications for entry for 2016–17 are oversubscribed by a factor of three even though none of the new housing for which the school was intended will in the event be ready for occupation at the start of the next academic year.

Achieving the broader vision of the school on a short timescale amid the shifting sands of government policy is a difficult balancing act. Since the school was given the go-ahead, funding per pupil is being reduced year-on-year in real terms; teacher education is being reformed so that universities are no longer at the centre of the process; nursery funding is under review, potentially making the planned school nursery a drain on school funds; the latter two instalments of government funding for the school's UTS status have been arbitrarily withdrawn and then happily reinstated; financial planning is necessarily short-term and a school designated officially as a free school cannot be 'free' without the financial resources to exploit that freedom. Perhaps this litany of concerns is merely the reflection of the disjunction between planning timescales and political timescales, or perhaps the difference between vision and reality. Be that as it may, the University of Cambridge now has the foundations of an excellent primary school and a key pillar of its new community. Its children will enjoy an excellent education. The ultimate vision is much broader. Now the hard work starts.

Finally, we end by saying something about the front cover of this book. Sharon McManniman is one of the school's parent governors and is a secondary art teacher. In the school's second term, Sharon and James Biddulph planned how to capture the essence of our new and growing school community through a piece of art. The book's front cover is the result of our collaborative efforts. The decisions originally made about the school's architecture were principled on democratic notions of education. Its circle shape, for example, is a symbol of this intention – circles being a universal metaphor for equality, collaboration, lowered hierarchies and unity. Those involved were sensitive in their choices of colour palette for the new school walls, rejecting advice to be bold (purples, reds, blues) and instead choosing colours that were warm: splashes of the Autumn and sprigs of the Spring; that is, what was wanted was a palette that related to nature, in the same way that the building's glass walls reduced the divide between indoor and outdoor learning. James Biddulph had often described the ways that 'the children will bring the colour' and this phrase started a discussion to inform the artwork. The result was that *And the Children Bring the Colour* became a collaborative art piece to which the UCPS staff and children, inspired by the art skills of Sharon, contributed. The textures and patterns, and the sections that looked unfinished, where the plan of the school can be seen, point to the newness of our community. The images on the cover of the children come in different shapes and different colours. The school's diversity is expressed. Its community is evolving. The artwork hangs in one of our learning streets (the name we give to the spaces in between the open-plan classrooms). It is large and it beautifully captures the personality of everyone in our school. Those working in the school come together every day to craft opportunities for inspired learning and teaching. They release imaginative possibilities. We know that there is much to do. Rome was not built in a day, we are told. But what we see each day, in the building of our Rome, are splashes, swathes and splatters of colour brought in by the children.

Acknowledgements

The authors wish to thank Dr Phil Gardner (Cambridge Faculty of Education) for his assistance in procuring some of the historical material cited in this introduction.

Notes

1 Prior to the adoption by the governors of UCPS in 2014, the school's working title was the University of Cambridge Training School (UCTS).

2 For the Sadie Tanner Mossell Alexander University of Pennsylvania Partnership School (founded in 2001), a K-8 school for the children of West Philadelphia that is linked to the University's Graduate School of Education, see http://webgui.phila.k12.pa.us/schools/p/penn-alexander. Dr Nancy Streim, co-author of the report for Gates, was one of the school's founders.

3 In the nineteenth and early-twentieth centuries, practising and model schools were attached to training institutions to provide near-to-hand classroom environments in which teacher novices could be trained and good practice modelled. Robinson's (2004, p. 72) assessment is that their history was 'limited and largely negative', and that they fell out of favour with the local education authorities established by the Education Act, 1902.

4 See http://www.ucls.uchicago.edu/about-lab/index.aspx. Subsequent to Dewey's association with Chicago, there were at least three other demonstration schools in major US cities: Seattle; Trenton, New Jersey; and Baton Rouge, Louisiana. See Loughland (2012, pp. 56–8).

5 See http://www.morley.cambs.sch.uk/our-school/about-morley-memorial-primary-school/

6 See http://www.brunswick.cambs.sch.uk/

7 A member of the Fielden family of Todmorden, West Yorkshire, a family of wealthy mill owners, see https://en.wikipedia.org/wiki/Todmorden.

8 Maria Montessori (1870–1952) was an influential Italian physician and educator, see https://en.wikipedia.org/wiki/Maria_Montessori.

9 See http://archiveshub.ac.uk/data/gb133-fed/fed/5.

References

Connell, F.W. (1980). A History of Education in the Twentieth Century World (Canberra: Curriculum Development Centre).

DePencier, I.B. (1967). The History of the Laboratory Schools: The University of Chicago, 1896–1965 (Chicago: Quadrangle Books).

Dewey, J. (1936). The theory of the Chicago experiment, Appendix II in Mayhew, K.C. & Edwards, A.C. (1936). The Dewey School: The Laboratory School of the University of Chicago, 1896–1903 (New York: D. Appleton Century), pp. 463–77.

Findlay, J.J. (1908). *The Demonstration Schools Record: Being Contributions to the Study of Education by the Department of Education in the University of Manchester, I* (Manchester: Manchester University Press).

Findlay, J.J. (1913). *The Demonstration Schools Record No. II: The Pursuits of the Fielden School* (Manchester: Manchester University Press).

Heffer, S. (2013). *High Minds: The Victorians and the Birth of Modern Britain* (London: Random House).

Loughland, T. (2012). Teacher professional learning in pursuit of the common good: A discussion of the role of demonstration schools in teacher education, *McGill Journal of Education*, 47(1): 53–68.

Martin, G. (2011). *Hughes Hall Cambridge, 1885-2010* (London, Third Millennium Publishing).

Mayhew, K.C. & Edwards, A.C. (1936). *The Dewey School: The Laboratory School of the University of Chicago, 1896–1903* (New York: D. Appleton Century).

Robertson, A. (1992). Schools and universities in the training of teachers: The demonstration school experiment, *British Journal of Educational Studies*, 40(4): 361–78.

Robinson, W. (2004). *Power to Teach: Learning through Practice* (London: Routledge Falmer).

Searby, P. (1982). *The Training of Teachers in Cambridge University: The First Sixty Years, 1879–1939* (Cambridge University Department of Education).

Selleck, R.J.W. (1968). *The New Education: The English Background, 1870–1914* (Melbourne: Sir Isaac Pitman & Sons).

Selleck, R.J.W. (1972). *English Primary Education and the Progressives, 1914–1939* (London: Routledge & Kegan Paul).

Simms, T.H. (1979). *Homerton College, 1695–1978* (Cambridge: Homerton College Trustees).

Streim, N. & Pizzo, J. (2007). *Investigation of Deep College and University Partnerships with Secondary Schools in the United States*. (Final Report to the Bill and Melinda Gates Foundation, December, 32 pp.).

1   Cambridge's global mission: A primary school at the heart

Jonathan Nicholls, Jeremy Sanders and Jonathan Rose

INTRODUCTION

The North West Cambridge Development (NWCD) was originally conceived in purely utilitarian terms as the answer to a need for future expansion space that would allow the university to maintain its excellence in research and teaching. Since then, the university has evolved an aspiration for the NWCD to be an exemplary urban extension that sets high environmental and design standards, and knits the university even more closely into the community and fabric of the city. The masterplan created by AECOM Design & Planning is an expression of that aspiration in physical terms, the University of Cambridge Primary School (UCPS) being the first and most obvious product.

In this chapter, we outline chronologically the progression from 1923, when the university purchased the site that has become the NWCD, to 2013 when Marks Barfield Architects was chosen as the architect for the UCPS. We then show how the vision for North West Cambridge has become an expression of ambition for the university's wider aspirations, and describe in some detail how the masterplan itself evolved through workshops, consultation and visits to key developments around the world.

CHRONOLOGICAL HISTORY

The story of the University of Cambridge's development of a new community in the City of Cambridge begins with the purchase of farmland from Trinity College in 1923. The university had leased Howe Farm and Gravel

Hill Farm from Trinity for its School of Agriculture since 1909. The decision was taken to buy the land from this willing seller after World War I, both as a mark of ambition for the School of Agriculture and for the long-term use of the university for future purposes that were unknown at the time. The farmland incorporated an experimental farm to which local landowners, Cambridgeshire County Council and the city contributed joint funding, given the importance of the rich peaty soils to arable and fruit crops in the Fens. This theme of the university working closely with local interests recurs in the vision and development of North West Cambridge, not as a closed community for university and college use, but as an urban extension of the city, connected to it and contributing significantly to its sustainable growth. A faint echo of the origins of the site will continue with the UCPS's ambition of growing some of its own food for and by its pupils.

The university's Department of Agriculture closed in 1972 and, although livestock husbandry remains a requirement for the Department of Veterinary Science, the future of the arable farmland soon became a focus for consideration as the university looked towards future expansion. As early as 1974, the then Vice Chancellor, Sir Peter Swinnerton-Dyer,[1] had proposed that major university buildings should be located in an ellipse whose centre incorporated the major developments in the heart of the city but whose foci were in the north west and the south east (in the area of the city now often referred to as the bio-medical campus, on which the University of Cambridge hospitals and associated research projects provided through the university and other partners are located). This proposal, often referred to as the Swinnerton-Dyer Ellipse, has underlain all future considerations of the strategic development of the university's lands. Its influence can be seen in the 1989 Report of the Long-Term Planning Committee (*Cambridge University Reporter*, 1988–9), which referred to the Ellipse and which looked in more detail at sites within it. Two years later, in 1991, a report of the Council of the Senate (*Cambridge University Reporter*, 1990–1) focused on all the land to the west of Cambridge between Huntingdon Road, Madingley Road and the M11 motorway (see Figure 1). This report established the formal university policy for the development of North West Cambridge and has governed all future policy for its use.

Two significant events took place in 2000. The first was a growing realisation in the university that its staff, and especially those whom it wished to attract to retain its world-leading position, needed access to affordable housing in a city where the economy was vibrant and housing stock was under increasing pressure. This was voiced in a Discussion (a formal

Figure 1: The NWCD site in its immediate Cambridge context.
(Image courtesy Getmapping PLC)

university process when reports are published for consideration in the university before decisions are taken on them by the Regent House, the governing body) in June 2000. That this was a more widespread concern is evidenced by the Council of the University (the principal executive and policy-making body of the university), which acknowledged this concern and reiterated it. The second significant event was the establishment of the Land Use Working Group to look in more detail at the development of North West Cambridge. The Working Group (chaired by the then Vice Chancellor, Sir Alec Broers – given its significance to the future of the university) employed EDAW, an international firm of architects and master planners, to look at indicative land uses for the site. EDAW was incorporated into AECOM in October 2009, having been closely associated with AECOM since 2005. AECOM remains the master planner for the North

West Cambridge site. This long-term relationship reached a high point when the NWCD won The Future Projects Award for Best Masterplan at the World Architecture Festival in 2014.

In 'The Plans for the Development of the University North West Cambridge Site: Notice' (*Cambridge University Reporter*, 2000–1, p. 466) the key issues for the future development of the university to 2016 were identified as providing for university expansion (based on projections of percentage growth for undergraduates, postgraduates and post-doctoral staff – the last as a proxy measure for research funding); siting such that future developments were to be close to existing academic sites to take advantage of proximity and to foster sustainable travel to work; the need to provide affordable housing for purchase and rent – with a reference to the then Government's *Regional Planning Guidance for East Anglia* that called for a further 22 000 residential units (over and above those already approved within existing local plans) in the Cambridge sub-region by 2016; sustainability to minimise environmental impact and to comply with legislation requiring high environmental standards; and research collaboration with external organisations. The Notice also referred to the need to take account of high-quality design for spaces and buildings, landscape settings, and the provision of associated infrastructure and social facilities, largely paid for by the sale or leasing of land on part of the site.

The importance of North West Cambridge was emphasised by an address given by the Vice Chancellor on 12 March 2001 in the Senate-House (the university's historic location for Discussions and important speeches) about the proposed development and the mounting in the same building of an exhibition by EDAW of the emerging ideas for the spatial use of the site.

Development of these proposals from this point onward was slowed because the site sat within the green belt, located partly within the city and partly in South Cambridgeshire. Therefore, master planning had to be undertaken in conjunction with both local planning authorities to determine the future green belt boundaries in the area. Such reviews are infrequent and the university needed to ensure that sufficient land would be allocated within the North West Cambridge site for development by anticipating the scale of expansion that might be required over the next 30 years or so. This story can be followed through subsequent reports (*Cambridge University Reporter*, 2002–3, 2003–4, 2004–5, 2007–8). The university's principles for the development remain largely unchanged from the Notice published in 2001, summarised above, but were amplified and made more specific by research carried out on housing needs for the university and by the inclusion of a requirement that community facilities should include a primary school and nursery (the former first appears as a concept in the Third Report: *Cambridge University Reporter*, 2004–5, p. 513).

By June 2010, the university had developed its proposals sufficiently that it could publish the 'North West Cambridge Project: A Green Paper' (*Cambridge University Reporter*, 2009–10, p. 1010), which set out in detail the proposed uses for the site, informed by a vision and purposes described below. It is striking that the university had not significantly altered its view of the uses for the site since 1989 and certainly not since the Notice of 2001. The concept that the proposed 3000 units of housing (of which half would be let at affordable rents and half offered for sale in the market) should be situated alongside community facilities had developed into a firm proposal that a local centre would be built as part of the initial phase of building to ensure that the first residents and those in neighbouring communities would have access from the outset to shops, a community hall, places to eat, and healthcare. School and nursery provision was now also established as an essential component of the new community. The anticipated child population was derived from statistical data in a report prepared by the university's Department of Land Economy. Based on that research, the masterplan included provision for a three-form entry (3-FE) primary school close to the heart of the site, adjacent to the community hall, and next to the major green space Storey's Field. It was noted that one possibility could be that the university would run the school. Secondary provision was not anticipated for the site but a contribution would be made to a new secondary school on the nearby National Institute of Agricultural Botany (NIAB) development site, just north of Huntingdon Road, which itself would provide significant new housing in the city.

The years following the publication of the Green Paper within the university were devoted to responding to the consultation, arranging and seeking approval for the governance arrangements for the development, the submission of outline planning permission for the masterplan, and the financing arrangements by way of new borrowing by the university through a public bond. These points are developed further below (and further details are in the *Cambridge University Reporter*, 2010–11a, including delegation to Council of the power to borrow up to £350m; 2010–11b; 2010–11c). Finally, in October 2012, a report was published for approval in the university seeking permission to commence the development by way of a Phase 1. Given the importance of this decision and the financial and other commitments to be made by the university, the question was put to the vote of the Regent

House (which has the authority to vote on significant matters), and was carried overwhelmingly in January 2013 (*Cambridge University Reporter,* 2012–13, p. 342).

Much work had been undertaken by those already responsible for the project prior to the final decision of the university in January 2013. Events, however, did not run sequentially. In August 2012, the Local Authorities' Joint Development Control Committee: Cambridge Fringes (which brought together the planning authorities of the City of Cambrdige, South Cambridgeshire and the County Council) had given consent to the submitted planning application subject to certain conditions that the university was confident could be met. Other planning obligations imposed on the university had also been agreed to in outline form.

This last point highlights the fact that not all the decisions taken about the development were solely driven by the university's desire to create an exemplar community. It is a well-established principle of planning in the UK under the *Town and Country Planning Act, 1990* that so-called section 106 agreements (referring to the relevant section of the *Act*) require site-specific mitigations for a development in order for it to be acceptable in planning terms. These may, for example, focus on restrictions on the nature of the development, require certain actions or obligations of the developer, and necessitate sums of money to be paid in respect of the provision of schools, community facilities, transport enhancements and other amenities. Through its negotiation with the planning authorities, the university was obligated in these respects, including the payment of sums for specified purposes against agreed trigger points. Some of these bore upon the amount to be paid for a new primary school and for secondary schooling. However, this was an obligation that the university was willing to embrace and, as chapter 2 explains, a combination of events and national policy provided the opportunity to go beyond the basic requirement of the planning authorities and conceive of a primary school that would bear the university's name and have a special pedagogical and research focus, consistent with the university's main purposes.

By its decision of 2013, the university committed itself to a first phase of mixed development that would comprise the following elements (the figures in brackets indicate the total for the whole development when fully built out):

- 530 units for rental to qualifying staff on a subsidised basis – in 2014, the number of units for subsidised rental in the first phase was increased to 700 (of 1500);

- 325 units of postgraduate student accommodation (of 2000);
- 700 housing units for sale on a market basis by residential developers under land sale agreements (of 1500);
- A food store and other shops;
- A primary school;
- A community centre;
- A nursery (1 of 3);
- Other community facilities including a senior living cluster with extra care;
- A hotel;
- Playing fields and informal open space;
- Landscaping.

The financial framework and criteria for the success of the project, together with an analysis of the risks, were set out alongside the details of the masterplan in the 2010 Green Paper. This is the largest development in the history of the university and its ambition required the launch of the university's first public bond (and first major borrowing from financial markets) of £350m in 2012. Delivery of the project was entrusted to a syndicate[2] – first mooted by the Green Paper –which has acted as a quasi-board within the university, with a mix of external experts and internal stakeholders both from the senior leadership of the university, the colleges and the academic community. The executive was recruited from the development and construction industry, and was complemented by major international consultancy firms for project management, cost analysis, transport and legal affairs. The university is not founded to be a developer. The arrangements put in place for North West Cambridge were designed to balance the need for commercial discipline in the delivery of the scheme with reassurance for the university's community that its ambitions for the strategic imperatives were being met. This was particularly true for those who would be most affected by the developments (for example the postdoctoral staff and the colleges, given the significant amount of new postgraduate accommodation planned for the site).

Phase 1 was divided into several lots and a competition was launched to find architects to lead the design for each lot apart from the school. The competition, informed by the vision set out in the Green Paper, was managed by Caroline Cole of Colander Associates,[3] and generated worldwide interest from practices large and small. The panel was chaired by Professor Jeremy Sanders, a member of the Syndicate and Pro-Vice-Chancellor (and second author of this chapter), and included architectural experts from the university and the city, and the principal master planner from AECOM (and third author of this chapter), Jonathan Rose.

The uncertainty over governance of the school required that the selection process be run in collaboration with the County Council using its standard procurement procedure: this mechanistic approach was not well suited to prioritising quality and inspiration, but the joint panel, which included the consultant headteacher to the project Dame Alison Peacock (the Wroxham School) and a Reader in the Faculty of Education, Dr Catherine Burke, were clear in their selection of Julia Barfield and colleagues from Marks Barfield Associates from the strongest possible shortlist of potential architects.[4]

THE UNIVERSITY'S AMBITION

The compulsion to develop North West Cambridge has at its core the pursuit of the mission of the university and its existential need to remain one of the best universities in the world, the better able to serve the needs of society. The 2010 Green Paper clearly set out this link:

> The University's mission[5] is to contribute to society through the pursuit of education, learning, and research at the highest levels of international excellence. It is this strategic purpose that is the motivating force behind the current proposals. The University faces increasing competition for the most able staff and students from across the globe and its reputation is affected by its ability to continue to recruit and retain the very best people in this environment. That is truer now than it was when the arguments for the development of North West Cambridge were first set out and the case will become only more pressing in the years ahead. The University intends to remain among the world's leading universities and North West Cambridge is a key component of realizing that ambition. The University's competitors in the Far East and North America are rapidly developing new research and teaching facilities that include high-quality residential accommodation for staff, research workers, and students. These universities are making such investments for the same strategic reasons as Cambridge and, as has been seen from recent field visits, are setting high standards for Cambridge to match. The consequence of doing nothing to address this competition will place the

University in danger of falling behind on the world stage. (*Cambridge University Reporter*, 2009–10, p. 1010)

The following three paragraphs of the Green Paper expanded on this vision in terms of social, environmental and financial sustainability:

In Cambridge there is a lack of good quality residential accommodation at affordable prices in the open market. One important factor in maintaining the University's ability to attract the world's best staff and students is a supply of affordable housing in modern and sustainable communities, including accommodation for students on the collegiate model, and scope for the development of new research partnerships in flexible accommodation in proximity. North West Cambridge offers the opportunity to contribute significantly to these needs and provide accommodation to internationally attractive standards on an affordable basis.

These are compelling reasons for promoting the development of North West Cambridge. But the vision for the masterplan goes significantly beyond this. The Project Board wishes to create a vibrant, urban extension to the City that predominates as a University quarter but one that is also a mixed academic and residential community supported by high-quality schooling, shops, community, and leisure facilities, connected internally and with the wider city by green spaces and pedestrian and cycle routes. The highest principles of energy and transport sustainability will be incorporated into the development so that not only will North West Cambridge support the academic and social needs of the University, it will be an exemplar of what can be achieved through contemporary technology, architecture, and urban planning. The underlying form sought through partnership between the University and local authorities is one of mixed-use neighbourhoods and North West Cambridge will reinforce that model in the way that it is developed out. It will also integrate with the development of West Cambridge and provide a coherent whole to the benefit of the existing residents, staff, and other occupants of that site, providing much-needed facilities that will assist development of the remaining areas of the West Cambridge site.

The University will have a long-term interest in the land at North West Cambridge; it will therefore wish to maintain control or influence development as much as possible. Any development must also be on financially acceptable terms, with tight management of income, expenditure, and capital flows. (Ibid.)

The postdoctoral staff who are likely to form the majority of tenants in the University's rental homes at North West Cambridge are a relatively new group of staff. They are working as researchers, predominantly in the areas of science, technology and medicine, usually immediately post-PhD, and the majority stay for one to three years en route to a permanent career elsewhere. They are recruited from all over the world, and are either paid from grants obtained by university academics or are on fellowships of their own. They are the creative and intellectual driving force behind the daily research success of Cambridge, and there is intense international competition to attract the best. Their numbers grow each year and in 2012 they became the largest staff group in the university. By 2015 their numbers had reached around 4000. By contrast there are 1800 permanently-appointed academics. Yet, historically, postdoctoral staff have been invisible in the university's *Statutes and Ordinances*,[6] and they have largely been excluded from college life and associated amenities such as accommodation. North West Cambridge aims to provide homes, an attractive environment and lifestyle. The accommodation will be designed in modern, open collegiate form, but exactly what that should mean socially and intellectually in the twenty-first century is open for discussion and exploration. In order to help catalyse this thinking, the Office for Postdoctoral Affairs was created by the university in 2013 and will be based in North West Cambridge from 2017.[7] The social organisation will evolve over the coming decades in response to new ways of working and living, and the architecture should be sufficiently flexible to respond to these unpredictable developments.

The university's long-term approach to North West Cambridge is quite different from that taken by a typical commercial developer. It would be irrational for a commercial developer to eschew profit and not to ensure that its owners, whether private or public shareholders, are remunerated for its activities. It might equally be irrational for such a developer not to prioritise quality and place-making in order to maximise its return. Some do. However, many developers will not retain a long-term relationship with a development once it is built; they will seek to create the largest amount of housing or other income-generating space that they can persuade the planning authorities to approve, while minimising their obligations. Much of the post-World War II development of Cambridge, for example, was undertaken as suburban housing without much regard for the need to create self-sustaining communities by integrated developments that included work places and amenities.

The University of Cambridge is a common law corporation, is authorised to act as a trust corporation and is an exempt charity. An exempt charity in this context is one that does not register directly with the Charity Commission of England and Wales but is regulated on the Commission's behalf by the Higher Education Funding Council of England. As a charity, the university is required to demonstrate public benefit from its activities and must act in accordance with its charitable objects as expressed through its mission statement (see note 5). The university and its sub-region, centred on the City of Cambridge, are bound together spatially, economically and intellectually. The university takes a long view of itself and its relationships. Its decisions are informed by research, informed debate and intellectual inquiry, and the development of North West Cambridge demonstrates the confidence that the university has in its own future and in its local community.

North West Cambridge presents a unique opportunity to enhance the life of both the university and the city: the challenge is to create a new place in a city that is already extraordinary. Informed by the masterplan, the architecture and public spaces of the highest quality need to create a sustainable community in a new local urban centre and in residential neighbourhoods that together will complement the historic city centre.

CREATING THE MASTERPLAN

The process through which the university's aspiration and ambition are translated into a deliverable masterplan in all its complexity has been a creative and highly iterative one. Similarly, the realisation of the masterplan is inevitably a long-term endeavour, not only in terms of the physical manifestation of new buildings, spaces and landscapes phase by phase, but also in establishing a series of open-ended social and other opportunities to support an ever-changing academic and urban community. From the outset of the masterplan process, the vision for a mixed and balanced community recognised that an exemplary new primary school located at the heart of the project would be essential to success.

As landowner and master developer of the site, the university has taken the leading role since the project's inception, creating the opportunity to engage with the City of Cambridge, and its existing and surrounding communities, through the whole process of development. Each phase will be realised through a unique partnering approach with the local authorities, including the primary school as the first completed building on the site, linking from and to this new part of the city at its foundation.

DEFINING QUANTITATIVE AND QUALITATIVE OBJECTIVES

As indicated in Figure 2, North West Cambridge will be embedded in a mixed community embracing different lifestyles and organised around a local urban centre that provides the practical necessities of daily life, shopping and schooling as well as social, sporting and green recreational opportunities. The entire development will set new standards of environmental and social sustainability, with an emphasis on safe pedestrian, bicycle and bus access. The architecture, public realm and landscapes will create a sense of place that is inspired by the historic city and yet is exciting, forward-looking and designed to face the changes in climate that are likely to occur in the future. (A number of the features mentioned below are also highlighted on Figure 2.)

Figure 2: The NWCD illustrative masterplan showing the primary school at the heart of the local urban centre. (Image courtesy AECOM)

This chapter has already noted the important population research of staff in the university undertaken for the development by the Department of Land Economy that influenced both the typology for the units of housing to be let at subsidised rentals and also provided the data that informed the negotiation with the County Council on the size of the primary school and the contribution to be made for a new secondary school (on the NIAB site to north of Huntingdon Road). The Syndicate has also drawn significantly on the advice and expertise of its advisory Quality & Sustainability Panel – which has provided scrutiny and challenge to the overall architectural vision for the development, the detailed designs for individual lots and buildings, and the measures taken to meet the high environmental standards that were an integral component of the development as a whole. The members of this Panel are distinguished in their fields and professions and include, among others, Professor Peter Guthrie, Director of the Centre for Sustainable Development in the university's Department of Engineering, as the Panel's Chair; Tristram Carfrae, Group Board Director with Arup; Pooran Desai of One Planet Communities; Diane Haigh, formerly Director of Design Review at CABE and an Associate of Cambridge Architectural Research; Dickon Robinson, Chair of RIBA Building Futures and Jeremy Newsum, Executive Trustee of the Grosvenor Estate and formerly Chair of the Urban Land Institute.[8]

The expertise provided through this advisory panel both from within and outside the university has been as vital as that of the members of the Syndicate. The international reach and experience of the master planners, AECOM, was also essential in understanding how the development could draw upon best practice elsewhere and influence key strategies such as the architectural competitions for the various elements in the development and the approach to sustainability and community infrastructure.

BENCHMARKING SUCCESS

The university has drawn on its own expertise honed by research in sustainability, architectural form, public art and housing, as well as a significant programme of visits by members of the master planning team, the executive and members of the Syndicate, to analogue sites in Europe and North America.

The statement from the Green Paper quoted earlier in this chapter about the international competition faced by the university and the investments made by its rivals in North America and East Asia underlines the desire for North West Cambridge to embrace lessons and features from the best similar projects internationally and in the UK. To that end, and guided by the knowledge of the university's own experts and that of AECOM, a series of study trips informed the evolution of ideas about North West Cambridge and what the university should seek to achieve to meet its vision. Those ideas and principles included the commitment to best practice in sustainable urban development, ensuring architectural coherence and the need to provide the essential elements to encourage community integration and belonging from the outset. In relation to peer universities, it was important to understand and compare their approach to delivering similar major capital developments.

Study trips were organised in Europe to Vauban in Freiburg and to Hammarby Sjostad in Stockholm. Further afield, particularly influential visits were made to the University of British Columbia in Vancouver, to Yale University, to Harvard and MIT. In the UK, the urban extensions at Poundbury in Dorset and Upton, near Northampton, were the subject of comparative study, while nearer at hand in Cambridge lessons from the new settlement at Cambourne and the proposed new settlement at Northstowe were valuable. The planning and development approaches taken at the other fringe sites in Cambridge were particularly instructive, specifically those to the south of the city at Great Kneighton and Trumpington Meadows.

MORE THAN A DECADE IN THE PLANNING

The planning process has been a lengthy one due to the site's original green belt status. Following the university's identification of need in 2001, the site was proposed for development in the Cambridgeshire and Peterborough Structure Plan in 2003. After this, the university and the two local planning authorities, Cambridge City Council and South Cambridgeshire District Council, worked together to satisfy the necessary planning and sustainability requirements that allowed the site to be removed from the green belt.

In autumn 2009, the planning inspectors published their report on the Area Action Plan (AAP) as jointly promoted by Cambridge City Council and South Cambridgeshire District Council. This document established the strategic planning policy for this site, including the need for the school, and other social and physical infrastructure such as public open space.

Over the following three years, the masterplan content and design were developed in close consultation with the local authorities and surrounding communities. This plan built on the framework laid out in the AAP, culminating in the Outline Planning Application and permission, which was granted in 2013.

In parallel with the required design, access and environmental statements, two key reference documents were prepared to articulate the university's quality and sustainability vision for the development overall, and provide the context from which the school design would emerge. The first, *Our Vision*, supported the 2010 Green Paper and was followed in September 2012 by the second, *What Kind of Place?*, co-authored with members of the Quality & Sustainability Panel, which continues to provide an overarching brief for the architectural character and quality of place envisaged by the university and its masterplan team.

MASTERPLAN PRINCIPLES AND THE '4 CS'

The masterplan design, planning and sustainability strategy has been led throughout by AECOM Design & Planning, together with Maccreanor Lavington, Wilkinson Eyre and a distinguished group of collaborating architects, landscape architects and partner developers, all working under instruction from the university as master developer and client.[9] In parallel, a wider multi-professional team has been mobilised to ensure that technical and financial objectives will be met on a phase-by-phase basis, including all engineering disciplines, property advisory, cost consultancy and project management.

The masterplan establishes the overarching principles for development, articulated in four themes, which, in consultation with the local authorities, synthesise the 4 Cs of *Connectivity*, *Community*, *Character* and *Climate*. By defining identifiable, walkable neighbourhoods, structured by a new public realm and landscapes, and brought together with clusters of academic and research activity in close proximity, a well-mixed new piece of the city will be created.

Connectivity

Central to the project's success and integration into Cambridge is the provision for safe cycling and walking environments throughout. The

Ridgeway, an extensive pedestrian and cycle network, will be created with public transport prioritisation along key routes to connect North West Cambridge into the wider city. Primary and secondary road networks linking Huntingdon and Madingley Roads directly will also ensure that North West Cambridge becomes an integral part of the city's movement system.

Following analysis and understanding of the existing site topography and predicting desired access lines, the Ridgeway is planned to form the core movement spine of North West Cambridge, thereby connecting all neighbourhoods to immediately adjoining spaces, and forming intuitive and convenient linkages onto destinations beyond the site boundary.

The archaeological survey undertaken prior to construction revealed underlying ancient patterns of human movement and settlement across the site. Marvellously, these coincide significantly with the overlay of the Ridgeway and new settlement designed at North West Cambridge, and establish continuity with the deeper history of the site.

Community

The masterplan forms well-scaled mixed residential and academic neighbourhoods, with a higher density local urban centre acting as the principal focus for community activity from the completion of Phase 1. The volumes of planned development have been carefully distributed in order to ensure a variety and mix of uses, with each neighbourhood honed to optimise specific local opportunities and cumulatively to make the most of the site's overall potential.

In addition to the primary school, excellent social infrastructure and public amenity space will be created, including a community centre and nursery, a major new central urban park and landscaped open spaces. The community centre will be managed through a joint trust with the City Council in the interest of all those who will use it, while an extensive parkland at the Western Edge will also provide a natural buffer landscape between the city and motorway, to collect and attenuate rainwater, enhance the biodiversity of the site and screen the development from the noise and visual intrusion of the M11.

Character

By bringing together an outstanding group of architects, landscape architects and engineers, there is a determination to create an authentic, contemporary new urban district that extends the qualities and special character of Cambridge. While North West Cambridge will provide new places and spaces of differing scales, these will build upon those that have worked well in the city both in terms of urban form, architectural and landscape character, and balance consistent materiality overall with individual detailing.

An architectural framework and design integration process has been established by the university to inspire each architect to pay careful attention to the scale, massing and detailing of their proposals in relation to others, and the emerging new built context. By integrating both the influences of modern technology and the natural environment on design, North West Cambridge will emerge as a distinctive contemporary extension to the city.

Climate

The NWCD project will achieve a very high level of environmental performance delivered through the masterplan and an infrastructure that will facilitate very low carbon living and working. This responds to the standards required by the university and local authorities, including compliance with the Code for Sustainable Homes (Level 5) and BREEAM Excellent as a minimum, with energy performance requirements achieved through a district heating system and one of the largest photovoltaic (PV) arrays in the UK, in order to meet 20 per cent of energy demands through renewable energy sources onsite.

Notably, the project also aims to mitigate climate change impacts at an urban scale by incorporating a site-wide sustainable urban drainage network and grey water main for recycling storm and rainwater within the landscape of the Western Edge. Nearly half of the site will be protected as open land, to balance ecological and natural habitat reinforcement with the new built environment.

THE NEW PRIMARY SCHOOL IN THE CONTEXT OF PHASE 1

The human capacity for division, for seeing the parts, is of staggering importance – second only to our ability to transcend it, in order to see the whole. (McGilchrist, 2009, p. 3)

On completion of Phase 1, North West Cambridge will offer all the components of daily life in one place, from living, learning and working to cultural, leisure and recreational opportunities, to support a very high quality of urban life. Phase 1 will establish a new place through a critical mass of social and other amenities, and help set the standard for the quality of place envisaged for the entire development.

In order to ensure that the UCPS would fulfil its role at the heart of the new community, three brief parameters were established prior to the appointment of the selected architects. Firstly, it was essential to select the best location in the masterplan, at the intersection of the local urban centre and the new public park at Storey's Field, where the UCPS would provide a key focus for the community, with easy access by walking, cycling and bus for all children, teachers and parents. Secondly, a site testing process established that all aspects of the school's requirements could be met on the preferred site. This culminated in the illustrative masterplan supporting the outline planning application, which showed how a provisional solution in terms of built form and open space could be delivered within the site boundary and proof-referenced best-practice design guidance, including *BSF Exemplar Designs: Concepts and Ideas* and local authority standards.

Finally, the strategic brief and vision for the UCPS was collected in close consultation with the Faculty of Education, including key inputs from Dame Alison Peacock (a distinguished headteacher, whose role is further described in chapter 2), Dr Catherine Burke (see chapter 3) and Professor Peter Gronn (co-editor of this volume) of the Faculty. This brief formed the starting point for the appointed architects as they began to engage in earnest with the school's requirements and how those would be integrated into the imagined future context of North West Cambridge, interacting with the wider design team.

Chapter 2 relates the intellectual and policy context for the establishment of the primary school as a free school and as the sole primary-level University Training School so designated by the Government in England. It also describes and analyses the influence of the research expertise in the university's Faculty of Education and of distinguished practitioners, such as Dame Alison, in providing an enriched brief for the architects. University policy, research and training excellence, and master planning were entwined in the genesis of the new school. The architectural story is told in more detail in chapter 3. That and the wider story of the origins of the North West Cambridge Development as examined in this chapter illustrate how a world-leading university, with long-term objectives and deeply-shared values of contributing to society at the highest levels of international excellence, has created a new place which transcends the normal priorities of a commercial developer. The UCPS exemplifies this outcome.

Notes

1 Sir Peter Swinnerton-Dyer is a distinguished mathematician and university administrator who had served as Chief Executive of the national University Grants Committee.
2 Syndicates have a long history in the University as entities with significantly delegated powers to run distinct activities. Both Cambridge Assessment (the University's provider of public examinations) and Cambridge University Press are managed by syndicates. Information about the executive team and the Syndicate for North West Cambridge can be found at: www.nwcambridge.co.uk. Recent decisions taken by the University will see the Syndicate become a Board with increased external membership.
3 Colander works closely with architects and engineers to enable them to plan for the future, and assists clients in finding the right consultants for their developments, see https://colander.co.uk/.
4 The Public Art Programme also began in 2013 and is described in detail at: http://nwcambridgeart.com/.
5 The mission statement and core values of the University can be found at: http://www.cam.ac.uk/about-the-university/how-the-university-and-colleges-work/the-universitys-mission-and-core-values.
6 This document provides the constitutional framework by which Cambridge governs its affairs, see http://www.admin.cam.ac.uk/univ/so/.
7 See http://www.opda.cam.ac.uk/.
8 Arup is a global firm of consulting engineers, see http://www.arup.com/; One Planet Communities is a network of globally sustainable communities, see http://inhabitat.com/one-planet-communities-the-earths-greenest-neighborhoods/; CABE is a construction and property group, see http://www.cabe.com.au/; Cambridge Architectural Research Ltd provides expert advice on buildings and the built environment, see http://www.carltd.com/; Building Futures is the future studies programme of the Royal Institute of British Architects, see https://www.architecture.com/RIBA/Campaigns%20and%20issues/BuildingFutures/BuildingFutures.aspx; Grosvenor Estate, headed by the Duke of Westminster, represents the business activities of the Grosvenor family, see http://www.grosvenorestate.com/; the mission of the Urban Land Institute is to provide 'leadership in the responsible use of land and in creating and sustaining thriving communities', see http://uli.org/.
9 Maccreanor Lavington and Wilkinson Eyre are architectural firms, see respectively http://www.maccreanorlavington.com/website/en/index.html and http://www.wilkinsoneyre.com/.

References

Cambridge University Reporter (1988–9). University development, 5405: 791.
Cambridge University Reporter (1990–1). The development of the West Cambridge area, 5471: 637.
Cambridge University Reporter (2000–1). The plans for the development of the University North West Cambridge site: Notice, 5837: 467.

Cambridge University Reporter (2002–3). Development of North West Cambridge: Notice, 5918: 695.

Cambridge University Reporter (2003–4). Second Report of the Council on the development of the University's land in North West Cambridge, 5939: 149.

Cambridge University Reporter (2004–5). Third Report of the Council on development of the University's land in North West Cambridge, 5992: 513.

Cambridge University Reporter (2007–8). Fourth Report of the Council on the development of the University's lands in North West Cambridge, 6107: 613.

Cambridge University Reporter (2009–10). North West Cambridge project: A green paper, 6194: 1009–28.

Cambridge University Reporter (2010–11a). Report of the Council on external financing for the development of its land holdings in North West Cambridge and other building projects, 6209: 403.

Cambridge University Reporter (2010–11b). Report of the Council on the governance arrangements for the North West Cambridge project and for the development of West Cambridge, 6218: 618.

Cambridge University Reporter (2010–11c). Report of the Council seeking authority to submit a planning application for University land at North West Cambridge, 6224: 760.

Cambridge University Reporter (2012–13). Report of the Council seeking authority to commence development of University land at North West Cambridge, 6282: 59.

DfES (2004a). *BSF Exemplar Designs: Concepts and Ideas*. London: DfES.

McGilchrist, I. (2009). The Master & His Emissary: The Divided Brain and the Making of the Western World (New Haven: Yale University Press).

2   Becoming a free school

Peter Gronn

In October 2014, the Registrary of the University of Cambridge received formal notification from the Deputy Director of the Free Schools Group in the Department for Education (DfE) that, in the view of the Minister for Schools, Cambridge had 'successfully met' the four conditions of approval that had been pending since the previous August, and that the university 'should therefore proceed' to (what is known in officialese as) the 'pre-opening phase' of its proposed University Training School (UTS). It was to be a free school. There were still some details to be finalised and agreed to in relation to trust membership and directorships, and in respect of operating budget projections, but significantly the Minister had also agreed to the government's capital contribution for the uplift from a 2.3-FE to a 3-FE school (Correspondence: Lang to Nicholls, 18 October 2013). A three-month interlude then followed until late January 2014, at which point the wider world was alerted by the *Sunday Telegraph* that the University of Cambridge was about to 'break new ground' by opening its own primary school and teaching children 'as young as four' (Paton, 2014). Not only did this announcement mark the end of about seven months of negotiations with the DfE on the university's final bid for capital funding, but it was also the culmination of just under three years of internal Cambridge planning and lead-up discussions with the DfE since it had initially broached the possible engagement of the university in English primary schooling. This chapter documents the key developments and milestones that occurred during that period and prior to the formal opening of the University of Cambridge Primary School (UCPS) in September 2015. At the time of writing, there are in England about 4500 free schools and academies (or approximately 22 per cent of all state-funded schools) – for some of their proponents a (or perhaps the) jewel in the school reform crown of the previous Coalition (2010–15) and current Conservative (2015–) governments. In light of the time frames just summarised, the more gung-ho of school reformers might be tempted to take these as confirmation of their worst fears about (what they see as) the glacial speed at which universities seem to move in getting from 'go to whoa' in major projects. On the other hand, the UCPS case documented below is significant as a timely reminder of the sheer scale of effort and coordination, and commitment of time, energy and resource that is entailed in the building of new innovative educational institutions along with the overall checks and balances that need to be in place in order to get such institution-building right.

HASTEN SLOWLY

The first feelers about a possible UTS at Cambridge were put out by the government when, in mid-March 2011, Sam Freedman (then an advisor to the Secretary of State for Education, Michael Gove) visited the Faculty of Education with his colleague Michele Marr (of the then Training and Development Agency – TDA). Freedman and Marr met with a group of six of the Faculty's senior leaders and, in light of the forthcoming closing date (May) for the receipt of applications for funding as part of the first round of approvals for free schools, they urged the Faculty group to frame a submission for a primary UTS. There was general agreement in the discussion that followed their departure that the lead time was impossibly tight. Clearly, with the timing all wrong in a number of ways, there could be no application from us for another 12 months at the earliest. On the other hand, we had not been caught entirely flat-footed, because my predecessor as Head of Faculty (Mike Younger) had attended (at the DfE's request) a meeting on the topic of UTSs and in February the TDA had circulated a briefing paper. Mike had also alerted colleagues to the package of the then incoming government's school reform measures (of which UTSs comprised one strand in the recent Schools White Paper, *The Importance of Teaching*) and, earlier that month, as a result of the focus in the White Paper accorded Finland's training schools, a Faculty delegation (which included Marr) had visited that country to view its training model first-hand (see chapter 7). By chance, the Freedman–Marr visit coincided with the handover to me as incoming Head of Faculty. Immediately after our meeting with them I did two things. First,

I conferred in the following week with the Early Years and Primary PGCE teaching team to discuss the possibility of a Cambridge UTS. Second, I met with the Director of the North West Cambridge Development (NWCD), Roger Taylor, to alert him to the government's soundings, the point here being that, as part of its North West Cambridge project, the university (as was suggested in chapter 1) was already committed to the opening of a primary school, as was required by the planning provisions of the S106. In fact, the university's intention to include in the development a primary school with capacity of up to 630 places had been public knowledge since at least June of the previous year (Exley, 2010). Moreover, earlier in that same year (February 2010), the Faculty had even signalled its willingness to help shape such a school as 'a professional development school' that would provide 'equitable educational opportunities and outcomes, within a pedagogical perspective informed by research and good practice' and that would act as 'a beacon for other schools locally and nationally' (Memoranda: Younger, 2010).

As part of a series of new measures envisaged for the training of teachers, *The Importance of Teaching* (Department for Education, 2010, paras 2.23, 2.25) was proposing the creation of training schools. Versions of these schools in North America and Europe were commended because they were claimed to act as 'a link between teaching and the latest academic research and innovation' (p. 24), with the implication being that training schools would enable trainee teachers to be exposed to more classroom practice than was asserted to be the case currently, as (according to the White Paper author) too little teacher preparation had been occurring on the job. Thanks to the Freedman–Marr visit, crunch time for a decision appeared to have come, except that what had changed since the initial flicker of Faculty interest in the previous year was that UTSs were now foreshadowed in *The Importance of Teaching* as having the status of either free schools or academies. As a result there were at least two reasons at that point for proceeding with caution. First, because free schools were not intended to be part of the maintained school sector and would be outside the direct control of local authorities, there was a potential structural (and ideological) stumbling block for those colleagues who had invested a significant proportion of their careers in strengthening relations with local authorities and improving state schools. Second, were it to link itself to a free school early in the roll-out of this initiative, the university risked being identified as unambiguously endorsing government priorities and thereby legitimating (what was at the time and has continued to be – see below) a contentious strand of public policy: free schooling. From the government's perspective, on the other hand, to be able to have Cambridge on board early in the piece – if only because of the outcome of the recent OfSTED (2010) inspection of its PGCE in which the Faculty's primary and secondary programmes had been rated as 'Outstanding' on all 22 criteria, with no recommendations made for improvement – and to have this commitment known publicly would be to land a very big fish indeed, and would provide a huge shot in the arm for the proponents of free schools.

A HOLDING PATTERN

A recent discussion of the university's view of its management suggests that it strives for 'a balance' between efficiency and democratic self-rule (Daunton, 2008, p. 291). With their minds attuned to the democratic side of that equation, the PGCE colleagues with whom I met were wary and (quite rightly) sought considerably more internal discussion about the government's UTS approach to us both within the Faculty itself and among the (approximately) 200 primary schools with which it had partnership agreements before a final undertaking to proceed could be communicated. Notwithstanding the exciting possibilities seen to be inherent in the idea of a UTS, to their way of thinking a series of issues – related, mainly, to the staffing of such a school, its governance, the composition of its pupil intake, the expectations of Faculty staff engagement in the school and implications for colleagues' research profiles, along with the potential for reputational risk – all required detailed discussion. PGCE (and subsequent senior leadership team) percipience prevailed and these colleagues' thinking formed the basis of a memorandum that I drafted for the Pro-Vice Chancellor (Education) in which I expressed support (with caveats) for a UTS at Cambridge.

When I spoke with Roger Taylor there was agreement that a submission to the DfE in 2011 was out of the question, because at that point (late March) his project team was still locked in discussion with the local authority (Cambridgeshire County Council) about the planning for the overall development.[1] It was only later in the year (November 2011) that the national legislative position in relation to the establishment of new schools was finally clarified when Parliament amended the *Education and Inspection Act, 2006* to read:

> If a local authority in England think a new school needs to be established in their area, they must seek proposals for the establishment of an Academy. (Education Act, 2011, schedule II, 2)

According to the DfE website, academies were defined as 'publicly funded independent schools, free from local authority and national government control' and free schools as 'all-ability state-funded schools set up in response to parental demand. They can be set up by a wide range of proposers, including charities, universities, businesses, educational groups, teachers and groups of parents'.[2] In respect of provenance, however, there were some subtle differences. Academies had been introduced by the previous Labour government as part of a closing-the-gap achievement strategy. But during the Coalition's period of office, academies were emanating increasingly from either sponsorship (e.g. by charities or religious groups) or conversion (from maintained schools deemed by Ofsted to be under-performing). Free schools, by contrast, were justified politically and by resort to Swedish educational market precedents, and proposals for them came from groups either disaffected with existing schooling provision or who resided in locations where there was no existing provision. In practice, however, the two school types were viewed (in our dealings with DfE personnel) as one and the same, in which case the umbrella term 'Academy' in the legislation included free schools. This default legislative stipulation became known as the 'academy presumption'.

In some parts of the public domain, the climate of expectations for free schools during this early period was very high. On the day before the 2010 election, for example, *The Times* (2010) had editorialised that the release of free schools from local authority control was virtuous for two reasons: new schools would be welcomed in an area (rather than being seen as threats to existing schooling supply) because then 'parents can more nearly match their preferences [for a school] to what is on offer', and because choice would act as 'a stimulus to schools to improve the standard of education that they offer'. As a result of the legislation, from the university's point of view a new school forming part of its NWCD, regardless of whether it was provided by the university itself or by another provider, would have to be a free school and would require approval as such. Fast forward to early 2012 and, with the legislative requirements now clarified, discussion about the university's options commenced between the Faculty's senior leadership team, the Development Director, the Registrary and the Pro-Vice Chancellor. What was still unclear from a planning perspective, however, was whether a County-administered competitive bidding process would be required for any proposed new school and, if so, whether as a result the university might then find itself in the (rather curious, or even invidious) position of having as part of such a process to frame a submission to build a school on its own land but for which (potentially) it might not be the successful bidder.[3]

SLINGS AND ARROWS

Academies (especially secondary academies) had been under fire in the final years of the Brown Labour government for their inability in some instances to meet their minimum GCSE targets (Woolcock, 2009), for example, or for gaming the league tables to boost those same GCSE targets (Richardson, 2010). But with the change of government in May 2010, and the promise of the new Secretary of State (Michael Gove) to give 'all schools' the 'opportunity to break away from local authority control and become academies' (BBC News, 2010), the tone of public comment stiffened and the sweep of the criticisms broadened. Expanded privatisation of state schooling through companies running the education departments of local authorities or being invited by councils to run individual schools, quite apart from the private sector's existing provision of financial, personnel and computer services to schools, was claimed to be at the heart of the Secretary's vision for free schools (Wilby, 2010). Moreover, by making many new and existing schools answerable solely to himself, the Secretary of State was said to be removing local democratic accountability and (in effect) nationalising the entire system (Newsam, 2010). By January 2011, there were reported to be almost 250 applications to establish free schools, with 35 having been given 'at least initial approval' and with the first clutch of eight approved for opening in September of that year (Doward, 2011) – although media reports suggested that these figures fluctuated from time to time. Among the criticisms of the new free schools were allegations that they were poaching pupils from existing state schools (Hurst, 2011) and, that by pandering to the predilections of middle-class parents, they were functioning as trojan horses for social division. There was also talk of legal action to prevent proposed free schools from opening (Boffey, 2011).

INTO THE BREACH

It was in this climate of increasingly shrill and polarising opinion that, in early May 2012, there commenced the first of what was to become a series of meetings over the next 16 months or so with representatives of the DfE, conducted either in-person or by conference calls, in addition to (a considerable amount of) between-meeting communications via telephone and email, correspondence and document submissions. Given the (presumed) likelihood at that stage in the timeframe of there being a competitive tendering process, and with the university understandably keen to maximise its chances of success, it began to work in tandem with the Faculty. For its part, the Faculty (with the endorsement of the Faculty Board and the Head of Faculty's key advisory groups) had agreed (if and when formally requested) to compose for the university a bid for a UTS to be approved as a free school. As far as the DfE was concerned, however, the Faculty's public face was to be seen to be hedging its bets in the absence of some clear official guidance about UTSs. The DfE's website, for example, did not provide a definition of a UTS and said merely that:

> The *Importance of Teaching* White Paper indicated that the Department would invite some of the best providers of initial teacher training (ITT) to set up University Training Schools. The intention is to establish a few pathfinders from those judged by Ofsted to have ITT provision that is rated outstanding.

And that:

> The university will be expected to provide the controlling influence on the University Training School. The university will provide outstanding initial teacher training and CPD [Continuing Professional Development] and undertake research.[4]

For reasons of cautiousness, then, in their initial meeting with the DfE (4 May 2012), Cambridge's representatives tried (although with only limited success) to obtain additional clarity about the UTS concept itself – with the point being made that, in comparison with Teaching Schools (a parallel Coalition initiative), the level and extent of the available DfE documentary steer on UTSs (including the nature of the application and approval process for them) was disarmingly minimal.

In late July 2012, the university signalled to the DfE its intention (as part of its S106 commitment to the County) to build a 2.3-FE UTS and left open the door for the upper limit to be extended to 3-FE (given its receipt of demographic advice about the absence of overall spare enrolment capacity among existing Cambridge primary schools). Its offer would be subject to receipt from the DfE of a capital grant (of approximately £3.6m) towards the funding of the 2-FE school, for which the university was liable for 75 per cent of the total cost, and for the underwriting of any additional costs incurred were the school to be built out initially to 3-FE capacity (Correspondence: Nicholls to Penny, 24 July 2012). The DfE replied in October. It reiterated that it would welcome receipt of a Cambridge proposal and flagged the possibility of this going forward as a 'UTS pathfinder, which would be processed outside of the annual Free Schools' round'. The DfE was also willing, subject to the assessment of the Education Funding Agency (EFA), to 'top up' Cambridge's funding agreed to with the County to permit the UTS to be a 3-FE school (Correspondence: Penny to Nicholls, 23 October 2012). Meanwhile, in early August, the Joint Development Control Committee: Cambridge Fringes had granted outline planning consent for the North West Cambridge project, 'subject to planning conditions and completion of a Section 106 Planning agreement' – and with the expectation of the signing of the latter in December 2012 (Memoranda: Faculty Report, 2012). By mid-November, the university confirmed with the DfE that it would definitely be submitting a proposal for a UTS. As a UTS pathfinder and in the absence of a developed approval mechanism for UTSs, the university was advised to utilise the existing documentation for prospective free schools (Emails: Penny to Gronn & Nicholls, 19 November 2012; Penny to Gronn, 20 November 2012).

At about this time, the fate of the proposed school moved back into the decision-making entrails of the university. The Council of the University was strongly supportive of the Faculty in framing a UTS submission (Email: Nicholls to Gronn, 25 September 2012), but the members of two key decision-making bodies, in particular, had to be satisfied if both the NWCD itself and the specific UTS proposal that comprised the initial core component of the Development were to go ahead. These were the General Board of the Faculties, which 'has charge' of university academic and educational policy, and the Regent House, a governance body that comprises all university officers and fellows of colleges, and which institutionalises the principle of 'participatory democracy' (Daunton, 2008, pp. 292–3). With regard to the Regent House, the Council sought authority to proceed with Phase 1 of the development (*Cambridge University Reporter*, 2012). Its proposal was submitted as a grace on 29 November.[5] Meanwhile, for the

General Board the present author (with the assistance of the Registrary and the Development Director) drafted a paper on the proposed new primary school and presented it at the Board's meeting on 31 October. The Board gave in-principle support to progress the proposal but sought assurance on three key academic matters: why a UTS was thought to be the best kind of school for the university; why it was in the university's interests to proceed with a UTS; and how and why the Faculty's research and teaching might be enhanced by the new school. The Board requested a more detailed paper from the Head of Faculty. Concerns had also been raised by the School of Humanities & Social Sciences (SH&SS), of which the Faculty is part, about any likely negative resource impact of the UTS on the Faculty (and as a consequence, therefore, SH&SS) both operationally and strategically. With these matters clarified to its satisfaction(that is, the satisfaction of the SH&SS), in early January 2013, a revised (seven-page) document was submitted to the Board.

INTO HIGH GEAR

While these formalities were underway, the Faculty was also being drawn into the North West Cambridge project planning cycle and procedures. These entailed regular stakeholder meetings (of project staff and representatives from a range of project consultant firms and Cambridge County Council) and (occasional) steering group meetings with the Council. In the case of the former, I represented the Faculty as its Head (along with various colleagues). Because sections A–C of the free schools approval documentation required detailed information about, respectively, the 'Outline of the School', the 'Education Vision' and the 'Education Plan', I also began a search for a primary school headteacher to be seconded as an external consultant to assist Faculty colleagues in kickstarting the drafting of this material. My efforts led to the appointment (initially) of Jan Cobley of the Lantern School, Ely, and Dame Alison Peacock of the Wroxham School, Potters Bar. Also, following a discussion at a Faculty-wide academic staff meeting, in mid-November I called for volunteers from among university and Faculty colleagues to attend an open meeting in December. This was intended as an opportunity for information gathering, exchange of views, questioning of key people, the building of momentum and, hopefully, the forming of an ongoing collegial grouping that might support, shape and fine-tune the work begun by the consultant headteachers. Alongside the building of this academic case for the school, in November–December 2012 the procurement process commenced for the appointment of the architect for the school, with the successful tenderer expected to be appointed by the end of March 2013. Here, the Faculty was especially fortunate to have Dr Catherine Burke, a colleague with internationally recognised expertise on which to draw in the areas of the history of childhood, and of school architecture and design, with whom the architect would liaise closely (see chapter 3). Two months later, in January 2013, the project consultants had received 150 expressions of interest.

By early 2013, then, there were at least four separate hares running down four distinct tracks, as it were, each with the potential (because they were so closely interrelated) to derail one or more of the others in the event of any unforeseen hiccups: articulation of a pedagogical model for the school; procurement of an architect and gestation of a design closely aligned with that pedagogy;[6] ongoing Phase 1 planning implementation, including community consultation about the NWCD project and school; and pathfinder UTS academic and business case discussions with the DfE. In respect of the latter, these were conducted on behalf of the university during 2012–13, following the initial meeting in May 2012, by varying combinations of Roger Taylor, Dr Jonathan Nicholls (University Registrary), Heather Topel (Deputy Director of the NWCD), Alison Peacock and the present author, along with data support and advice on the business case for the school provided by Richard Williams and Gleny Lovell (external educational consultants), and the secretarial support of Vicky Mays (North West Cambridge project). Meetings with the DfE (and EFA personnel) were amicable and mostly productive. On the other hand, however, the initial lack of official clarity about the UTS concept and ground rules was compounded by one mildly frustrating feature of the overall engagement: a lack of continuity between, and the increasing number of, civil servants with whom Cambridge was having to work. This churn of personnel (about 20 for the entire period) at Sanctuary Building meetings in London resulted in lapses and gaps in collective memory, the consequent need for occasional repetition of arguments and data presentation, and a diminution of a sense of urgency, particularly as the ongoing discussions were being overtaken by wider North West Cambridge project planning imperatives and deadlines. In fairness, these concerns were mitigated significantly by the DfE's appointment in November 2012 of an outstanding young civil servant as Cambridge's UTS Lead Contact.

At its January 2013 meeting, the General Board agreed that the Faculty's pathfinder UTS proposal 'represented an excellent opportunity for the Faculty and the University'. It authorised the full development of the proposal for submission to the DfE to be approved by the Registrary, the Head of Faculty, the Head of SH&SS and the Pro-Vice Chancellor of Education (General Board, 2013). With the four imperatives just summarised in mind, the Board had been reassured that the draft deadline for the bid to the DfE was to be the beginning of March 2013 – that is, a little shy of two years since the Freedman–Marr visit. In the event, this proved to be a hopelessly ambitious target date, given the extent of specialist drafting required for various sections of the document and the need for their integration; the necessity for subsequent Faculty-wide discussion, the amendment of and revision to the draft document; consultations with partner primary schools and headteachers, and community groups (e.g., residents' associations, faith bodies); liaison (over governance-related matters) with the university's Legal Services Office and the university's solicitors; the obtaining of Faculty Board approval; and term and Easter breaks. For these reasons, Cambridge's 146-page bid (Documents: Submission, 2013) for a 3-FE purpose-built primary school did not arrive at the DfE until late June 2013.

THE UCPS AND THE NATION

A key outcome of internal Faculty discussions on the academic case for the school in the months immediately preceding this date was agreement on a vision for the UCPS. As intimated earlier in the introduction to this book, this vision combined three functions: primary education, provision of initial teacher education (ITE) placements and research. Part of the university's core mission quoted in chapter 1 – to 'enhance the ability of students to learn throughout life' – was the departure point for the proposed vision, in which the school was framed as 'an inspiring learning community centred on a research-informed approach [for which the possibilities and problems are discussed in chapter 9] which aims to provide a high quality and depth of education for children and families' and 'a ground-breaking and innovative learning community with an explicit focus on exemplary teaching and learning practice'. It was this research function that was intended as the school's distinctive UTS element. Significantly in this regard we said that, 'through a research-informed approach to leading the way in respect of such exemplary practice', the UCPS aspired to varying levels of impact: local, regional and national, so as to align with the anticipated UTS contribution sought by the government and DfE – hence, as noted in the introduction, the choice of this book's subtitle wording – and international, in keeping with the university's research-intensive expectations of remaining at the global forefront of knowledge creation (Documents: Submission, 2013, p. 13).

In particular, we stipulated four dimensions of the UTS component of the school in which, operating as a research centre, it would:

• undertake basic and applied educational research to facilitate the uptake of research-informed classroom-level and school-level practices, and

• co-ordinate research by colleagues from academic units in Cambridge with specialist expertise and interests in enhancing the development and well-being of children.

And, with the Faculty of Education and partner schools, it would:

• facilitate the exchange and transfer of basic and applied research knowledge of education, to help build overall national capability for primary school improvement, and

• provide a hub for teacher education programmes and dissemination of professional knowledge, to help shape national standards of teaching and learning practice. (Documents: Submission, 2013, p. 14)

While the above list may seem to be light on details – that is, of specific instances of projects and programmes – the intention was to outline a credible overall strategy, while trying to avoid limiting the discretion of the future UCPS headteacher and staff, the Faculty and its partner schools, and the work of a research (or, as we termed it then, clinical) professor expected to be appointed to oversee UCPS-based research (Documents: Submission, 2013, esp. pp. 14, 56, 60, 79). Taken together, the outcomes of these endeavours were anticipated to yield what – following a helpful suggestion made in discussion by DfE colleagues – we termed a national (and East of England regional) educational 'dividend'. To this end, we suggested a series of potential UTS initiatives that might include collaboration with:

• research bodies, professional associations and other agencies to augment the existing research evidence base for teaching and learning, and

- professional agencies such as the new College for Teaching (see chapter 10) to assist with standard-setting and professional learning
- regional groups in identifying school improvement needs, priorities and strategies, and strengthening teacher school improvement networks for professional learning, and alliances of Teaching Schools. (Documents: Submission, 2013, pp. 60–1)

Finally, the underlying rationale for the vision for the UCPS's proposed curriculum, pedagogy and assessment was anchored in two major national research studies: the *Cambridge Primary Review* (Alexander, 2010),[7] including the *Review*'s approach to the English National Curriculum,[8] and the principles of the ESRC-funded Teacher Learning & Research Project (see chapter 10).

GETTING TO THE POINTY END

By late April 2013, the vision and the detail of the proposed curriculum had been agreed to by Faculty colleagues (following the internal circulation of up to 10 draft versions) with the most recent draft incorporating some suggestions made by the DfE's representatives. The significance of this dual Faculty and DfE endorsement was two-fold. First, the agreed draft version could be made available (and it was) to firms shortlisted for interview as the prospective UCPS architects, following which meaningfully-informed negotiations could commence with the successful architect about a specific building design that would facilitate the realisation of the UCPS's pedagogical aspirations. Second, detailed work could also begin on the capital and revenue funding estimates for the UCPS. These, in turn, required firm evidence of pupil demand and anticipated enrolment targets, a fully costed staffing profile and construction costs. It was about this time (March–April 2013), for the purposes of calculating UCPS revenue funding, that we had begun working with successive versions of the DfE's funding rates financial template – a spreadsheet tool which required indicative annual estimates projected forward for an eight-year period. Credible revenue funding calculations depended on robust pupil data, except that here we were flying blind – principally because in the development site construction schedule the school was to be the first completed building and yet by its opening date it would not have a substantial residential base from which to attract pupils.[9] On the other hand, a couple of factors were working to our advantage. A recent report of the National Audit Office had suggested that by 2014–15 there would be a national shortfall of 240 000 primary school places in England. We were aware also from the County's admissions service that, for the forthcoming school year, there was likely to be an over-demand for, but an under-supply of, primary school places in areas adjacent to the NWCD. As part of our bid to the DfE, then, both sources of information were cited (Documents: Submission, 2013, pp. 72–3), and, coupled with North West Cambridge project survey data on anticipated residential uptake in the development, provided the bases on which (with our consultants) we devised a series of plausible low, medium and high pupil enrolment projections that included in each case commensurate staffing requirements and operating funding estimates.

Taken at face value, the devising of such an enrolment calculus may appear benign and pain-free. In reality, however, unless we were prudent we risked running foul of both national policy and local school politics. On the one hand, the English schooling system under the Coalition was evolving into a hybrid mix of (and tension between) three structural control mechanisms in the relations between schools and the government: hierarchy, markets and networks (Gronn et al., forthcoming). Markets were very much in play in respect of the UCPS's prospective admissions policy, as we noted in our documentation. Here, from the government's perspective, parental choice was philosophically overriding in respect of free schools. According to the dictates of market demand, therefore, as a free school the UCPS would be required, we informed the DfE,

> [to] operate as an atomized unit with other schools as similarly atomized units that are part of a demand-driven competitive market. In these circumstances, the viability of the [UCPS], and schools with which it is likely to be in direct competition for pupil numbers, stands or falls, in market terms, on its ability to cultivate and sustain parental and family demand. (Documents: Submission, 2013, p. 57)

But our particular dilemma was that the UCPS would be a dual-identity school: while we were officially designated as 'free', we were also advancing a national mission. And 'national' (as I have just indicated) also entailed being a good citizen regionally and locally. While the set of assumptions underpinning this approach was antithetical to, and irreconcilable with, markets, it was consistent with the building of networked relationships as part of the so-called middle tier of the system, now that local authorities were increasingly vacating that middle tier and being marginalised:

> [A]t the core of the [UCPS]'s training and research mission is the prin-
> ciple of partnership. 'Partnership' entails mutuality of interests, in
> which relations among schools are grounded in the principle of inter-
> dependence, not competition. (Documents: Submission, 2013, p. 58)

We were clear in our view to the DfE that, if push came to shove and we
were required to privilege either markets or networking and partnering,
then networked relationships simply had to trump marketisation. This
UTS mission imperative was reinforced by the policy of the UCPS governing body (and the university) for the school to be a good citizen in the
north-west locality. Given the UCPS's need to define for itself a catchment
area – which, as is true of all new schools, unavoidably entailed the excision
of parts of the catchments of existing neighbouring schools with whom it
was intent on building good relations (and with whom in some instances
the Faculty was already partnering) – the last thing in these circumstances
that the UCPS wanted to do (and could afford to do) was to alienate its
neighbours. For as long as the adjacent schools were over-subscribed and
in high demand, however, any potential tensions generated by the arrival
of the UCPS as a 'new kid on the block' could be mitigated.

DOWN TO THE WIRE

In late June 2013, prior to the Summer vacation period, Cambridge submitted its application for a free school, including a request for a capital contribution sufficient to build a 3-FE UTS, with a view to it being open for the
2015–16 school year. Between June and November there was considerable
tick-tacking between Cambridge and the DfE, including the compilation
by Faculty colleagues and university officers (at the DfE's request following a late July meeting) of an additional 42 pages of material (Documents,
Addendum, 2013) prior to final agreement being reached. The information
sought included finance (e.g. cost metrics used in space calculations for the
UTS component of the school, possible UTS income streams, the leadership
and staffing structure model), governance (e.g. recruitment profiles and
skills-sets envisaged for governors) and admissions policy (eg. achievement
of a socially diverse pupil intake). On receipt of this material, in August
the Schools Ministers stipulated four conditions (which reinforced some
of these points) to be met prior to their granting of approval: revision of
the draft UCPS admissions policy to achieve 'a broader pupil intake which
represents a wider demographic'; UCPS and school partner engagement

with School Direct;[10] the university to underwrite UCPS budget deficits and appointment of additional trust members with 'prior business experience'. In addition, some scaling back of the UTS facility was sought (Correspondence: Hollom to Nicholls, 16 August 2013).

Taken at face value this was a tall order. But with some nipping, tucking and tweaking (e.g. a 10 per cent reduction in projected UTS space, further undertakings with regard to School Direct), and assurances that (if the subtext of the admissions point was really a concern that the UCPS not be merely a school for the university) less than a third of pupils would be from university and college staff, and that the ranking of government pupil deprivation measures (such as eligibility for free school meals and the Pupil Premium) would be positioned higher in the admissions code, most of the ministerial concerns were met (Correspondence: Nicholls to Hollom, 10 September 2013). While the budget (including agreement on the capital grant) remained a sticking point, it was after additional fine-tuning following internal Cambridge consultation (Correspondence: Nicholls to Lang, 10 October 2013) that ministerial agreement was forthcoming. Given that this agreement came in the same month that free schools were receiving a particularly bad press – Ofsted was reported as having declared a free school in Derby to be 'dysfunctional' (Watt, 2013); Schools Ministers were reported as having approved reduced checks on free school proposals (Mansell, 2013); and a free school headteacher in a high profile London school had resigned after only seven months in post (Syal, 2013) — this was a particularly good outcome. Ministerial agreement was reported to the General Board in November. The remaining items of unfinished UCPS business were to be completed prior to the signing of a funding agreement by the Minister and the university. At that point, the key tasks to be completed by the trustees in time for summer 2014 included the expansion and finalisation of the membership of the trust, completion of the staffing profile and operating budget, appointment of the headteacher and an assistant headteacher, and the undertaking of a series of community consultations. By mid-November 2014, construction of the school was under way and, in collaboration with the headteacher, the trust commenced the finalisation of financial plans and the drafting of numerous school policies. With the requirements of Ofsted's pre-registration inspection and the DfE's readiness for opening meeting satisfactorily negotiated in June 2015, the final two official pre-opening hurdles had been surmounted.

CONCLUSION

In the journey of institution-building recounted in this chapter, the totality of the information provided is akin, in visual terms, to the landscape of an iceberg that sits above the water. Considerably more of the diurnal nitty-gritty from the murky depths below the waterline, as it were, might have further embellished the rhythm and momentum of the account, but at the cost of readers being submerged in a sea of unfathomable details. Sufficient detail has been revealed of what occurred over the course of four years or so, however, to reinforce a valuable lesson that is a strength of a great university. If ever tangible evidence is required to convince wary sceptics of the power of the combination of patient and painstaking consultation, wide-ranging collaborative effort, the identification and the harnessing of collective human talent, attention to detail, persistence, the availability of a deep reservoir of sheer good will, but perhaps most of all a climate in which colleagues are simply trusted to get on with the job in hand, then the UCPS stands as a living testimony to such hopes and aspirations. When initially the enthusiasts for this project were given an open-ended or blue skies opportunity to devise a school, there was no blueprint for how to go about it. And, with hindsight, and the dictates of imagination and the release of creativity in mind, this is just as well. At the same time, however, because the Cambridge team was acting within the constraints imposed by a particular public policy and did not have the luxury of endlessly available resources on which to draw, the sky was never the limit for it. Ultimately, the enthusiasm of the children for the outcome of the team's endeavours, especially the quality of the learning that they experience, will be the yardstick for determining whether that Cambridge team got it right.

Notes

1 Even though a bid for 2011 was not possible, the Faculty was still being lobbied by the TDA in May of that year to commit to a 2012 round bid. We declined, our view at that time being that if we were to proceed, we would do so at a time of the University's choosing.

2 See http://www.education.gov.uk/vocabularies/educationtermsandtags/106, retrieved September 2012).

3 Absence of certainty about the school provider and time delays, of course, would not help residential developers when bidding for sites in the Development. Later in 2012, the County confirmed that it would only administer a free school competition if the University decided that it would not submit a bid for a school.

4 See http://www.education.gov.uk/schools/leadership/typesofschools/a00210474/uts, accessed September 2012).

5 As noted in chapter 1, the outcome of the ensuing postal ballot was overwhelmingly in the affirmative (*Cambridge University Reporter*, 2013).

6 An academic letter writer to the editor of the *Guardian* (5 January 2013), for example, claimed that in research in diverse schools, 'built environment factors' had been found to account for 25 per cent of the variation in the learning rates of approx. 750 pupils.

7 A four-year (2006–10) Esmée Fairbairn Foundation-funded investigation in which a team of Faculty of Education researchers, directed by Professor Robin Alexander, Fellow of Wolfson College, Cambridge, undertook the most comprehensive analysis of English primary schooling since the Plowden Report of 1967.

8 Utilised in January 2015 by the UCPS governors as the basis of an in-house curriculum development seminar.

9 With the exception of some possible pupil admissions from the small number of residences on the nearby West Cambridge site.

10 An ITE trainee recruitment scheme in which schools recruit prospective trainees (via either a salaried or non-salaried route) in which schools offer training either as an accredited SCITT (School Centred Initial Teacher Training) programme or through a partnership with an accredited provider (e.g. a university PGCE).

References

Alexander, R. (ed.) (2010). *Children, Their World, Their Education: Final Report and Recommendations of the Cambridge Primary Review* (London: Routledge).

BBC News (2010). Schools are promised an academies 'revolution', 26 May 2010 (BBC News website).

Boffey, D. (2011). Gove's free schools will divide pupils by social class warn headteachers, *Observer*, 12 June 2011.

Cambridge University Reporter (2012). Graces submitted to the Regent House, 6287: 173.

Cambridge University Reporter (2013). Result of ballot on grace 1 of 28 November 2012, 6295: 342.

Correspondence (author's files): Lang to Nicholls, 18 October 2013; Penny to Nicholls, 23 November 2012; Nicholls to Penny, 24 July 2012; Hollom to Nicholls, 16 August 2013; Nicholls to Hollom, 10 September 2013.

Daunton, M. (2008). Running the university: Modern management in a medieval framework, in Pagnamenta, P. (ed.), *The University of Cambridge: An 800th Anniversary Portrait* (London: Third Millennium Publishing), pp. 291–4.

Department for Education (2010). *The Importance of Teaching: The Schools White Paper 2010* (London: HMSO).

Documents (author's files): Submission (2013): Storey's Field primary school – The University of Cambridge Training School; Addendum (2013) to 'Storey's Field primary school – The University of Cambridge Training School', 28 July.

Doward, J. (2011). Cameron predicts education revolution as the first eight 'free schools' win approval, *Observer*, 30 January 2011.

Education Act (2011). London: HMSO.

Emails (author's files): Nicholls to Gronn, 25 September 2012; Penny to Gronn & Nicholls, 19 November 2012; Penny to Gronn, 20 November 2012.

Exley, S. (2010). University wants primary school under its own brand, *Cambridge News*, 25 June.

General Board (2013). Minute 12.10b.B3, 9 January.

Gronn, P., Ilie, S. & Vignoles, A. (forthcoming). The political economy of leadership, in D. Waite & I. Bogotch (eds), *The International Handbook of Educational Leadership* (New York: Wiley-Blackwell).

Hurst, G. (2011). New free school 'poaching pupils' in a struggle to fill its first form, *Times*, 31 May 2011.

Mansell, W. (2013). Ministers approved reduction in checks on free schools, *Guardian*, 24 October.

Memoranda (author's files): Younger, M. (2010). A University Training School in Cambridge? A position paper following discussions with DfE and TDA; Faculty Report (2012): North West Cambridge Project – University Training School.

Newsam (2010). Letter to the editor, *Guardian*, 20 July 2010.

OfSTED (2011). University of Cambridge: Initial Teacher Education inspection report (www.ofsted.gov.uk).

Paton, G. (2014). Primary pupils at university, *Sunday Telegraph*, 26 January.

Richardson, H. (2010). Academies accused of dumbing down, 26 May (BBC News website).

Syal, R. (2013). Headteacher of free school appointed with no qualifications quits after seven months, *Guardian*, 10 October.

The Times (2010). Free schools, 5 May (editorial).

Watt, N. (2013). School at heart of education reforms row is dysfunctional and in chaos, says Ofsted, *Guardian*, 17 October.

Wilby, P. (2010). Brand new world, *Education Guardian*, 25 May.

Woolcock, N. (2009). Third of academies are failing to meet minimum GCSE targets, Balls admits, *The Times*, 23 September.

3 Creating a space for irresistible learning

Catherine Burke, Julia Barfield and Alison Peacock

> *It must be a place which permits the joy in the small things of life and democratic living.*
>
> (Mary Medd, cited in Burke, 2013, p. 219)

INTRODUCTION

How does one create a school where the philosophy of practice and architecture are aligned? What form should the building take in articulating a view of the child as an agent in her or his own learning, where dialogue is recognised as essential to high-quality teaching and where the pupils' views, ideas and perspectives are respected and supported? What kind of building design suggests a thriving multi-generational democratic learning community that is inclusive, open and welcoming? How can excellence in educational experience be made compatible, through design, with the creation of a home-from-home, a place that is comfortable, warm and nurturing? How should the building address the educational needs of the school community while offering state-of-the-art training facilities for the next generation of teachers?

As has been indicated in the earlier chapters, the University of Cambridge Primary School (UCPS) is the first building to be completed on the site of the North West Cambridge Development (NWCD). At capacity, it will house over 700 children aged from four to 11 years of age. The final design allows for the model of schools within a school to be realised through three linked clusters, each containing everything needed to support the well-being and education of mixed-age communities of six to 11-year olds and their teachers. Alongside these clusters of classrooms and a 'shared learning street', specialist rooms provide spaces available for the entire school community. The building is a bold circular presence in the landscape, presenting itself as a modern, innovative structure that sits at ease within the developing community. How was this achieved? In this chapter, we explain in detail how the vision for an education that has the highest aspiration for every learner informed the design of the building and outdoor landscape.

RESEARCH-INFORMED DESIGN

The challenge and opportunity for the UCPS is to demonstrate through practice what can be achieved when research-informed design seeks to create an excellent educational experience for every child. The demonstrated everyday practice of this school intends to influence change at national and international levels. Through a longitudinal study of technology-enhanced pedagogy and place, the design seeks to support and generate wide scale transformative practice. The vision for the Development is explored elsewhere in this book but it is important to recognise that the school's ethos needed to resonate with that of the entire North West Cambridge project. Children are at the heart of a community and the school aims to bring into being the core principles of living a good life in a high-quality, sustainable environment.

After a competitive process of bidding to build the school, Marks Barfield Architects was selected as the firm most attuned to the task of creating an environment that would respond dynamically to the needs of children and teachers whilst also offering an open environment for those seeking to learn about transformative pedagogies. The Marks Barfield design team spent time carefully listening to advice given by Dame Alison Peacock, and asking questions about the educational vision. The partnership between educator and architect was dynamic and highly rewarding. This partnership sought expertise and was inspired by the history of school design and the views of children brought to the process by a decade of research on these matters carried out by Catherine Burke. A wonderful dialogic process that included site visits and testing of ideas began.

Marks Barfield Architects is frequently told that practice is difficult to categorise. Each project is very different from the last but all are characterised by an approach that strives to stay free of dogma and preconceptions, and open to possibility and change. Their designs, therefore, often lead to unexpected solutions. The UCPS is a prime example of this approach. From the outset, Marks Barfield sought to understand and allow the educational vision and aspirations to take the lead and inform the architectural direction. The design for the school is the result of a close creative collaboration over many months between the authors of this chapter – Julia Barfield of Marks Barfield, consultant headteacher Dame Alison Peacock and educational historian Catherine Burke. Lessons learnt from extensive research of school precedents – historical and contemporary, in UK and globally – informed the design.

A VISION FOR TWENTY-FIRST CENTURY LEARNING

We need educational intuitions that can:

- teach us how to create, draw upon and steward collective knowledge resources;
- build intergenerational solidarity in a time of unsettled relationships between generations;
- help us figure out how to deal with our new and dangerous knowledge;
- act as midwives to sustainable economic practices that strengthen rather than hollow out local communities across the globe;
- nurture the capacity for democracy and debate that will allow us to ensure that social and political justice are at the heart of the socio-technical futures we are building. (Facer, 2011, p. 103)

Drawing from the best of knowledge and experience in envisaging an educational environment that meets the needs of present and future generations of children, Marks Barfield were able to build a strong relationship with a range of educational advisers in this project. Alison Peacock's work as a teacher, writer, specialist on pupil voice as part of the *Learning without Limits* projects (2012, 2016), and network leader for the *Cambridge Primary Review* (2010), was highly valuable and thoroughly applied in the design process. Alison articulates a clear vision for primary education which centres on the key principles of:

- Trust
- Co-agency
- Inclusion

These principles apply equally to children and adults, and underpin a culture of lifelong learning that seeks to build equity, empowerment and expertise. In essence, these principles suggest that the school should be a safe, secure and nurturing environment, inwardly containing but outward-looking and ambitious. There should be a balance struck between nurture and independence, between rigour and freedom, and between inclusion and openness. Inclusion was interpreted to mean that every child and adult should be valued for their individuality as opposed to a narrow identity viewed through the lens of test scores. The school's design needed to reflect an open, inclusive pedagogy as opposed to one that defined and designated certain areas for the majority, and other areas for those labelled as having special needs. Trust was to be at the heart of a school that aimed to be non-hierarchical and highly democratic, where all children would be listened to, and their views and preferences taken seriously. Experience shows that when children are trusted and know this, there is a positive impact on all aspects of their learning. It was important, therefore, that the design of the building communicated a strong recognition of the benefits that would accrue from trusting young learners rather than one that merely was about confining them.

Spaces for play, for enquiry, for reflection and for exuberance would reflect respect for the extensive variety of ways in which a child might be engaged in school life. A careful balance needed to be struck between a design that encouraged respect for individuality as well as community. The building should enhance opportunities for listening, shared decision-making and dialogue. Co-agency requires that everyone's voice should be valued and that decisions should be reached through dialogue and collaboration. It was vital, therefore, to ensure that both formal and informal opportunities could be easily created for dialogue to take place between children of all ages and adults. This might occur in the classroom, beyond the classroom in shared areas, in the dining hall, or outdoors in a range of spaces. Families and the wider community should be enabled to easily find their place in the school and there should be built-in opportunities for dialogue and exchange, be it in a comfortable and calm dining area at lunch time, at the beginning or end of each day, or as part of celebrations and performances where pupils' participation in, and generation of, the arts would be recognised.

The importance of subject knowledge and specialist pedagogy is at the heart of the ethos of a school dedicated to excellence in the learning experience and so it was also important to provide as much opportunity as possible for all children to have access to specialist facilities. These opportunities might be supported by the appointment of specialist staff who may teach across many classes. A science, technology, engineering and mathematics specialist, for example, could be employed to teach all Key Stage 2 classes.

Resisting notions of fixed ability, we were conscious that children of different ages would learn in close proximity to each other, offering the potential for younger children to be inspired by older children, and for all children to support each other as a learning community. The aim was that learning should take place everywhere. This illustrates the vision for the school as one in which all individuals know that they are valued. Opportunities for children to surprise themselves and others would be optimised, and enable liberating achievements. Such provision would offer a very different ethic from one relying on predetermined outcomes dominated by performance in English and mathematics, often to the exclusion of other curriculum subjects.

It is well recognised that the immediate outdoor environment is a significant resource in supporting play, learning and the vital opportunities for socialisation that all children need. It was important in this school, therefore, that there should be easy access to the outdoors from each learning area, to encourage and enable the learning to spill out beyond the classroom but also to ensure that children did not feel confined or boxed in. Forest School is an approach to outdoor learning first developed in Scandinavia, in which children learn how to appreciate nature and the outdoor environment by interacting with it through play, enquiry and physical engagement. The decision to plant a wildwood and to include running water, large rocks and a variety of planting emerged from an imperative to provide an outdoor environment that was free-flowing and non-sterile.

Unlike other English primary schools, as a University Training School (UTS) the UCPS is likely to have higher numbers of adult visitors whose presence should not impact on the quality of the learning experience for children. Spaces for formal professional learning activities such as seminars and lectures, therefore, needed to be provided. When the school is fully enrolled, for example, up to two-thirds of classes might, potentially, host a trainee teacher. Additionally, many trainee teachers are likely to visit the site as part of their training with the Faculty of Education. The building, therefore, needed to provide access to the learning clusters without interrupting activities by facilitating high visibility of the daily life of the school. This was achieved via the gallery and windows into the hall. It was vital that neither teachers nor children should feel that they were trapped in an observation unit – the open nature of the classrooms and provision of the learning street would enable a free-flow space. The UCPS is designed to offer a shared opportunity to understand learning and pedagogy in action. Rather than provide technical observation rooms, the decision was taken to imbue the entire building with the ethic of openness. It was intended that anyone visiting the school to study the children's experience of primary education should be able to see this readily without disturbing the flow of learning. This strongly suggested a design that ensured that classrooms would be open and that shared learning spaces would attract pupils naturally. Children might begin learning within the classroom but enjoy the independence to extend their study beyond the classroom into shared indoor and outdoor spaces. Such ease of movement between settings would result in powerful informal learning taking place between children of different ages or with adults, with children also studying.

Children need to feel safe and secure in their schools. They also need to experience a sense of freedom and ease of movement, 'a safe haven, not a prison' (Burke & Grosvenor 2003, p. 113). The broken circle of the UCPS buildings suggests a protective nurturing space. The school areas are not gated or restricted. Although the perimeter of the overall site is fenced, there are many spaces in the grounds that enable exploration. This feature will increase as the building becomes lived in and such areas are developed further.

THE DESIGN RESEARCH

> An unarticulated rectangular classroom lends itself best to instruction, the unidirectional transfer of knowledge that forms the basis of teacher-fronted lessons. ... An articulated space by contrast is less easily survey-able and provides more places for different groups or individuals to engage in different activities simultaneously in a room without being unduly distracted by each other. So the number of options are greater here, there being several centres of attention rather than just the one. (Hertzberger, 2008, p. 24)

The research undertaken for the design was a process of learning from the past and present while looking to the future. We spread the net wide, studying more than 25 schools, striving to be open to, and informed by, ideas and evidence from around the world. Architects who had made school design their specialism were studied in detail with the object of being able to learn from the best that had been achieved, past and present. Those whose buildings offered valuable knowledge were Herman Hertzberger (Netherlands), Bruce Jilk (Finland/Iceland), Peter Hubner (Germany), Teznka Architects (Japan), Mary and David Medd (UK), Colin Stansfield Smith (UK), Arne Jacobson (Denmark), Perkins and Wills with Eero Saarinen (USA), and Walter Gropius with Maxwell Fry (UK).

The late David Medd had left a valuable legacy shortly before his death in recording revisits to schools, the designs of which he and his wife Mary had helped realise. Marks Barfield were able to access the booklet, with accompanying films, *Principles and Values of Primary School Design*. The efforts and achievements of architects past and present in providing spaces that offered flexibility, suggested easy movement, linked inside and out, and created a warm and welcoming environment for living and learning, were recognised to be relevant today and brought to the design table. Powerful ideas integrated into the design of the classrooms were the Medds' approach of identifying what they called the 'ingredients' of learning spaces and their physical attributes, alongside Hertzberger's ideas about the articulated classroom.

The L-shaped classroom at Crow Island School, USA (1941), for example, found its way into the design thinking, while the ideas from Bruce Jilk and Stansfield Smith about shared learning spaces and degrees of openness were also influential, as was the purity of form of Teznka's Fuji kindergarten in Japan and the masterful use of natural light and detailing of Jacobson. Henry Morris's Cambridgeshire village college schools were also influential, leading to a study of courtyard precedents – both of Cambridge colleges and the village colleges – to inform the scale of a courtyard appropriate for a modern primary school. Visits were made to observe eight schools in the UK – including Alison Peacock's school in Wroxham, to learn the lessons of what works and what doesn't. Invaluable parts of the research process were the conversations that the visits generated between members of the design team. A research day was also spent with Professor Keri Facer (of Educational and Social Futures, Bristol University), to ensure that thinking about possible educational futures, and prospective innovative learning and teaching technologies, were also integrated into the process. Finally, but perhaps most importantly, the views of children were brought into the process via *The School I'd Like* initiative whereby pupils' visions of how the built environment might be changed to bring about an educational experience suitable for twenty-first century learning were articulated.

HISTORICAL PRECEDENTS

The promotion of excellence in primary education through the design of the built environment has a rich and valuable history. In particular it has long been recognised that serious and sustained dialogue between educationalists and architects is the foundation for the creation of visionary school design. In Cambridgeshire, Henry Morris, who was Chief Education Officer from 1922–54, was driven by an idea of reforming education through the provision of the best and most innovative architecture of the time. His village colleges, which form a ring around the outskirts of the City of Cambridge, including Sawston (1930) and Impington (1939), were important precedents. Designed by the best modernist architects, including Maxwell Fry and Walter Gropius, Impington, in particular, articulated a view of the school building as providing educational opportunities for all, from the cradle to the grave. For Morris, like many others of that generation, the school building could be regarded as a teacher, conveying through the beauty of its design a high regard for those who inhabit its spaces day by day. He was a visionary and was completely convinced of the essential value of the built environment in providing the best quality education for all. In an oft-quoted passage of his memorandum, he declared:

> The design, decoration and equipment of our places of education cannot be regarded as anything less than of first-rate importance – as equally important, indeed, as the teacher. There is no order of Precedence – competent teachers and beautiful buildings are of equal importance and equally indispensable ... We shall not bring about any improvement in standards of taste by lectures and preachings; habitation is the golden method. Buildings that are well designed and equipped and beautifully decorated will exercise their potent, but unspoken, influence on those who use them from day to day. This is true education. The school, the technical college, the community centre, which is not a work of architectural art is to that extent an educational failure. (Morris, speech delivered at the opening of Impington Village College 1939, cited in Jeffs, 1999, p. 58)

During the immediate post-World War II period in England, the necessary reconstruction carried out included a large-scale school building programme directed by the Ministry of Education. Among the architects recruited to serve the government at the time were the husband and wife team David and Mary Medd (née Crowley). They advanced the art of school design over the following decades in dialogue with leading educational administrators in the regions, including Morris in Cambridgeshire, John Newsom in Hertfordshire, Sir Alec Clegg in the West Riding of Yorkshire and Stuart Mason in Leicestershire. Schools for the younger child, including nurseries, became their specialism, and Mary Medd in particular had a deep understanding of education and the potential of the built environment to support democratic practice. In the early 1970s, reflecting on their method of design rooted in a dynamic view of the child and their environment, the Medds explained that:

> If children were learning at different rates and in different ways, it was little wonder that the homogenous character of the conventional classroom had to be destroyed, that the rigid structure of the old classroom-corridor school had to be changed. It could not respond. (Medd & Medd, 1971, p. 9)

Creating a common vocabulary of design through close observation and serious engagement with progressive educational specialists, the Medds left a rich and relevant legacy. This included practical development of the articulated classroom as well as the use of circulation areas providing nooks and bays supporting individual or small group activities. The importance of the provision of well-equipped spaces within general work areas where construction might be encouraged was reflected in the schools that they designed. The vital connection between inside and out, and the careful provision of access to areas for play, construction and other learning activities in spaces protected from the elements, was built into their infant and primary schools.

'THE SCHOOL I'D LIKE'

At the heart of the primary school lies the child.
(Central Advisory Council for Education, 1967, p. 7)

In 2001, a survey was carried out in collaboration with the *Guardian* in the UK. *The School I'd Like* was presented as a competition and it invited all children of school age to describe in any format the school that they would like. The idea was to compare the findings of what children said in 2001 with the summary of an earlier initiative carried out by the *Observer* in 1967 (reported by Edward Blishen, 1969, in a small Penguin book: *The School*

That I'd Like). A similar competition was organised in Australia with the *Sydney Morning Herald* and the Melbourne *Age* (2005). What was evident in the thousands of varied responses were the many ways in which children and young people from both hemispheres presented their ideas with reference to the built environment, with much emphasis on beauty, spirit, humanity, warmth, colour and playfulness, and where the arts would take a central position in the curriculum. Here are some examples which came from across the primary school-age group. Their priorities were unanimous and their ability to articulate a new vision of education for the twenty-first century was inspiring:

> My dream school would be a school which would let me explore the world and tell me human knowledge. To achieve this [the] ideal school would be located in three different places: underwater, underground and in space. At the start of every year, the children will choose the topics they are most interested in [There are no compulsory timetables]. (Guatier, primary age)

> There will be lots of windows. The classrooms will be circular (so there won't be a naughty corner) with desks that sit next to each other. The desks will have a part for your stuff. There'll be posters of star constellations on the walls. There will be hundreds of thousands of books on the wooden bookcase. There will be two doors, one leading to the playground. (Joe, 9, Clacton-on-Sea)

> I want lots of colours. (Liam, 4, Barnsley)

> The school I would like would be in a beautiful park, with a river running by. The building would be very modern with lots of windows. Some of the windows would be made of stained glass. In the school grounds there would be a glass dome which would be warm inside and decorated with tropical plants. (Hannah, 8, Godalming)

> The type of school I would design would be light and airy with solar panels on the roof to provide heating and hot water. There would be patio doors in each classroom opening on to a large courtyard, with a glass covered way all around so the children could still go out when it rained, big enough to play under with tables and chairs so that it could be used as a picnic area in the summer ... inside the school there would be two teachers in each classroom so that the children would get more attention. (Emma, primary age, Reading)

MAKING THE SCHOOL: THE SITE AND ITS CONTEXT

The UCPS occupies a pivotal site within the North West Cambridge masterplan (see the aerial images in the introduction). Its design needed to respond as thoughtfully to its context as to the educational brief. The site, situated between the wider landscape of Girton's Gap and Storey's Field to the east and the townscape to the west, provides an interface to the south with the town centre beyond. Each of the four boundaries warranted a specific response. The townscape interface needed to help define the street edges, create a strong civic presence, and frame and punctuate views from the surrounding streets. The relationship between the UCPS and the nearby nursery and community centre was seen as key to the successful formation of the lifelong learning community cluster. The building and public realm at the entrance to the UCPS needed to clearly signal the entrance, create an identifiable space – or school yard – and link into the nursery and community centre entrance. As the northern and eastern edges are more pastoral, the landscape would respond accordingly.

THE KEY DESIGN DRIVERS

... the idea of articulation is very important. The space should be articulated in the sense that you are sort of protected, but feel part of each other. It's a sort of balance between concentration on what you are doing and being part of the whole.[1]

Within an arrangement that saw the creation of three inter-age clusters of six classrooms – Year 1 to Year 6 – breaking down the size of what is a large school into smaller communities of 210 pupils, the educational vision together with lessons learnt from the research led to the definition of the key design drivers that informed and guided the design process:

- All classrooms were to have direct, level access to the outside, thereby creating fluidity between inside and outside, enhanced by the provision of covered external learning space;

- articulated learning spaces and classrooms were to be the building blocks of the three clusters making up the school; these were designed to accommodate varying sizes of pupil groups, supporting and suggesting varying types of formal and informal learning activities (general work areas, practical areas, specific quiet areas); small, attractive and calm group rooms that could be closed off from surrounding areas were to be provided to support intervention work;

- a shared internal double-sided learning street connected loosely to class-rooms through wide openings was intended to offer additional varied learning areas; absence of doors to classrooms would provide ease of access for informal observation by the research, and teacher training personnel and their mentors; this efficient use of circulation space was intended to also encourage cross-fertilisation of ideas among teachers and other professionals, as well as encouraging inter-age learning by means of a bright welcoming break-out space;

- a courtyard connecting all parts, serving as a unifying symbolic demo-cratic centre-point of the school and allowing for recreation and perform-ance would provide the lungs and heart of the educational environment; enclosed and intimate, but opening out to the public realm and to the school yard beyond, this attractive area would provide views out onto the landscape to the north and east;

- the creation of an early years cluster – nursery and reception – with its own entrance from, and playground linked to, the nursery to the south; a rich landscape designed to foster connection between people, plants and nature with habitat areas, ecological planting and food growing was intended to provide opportunities for formal and incidental child-led learning, to inspire and engage; this would include a specific Forest School area to enable experiential learning in a woodland environment – a wildwood;

- finally, the building would provide a strong civic presence to the nearby streetscape, also visible from Ridgeway Place and the local centre, cre-ating shared public space with the nursery entrance and community centre; central communal spaces (e.g. halls, library, studio, specialist learning spaces) were to be designed so that they could be accessible to the wider community.

THE DESIGN CONCEPT

The design process started from the inside out, by identifying all the ingredients needed to create the ideal classroom spaces, both indoors and

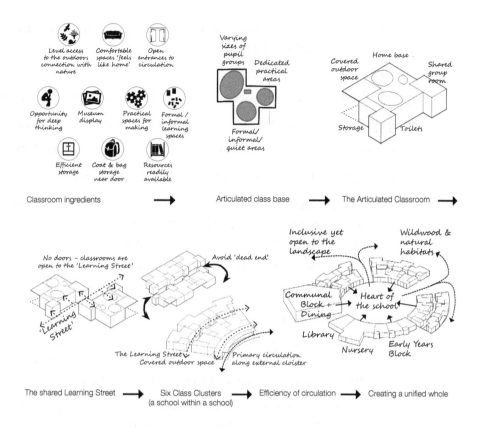

Figure 1: Design process. (Image: © Marks Barfield Architects)

outdoors. An articulated ideal classroom was created and became the building block for the school. General features of ventilation, good acoustic separation and good daylight were designed into the plan, the latter achieved by high ceilings and roof lights. With regard to the articulated classroom, the ingredients identified were:

- Open entrances to shared circulation space;

- direct level connection with outside and covered outdoor learning;

- practical, active space for making – robust flooring with access to water and power;

- an area for disciplined learning and powerful thinking;

- comfortable, soft 'feels-like-home' space, quiet spaces for reflection, whole-class sitting area for story-telling;

- nooks and crannies – small spaces offered by the contours of the building for withdrawal and/or play;
- efficient storage rooms;
- places to display work in a museum-style onto the learning street;
- coat, lunch box storage in close proximity to the door to the outside;
- resources readily accessible to pupils to encourage independent learning.

More general factors for the whole school environment were:

- A rich, stimulating, fun, not risk-averse landscape design with a wild-wood, an orchard and vegetable plots with water run-off from the roof channelled into a rill where children can play;
- strong presence and high ambition, accessibility and inclusion;
- sustainability;
- a school with a heart (i.e., a hall and courtyard);
- variety in learning spaces – formal and informal; a practical and pupil-led school divided into smaller communities – schools within the school, craftsmanship encouraged – learning through doing;
- ownership enhanced through possibilities whereby pupils and teachers might create or influence their own surroundings;
- a child-centred and scaled environment;
- a sense of being part of one world.

Two classrooms were placed either side of a generous corridor, thereby creating a shared learning space while also providing a more efficient overall use of space. Six classrooms were then combined to make a cluster, in effect becoming the 'school within a school'. The desire to create clusters intended to support democratic learning communities within a non-hierarchical school led directly to the circular plan and the creation of the unifying circular courtyard. The courtyard itself was inspired by the University of Cambridge's historic college courtyards as well as Henry Morris's Fountain Court at Sawston Village College (1930), although it differs from traditional courtyards in that it is open to the entrance, playground and landscape beyond. The typology of circular-formed buildings has its roots in many cultures and occurs historically as well as in contemporary buildings. It was also a form that many children and young people articulated as their desired school plan in the collection forming *The School I'd Like* (2003, 2015).

A scale comparison exercise concluded that a 50-metre diameter courtyard would be appropriate for the UCPS.

The articulated classrooms succeed in creating a variety of flexible spaces for different types of learning activities, with nearby group rooms allowing for individual and smaller group activities. The informal learning spaces in the light-filled shared learning streets are an extension of the classrooms, the height of which enables natural ventilation via the stack effect. The inherent efficiency of a circle, combined with the principal circulation as an external glazed cloister enabled the creation of a dining area and additional learning spaces – which is not normally possible within the government's area guidelines (Department for Education, 2007).

Within the communal block, a triangular double-height space opens up between the ground and first floors at the point at which the rectilinear geometry of the street-facing block meets the circular geometry of the learning areas. This allows natural light and ventilation to penetrate deep into the dark areas of the dining area and expresses the essential geometry of the building.

MATERIALS

A small, simple palette of durable materials that are harmonious within the context of the masterplan and the wider context of Cambridge has been used. Natural, self-finished, robust materials were chosen wherever possible to allow for low maintenance and to assist long-term sustainability. The principal materials are light, warm, buff-coloured brick; high-performance aluminium glazed cladding; fenestration and roof lights; and a high-quality metal standing seam roof. The prominent two-storey communal block received special attention by incorporating soldier courses and some patterned brickwork on the protruding vertical element in the form of split bricks that give texture to the elevations.

Glazed cladding and fenestration has been used to reflect the spaces within. Animate façades maximise natural light and external awareness to create a distinct identity appropriate for the high ambition of this unique school. The soft grey-green colour of the fenestration was chosen to complement the natural materials. The cloister is constructed of finely detailed elements of steel with glass panels, with solar shading incorporated into the southern side and integrated artwork. The authors worked with artist Ruth Proctor to develop artwork integrated with the architecture and consistent with the school's vision. Proctor created a concept entitled 'We are all under the same sky', which has involved people taking photographs from all over the world of their sky at a certain time. These are displayed on the glazed cloister around the courtyard.

THE DESIGN IN CONTEXT

The two-storey communal block presents the distinctive civic face of the building. It responds to the rectilinear geometry of the masterplan, and is orientated to help define and hold the street line of Eddington Avenue. It contains all the common areas of the building, the administration, the school hall, dining area, specialist teaching areas and UTS rooms, and is close to the main entrance, thereby allowing ready access to the community centre. The communal block has been carefully positioned so that it is on an axis with Turing Way looking east. This enables it to be a highly visible and distinct focus for those entering from the north along Turing Way. The double-height hall is expressed on the outside with a 6-metre high window that displays an image of the Milky Way (recently taken by the neighbouring university's Institute of Astronomy as part of its stellar mapping exercise). The boundary wall cycle store that runs from the corner of the day nursery is made predominantly of brick and also runs parallel to Eddington Avenue to re-enforce the street edge. A schoolyard with seating has been created at the main entrance to the school. On sunny days its western orientation will mean that it will be a warm, sunny place at which to meet.

A major visual axis has been created, running through the whole site from the entrance, and through the courtyard to a focal raised point in the school landscape and beyond to the Storey's Field and the park. This axis anchors the school in its wider semi-rural context. The entrance is clearly signalled by the entrance canopy, crowned by a prominent yet delicate school sign. This entrance and threshold area of the UCPS provided an opportunity to introduce a symbolic decorative feature. Alison Peacock made reference at the very beginning of the design process to the iconic globe in Robert Owen's pioneering New Lanark School of the 1820s. The globe – also used at the École de plein air de Suresnes in France in the 1930s – has been conceptualised as a powerful practical and symbolic reference point in a child's journey through education into the wider world. It also references the UCPS's likely international intake. With this in mind, a symbolic global map has been integrated into the design of the main gate.

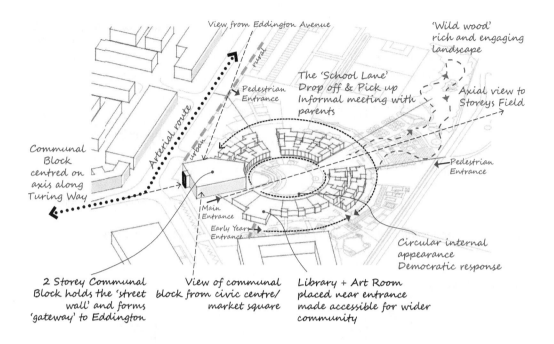

Figure 2: Civic response. (Image: © Marks Barfield Architects)

A visitor to the school will see the two-storey rectilinear block that clearly defines the entrance; however, only on entering under the portico will the circular form of the courtyard and building be revealed. The generous openings in the circular courtyard out to the entrance and the landscape ensure that the school is outward-looking, yet at the same time what is experienced is a sense of enclosure.

SUSTAINABILITY

The UCPS has attained an Excellent BREEAM rating which puts it in the top 10 per cent of the UK's non-domestic buildings. The requirement for 20 per cent on-site renewables means that photovoltaic arrays cover the south-facing portion of the circular roof form as well as the roof of the two-storey hall. The school is largely naturally ventilated and has hit-and-miss bricks on its western elevation to allow fresh air intake.

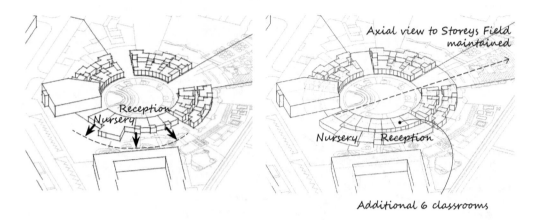

Figure 3: Future adaptability - example: enlarging the school to receive 4-Form entry.

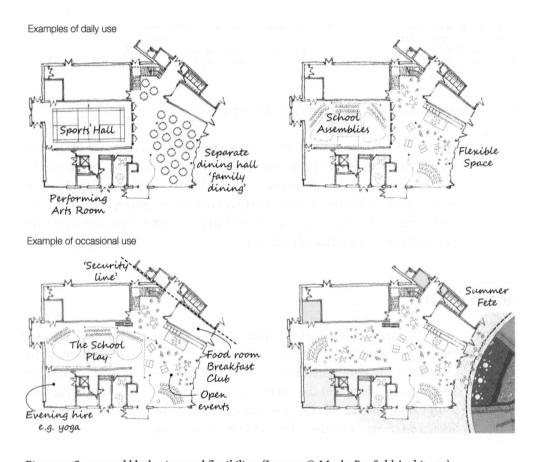

Figure 4: Communal block – internal flexibility. (Images: © Marks Barfield Architects)

FUTURE ADAPTABILITY AND FLEXIBILITY

Children's needs for fundamental features in school environments are pretty consistent over time: they want to be listened to, take an active part in their own learning, help to shape their environment inside and out, and have comfortable, cosy spaces where they can curl up with a book or stretch out to complete a task alone or with others. They want a creative, talented, friendly teacher who is trusted to keep them secure and support their development. However, adult ideas about education and how it is best achieved can and do change. The built environment can then become an obstacle to reform. In the event of the need to enlarge the school, for example, to receive a 4-FE intake, it has been made possible in this eventuality to locate an additional six classes in the inner ring, and relocate the art room, nursery and reception classes to the outer ring and enlarge as required. Internal flexibility is enabled by the use of the steel structural grid which allows walls to be changed, independent of the structure. The distribution of classes within the clusters is also flexible. In effect, the school can be organised in the traditional horizontal manner with classes of the same age together, vertically to enable inter-age learning, or alternatively it can be organised to co-locate Year 1 with early-years children and distribute the remaining years as inter-age.

'WHAT IS AND WHAT MIGHT BE'[2]

In many ways, the design of the UCPS building and its representation of relationships of learning and teaching correspond to the characteristics of children's ideas offered in 2001 for *The School I'd Like*. In 2011, the *Guardian* returned to the question of what matters to children in their schooling, by drawing together a revised Children's Manifesto.[3] Not surprisingly, because children's needs are pretty consistent, these more recent suggestions and pleas struck a similar tone to those first published a decade earlier. Children requested that their ideas be respected and there were many practical suggestions, but in brief they wanted their education to be (in their own words): 'active', 'calm', 'comfortable', 'creative and colourful', 'expert', 'flexible', 'friendly', 'inclusive', 'international' and 'technological'. They wanted a listening school in which learning happens everywhere including beyond the school gates. A perfect school would also have the following features:

- No homework (all the work would be finished at school);
- a flexible timetable;
- an hour-long lunch break;
- pets;
- first-aid lessons;
- a choice of uniform to express one's personality;
- after-school clubs in all sorts of subjects;
- hot dinners;
- an iPad for each pupil;
- a football field;
- fewer tests (but not no tests at all).

Whether the UCPS is able to come close to the radical agenda suggested by these young voices will depend to a large extent on whether the building indeed houses a school devoted to dialogue and a recognition of what matters to children in their educational experience. There is hope that inspired leadership informed by an historical sensibility and a high level of energy will indeed create a showcase of what is possible to achieve through learning without limits. Whether the UCPS fits the child in the way that is intended will depend on the capacity of teachers now and in the future to practice their art fully, and with a wisdom that is rooted in a respect for the children as agents in their own learning and creators of their own worlds.

Acknowledgements

The authors wish to acknowledge and thank the following individuals and organisations for their contributions to the design and construction of the school: architect: Marks Barfield Architects; landscape architects: Colour UDL; structural engineers: URS (now AECOM), Parmarbrook; mechanical and electrical engineering consultant: Briggs & Forrester; Building Services Design, URS (now AECOM); quantity surveyor: Gardiner & Theobald; Acousticians: URS (now AECOM); main contractor: Willmott Dixon; artist: Ruth Proctor; Contemporary Arts Society; furniture: Hampshire Council Architects; project manager: Turner & Townsend; and supervisor: Calford Seaden.

Notes

1 Herman Hertzberger, in conversation with Catherine Burke, Emma Dyer and Dominic Cullinan, Amsterdam, September 2015.

2 Holmes (1911). Edmond Holmes was a school inspector who resigned from his post as he realised that what he was expected to measure and account for bore no relation to true education, see http://www.educationengland.org.uk/documents/holmes/whatis.html.
3 For the 2001 Children's Manifesto, see http://www.theguardian.com/education/2001/jun/05/schools.uk7; for the 2011 Children's Manifesto, see http://www.theguardian.com/education/2011/may/03/school-i-would-like-childrens-manifesto.

References

Alexander, R. (ed.) (2010). *Children, Their World, Their Education: Final Report and Recommendations of the Cambridge Primary Review* (London: Routledge).

Blishen, E. (1969). *The School That I'd Like* (London: Penguin).

Burke, C. (2013). *A Life in Education and Architecture: Mary Beaumont Medd 1907–2005* (London: Ashgate).

Burke, C. & Grosvenor, I. (2015). *The School I'd Like Revisited*, revised edition (London: Routledge).

Burke, C., Clark, A., Cullinan, D., Cunningham, P., Sayers, R. & Walker, R. (2011). *Principles and Values of Primary School Design* (Cambridge: Association for Cultural Exchange).

Central Advisory Council for Education (1967). *Children and Their Primary Schools: A Report of the Central Advisory Council for Education* (England) (London: HMSO).

Department for Education (2007), *Building Bulletin 99* (Briefing Framework for Primary School Projects Incorporating primary school revision to BB82: Area Guidelines for Schools).

Hart, S., Dixon, A., Drummond, M.J. & McIntyre, D. (2004). *Learning without Limits* (Maidenhead: Open University Press).

Hertzberger, H. (2008). *Space and Learning* (Rotterdam: 010 Publishers).

Holmes, E. (1911). *What is and What Might Be* (London: Constable).

Medd, D. & Medd, M. (1971). Designing primary schools, *Froebel Journal*, 19: 9.

Peacock, A. (2011). Circles of influence, in E. Sanders (ed.), *Leading a Creative School: Learning about Lasting School Change* (London: David Fulton), pp. 29–41.

Peacock, A., Swann, M., Hart, S. & Drummond, M.J. (2012). *Creating Learning without Limits* (Maidenhead: McGraw-Hill).

Peacock, A. (2012). Developing outward-facing schools where citizenship is a lived experience, in J. Brown, H. Ross & P. Munn (eds), *Democratic Citizenship in Schools: Teaching Controversial Issues, Traditions and Accountability* (Dunedin: Academic Press), pp. 120–33.

Peacock, A. (2016). *Assessment for Learning without Limits* (Maidenhead: McGraw Hill).

4 The potential influence of the University of Cambridge Primary School in the English school-led, self-improving system

Alison Peacock

A PERSONAL PERSPECTIVE

This chapter offers an individual, personal narrative that explains why the opportunity to support the application for a new model of school built at the heart of the University of Cambridge became an irresistible prospect. I had been a primary headteacher for over a decade when I was approached by the Faculty of Education to work with a team to create a vision for a new model of a University Training School (UTS). Although I am still a headteacher, I also occupy the territory described as System Leader.[1] My school, a stand-alone academy, is a designated Teaching School[2] with a large alliance network of associated schools. Until recently I was a member of the Teaching Schools Council.[3] I am a member of several Department for Education (DfE) committees and a trustee of Teach First[4] and Open Futures.[5] Additionally, I am a member of the North West London and South Central Headteacher Board for the Regional Schools Commissioner.[6] Somewhat uniquely, however, I have also spent my career actively engaged in educational research and the dissemination of groundbreaking educational review and theory.

My professional experience has always been enriched through engagement with university colleagues in pursuit of an education that is meaningful and purposeful for every child. In 2010, the eagerly awaited final report of the *Cambridge Primary Review, Children, Their World, Their Education* (Alexander, 2010) was published. I was privileged to work alongside Professor Robin Alexander to establish a national network to disseminate the *Review's* findings and policy recommendations. Alexander's work provides the most informed and wide-ranging review of primary education since the Plowden report, *Children and their Primary Schools* (Central Advisory Council for Education, 1967). The *Cambridge Primary Review* offers comprehensive recommendations about all aspects of primary education and is underpinned by core aims and principles that seek to promote equity, empowerment and expertise. It is my belief that initiatives such as the development of the first specialist primary UTS may enable some of the core recommendations of this work to move towards reality.

As a participant in the first *Learning without Limits* study (Hart et al., 2004) and an insider researcher in *Creating Learning without Limits* (Swann et al., 2012), I realised that principled action and leadership can enable inclusive learning for *all* pupils and teachers. These principles aligned with those of the *Cambridge Primary Review* and focused on the importance of developing:

- trust
- co-agency
- an ethic of 'everybody'.

My involvement with research and my experience in schools has convinced me that much can be achieved when educationalists build expert knowledge inspired by belief in the educability of everyone. This hope, ambition and relentless optimism underpin my horizon scanning of the current educational landscape in England. From my perspective, there will always be too much to do (ask any teacher). However, if initiatives such as university-linked schools can begin to support and inspire the alignment of core values and practice towards greater quality for learners, we have a duty to explore this and fan any flickering flames towards success.

THE CONCEPT OF UNIVERSITY TRAINING SCHOOLS

The Schools White Paper *The Importance of Teaching* (Department for Education, 2010) first mentioned the prospect of UTSs. This initiative has come to fruition in two purpose-built schools to date. The school that we are focusing on here is a large primary school with a nursery. Not only is this building a brand new purpose-built school, but it also seeks to provide maximum opportunity for as many teachers as possible to learn through the first-hand experience of visiting the school in operation. Its aim, in essence, is to provide a living, breathing example of pedagogical excellence and educational leadership forged through local, national and international collaboration inspired by engagement with research. In chapter 3 we described the process of school building design informed by educational principles. Whilst conceptualising the way that the University of Cambridge Primary School (UCPS) works, it is important to understand the *Learning without Limits* principles that underpinned the design.

When conducting research for *Creating Learning without Limits* (Swann et al., 2012) we identified seven key leadership dispositions for building an inclusive culture of challenge and success. They relate to leadership in the broadest sense and include young people as leaders alongside class teachers and senior leaders. These dispositions are summarised in Table 1:

Table 1: Seven key leadership dispositions (Swann et al., 2012, p. 88)

Seven key dispositions that increase the capacity for professional learning.		States of mind that inhibit learning
Openness to ideas, to possibilities, to surprise	not	belief that there is one right way, that outcomes are predictable
Questioning restlessness, humility	not	reliance on certainties and ready-made solutions
Inventiveness creative responses to challenges	not	compliance with imposed models and materials
Persistence courage, humility	not	settling for easy answers, rejecting complexity
Emotional stability taking risks and resistance	not	fear of failure, fear of trying new things
Generosity welcoming difference	not	deficit thinking, desire for uniformity
Empathy mutual supportiveness	not	fear, defensiveness, blame

An extension of this thinking now applies to the design of the UCPS. These dispositions can also be seen to relate to the process of professional learning in collaboration, whether this is as a novice or an expert teacher. Instead of building a school with observation rooms and screens, for example, the decision was taken to create a centre of learning that would appeal to both children and adults. The leadership disposition of openness is embodied at the new school through the free-flowing nature of the classrooms into a 'learning street' and through shared facilities that allow children and adults to work side-by-side. Seminar rooms and space for professional learning conferences provide a state-of-the-art opportunity for research and practice to become entwined. The challenge for the new UCPS will be to ensure that leadership and teaching is highly effective not only (and most importantly) for the children but that the approaches adopted can be clearly understood by both the novice and expert observer. The clear articulation of principle and practice will need to be evident to all participants, including the children. My own research at the Wroxham School (Peacock, 2016) has found that children are often key advocates for successful pedagogical change and as such enable visiting teachers to become convinced of the efficacy of practice.

ENGAGEMENT WITH RESEARCH

The establishment of the Education Endowment Foundation (EEF),[7] under the leadership of Kevan Collins, and publication of the Sutton Trust[8] – EEF Teaching and Learning Toolkit[9] has provided a welcome incentive for school leaders to become more interested and knowledgeable about educational theory. In addition, the advent of educational debate via social media such as blogging and twitter has led to system-led initiatives such as researchEd,[10] Teach-Meet[11] and TED talks[12] that open debate about educational issues for anyone with internet access. The landscape has shifted dramatically in the last decade, with teachers now much more inclined to read, discover and debate pedagogical practice online. Within this arena, the introduction of influential highly regarded university-linked schools where fads and ill-informed ideas will be resisted in favour of approaches based on grounded research studies will become increasingly important. The trick will be for such university-linked schools to join the online communities and present their own stories of practice and impact. To this end, investment in web resources such as films, podcasts and research-informed blog articles will be an important way of enhancing the influence and system-wide impact of UTSs in particular.

EDUCATIONAL HEROES

As an influential pioneering institution, the UCPS could play a part in motivating new colleagues to join the profession. For my own part, I was motivated to become a teacher because I disliked school when I was a child. I was convinced that there had to be a more humane way of teaching. I began my career by trying to influence school-wide decisions from within my classroom. As a new headteacher I worked to change the culture within classrooms throughout the school by supporting and building the confidence, professionalism and expertise of teachers. As the head of a Teaching School I have tried to establish an alliance of schools where the dominant culture is one of dialogue and empowerment rather than improvement. Of course, school improvement is essential. My point is that to improve without seeking to build professional agency and expertise can only have limited impact. Little of this could have been achieved at each stage of my career without connecting with colleagues beyond my school. Whilst teaching I studied for a Master's degree at the University of Cambridge and engaged with small-scale research studies. Prior to taking up headship as well as studying for my headship qualification, I read as many books on leadership as possible. The point here is that in order to find *another way of seeing*, to make the familiar strange, it is necessary for teachers to connect beyond their own school setting. This may be through reading, via social media, by attending lectures, by engaging in debate or through conducting research. Professional learning feeds the mind, reduces any sense of isolation and builds courage for change. As it emerges in the English educational landscape, the UCPS promises to inspire colleagues near and far to learn more about its pedagogical approach, its curriculum and its assessment methodology.

A SELF-IMPROVING SYSTEM

Over the past five years, initiatives taken by the government have tended to diminish local authority control in favour of a school-led system. The introduction of Teaching Schools, free schools and academy groups and chains has shifted the locus of control for school leadership and performance towards headteachers. As a school leader, the autonomy available to me as headteacher is hugely welcome. The disruptive concept of a self-improving system provides confident leaders with the opportunity to develop new partnerships and to respond as appropriate to the needs of their school communities. A culture of ideas at the centre of school leadership is desirable and motivating, as long as inequity does not become an unintended outcome. However, there is a real risk of a 'survival of the fittest' marketised view of schools, especially where there are falling rolls and where the greatest challenges exist in deprived communities. The group that has been least likely to embrace structural change is the substantial number of small primary schools throughout the country. This may be because structural reform is much less attractive to small organisations that have previously enjoyed the support of local authority advisers and services. The model of university-linked schools should be one that supports collaboration and innovation amongst such groups of schools through outreach, professional learning offers and leadership forums.

The idea of greater collaboration is helpful, except where schools through no fault of their own find themselves working in competition for survival. Place allocation and planning is an activity that is most suitably carried out at the macro (or regional) level and this is an area that is often inaccurate and unreliable. Ironically, although the new UCPS seeks to work in partnership and collaboration with others, one of its greatest challenges in the early days will be to do so without draining pupils from neighbouring schools.

HIGH-STAKES ACCOUNTABILITY FOR LEADERS

Alongside increased autonomy comes even greater accountability. Throughout the period of my headship since 2003, there has been a seemingly relentless move towards increasingly high-stakes pressure to constantly raise standards. This accountability rests inexorably with school leaders. Gradually, since local management of schools (LMS) was first introduced in the 1990s and gave school leaders the power to control their own budgets, schools have become more like individual businesses. The theory here is that high levels of freedom need to be countered by high levels of accountability. In reality, my experience of working with many primary headteachers across England is that the excessive fear of a poor inspection outcome encourages a lack of innovation. Additionally, a focus on test results in English and mathematics often leads to an unacceptable narrowing of the curriculum. The UCPS, therefore, will first need to prove its worth to the profession by navigating the demands of the accountability framework. Once achieved, this success will provide the badge of honour needed to begin influencing change.

A prime challenge for the new UTSs will be for them to use the high autonomy afforded them as the very means to achieve the inspection status that will enable innovation to continue. Professional courage will grow across the country once it becomes possible to observe real-life practice that has been validated by inspectors. Every aspect of a school will become a means of illustrating to teachers what may be achieved when principled inclusive leadership offers high ambition through the full breadth of the curriculum, expertly taught.

SCHOOL-LED INITIAL TEACHER EDUCATION

There is increasing competition amongst Initial Teacher Education (ITE) providers. School-led providers have been encouraged to establish SCITTs,[13] whilst Teaching Schools are expected to recruit trainees via School Direct (see chapter 2, note 10) in partnership with universities. The current recruitment picture for teacher training is confused and in some cases risks closure of existing provision and severe under-recruitment in others. The arrival of UTSs amongst the plethora of existing ITE routes provides yet another layer of complexity. At the time of writing, there is no way of predicting how this confusion will be resolved except to say that, at a system level, the allocation of pupil places feels at best haphazard and at worse in crisis. The vision for UTSs should be one of quality-first ITE experience with opportunities to learn first-hand from the best practice. This approach already works with the most outstanding ITE providers, but should be enhanced through ready access to a university-linked school where quality can be guaranteed and is easily to hand.

EARLY CAREER DEVELOPMENT

UTSs will be perfectly positioned to provide ongoing support and inspiration to newly qualified and early career teachers. The opportunity of studying for a Master's-level accredited course is much more likely to form an attractive proposition if this takes place within an accessible school environment. Similarly, the option of continuing to develop subject knowledge is most likely to be successful if lessons learnt can be taken (literally) from examples within classrooms of the highest quality. The UCPS has purpose-built offices to enable appropriate senior academic staff to be based at the school. The opportunity for researchers and practitioners to work side-by-side is of itself likely to inspire a thirst for enquiry and continuous improvement.

PROFESSIONAL LEARNING

If the profession enables the most enlightened teachers to become those who in turn lead and inform others, then the community has the best possible chance of improvement in the education system. There is a need for positive educational role models. The teachers required are those who read educational research, who question findings, who rigorously respond to the needs of their pupils and are constantly seeking to find a way through for every child. These teachers in turn need to be informed and inspired. They also need to be listened to and to engage in debate. The alternative is a passive, unthinking workforce as opposed to a lively free thinking and passionate profession of educators. The DfE is consulting on the development of professional standards for CPD (continuing professional development) as the importance of enabling teachers to engage in lifelong learning cannot be overstated. With its purpose-built conference facilities, the UCPS will be ideally placed to work in partnership with local Teaching Schools to develop professional learning that is bespoke to the needs and wants of schools across the East of England. Birmingham and the Midlands will be similarly served by the University of Birmingham School. Teaching Schools across the country working in partnership with universities could extend this offer still further.

BUILDING SUBJECT KNOWLEDGE AND EXPERTISE

One of the recommendations of the final report of the *Cambridge Primary Review* (Alexander, 2010, p. 496) was that the full breadth of the curriculum should be an entitlement for every child and that each domain should be taught by teachers with a 'grasp of principles grounded in evidence, together with the appropriate pedagogical content knowledge and a broad repertoire of strategies and techniques'.

The revised National Curriculum (Department for Education, 2013) raises the bar for age-related expectations, particularly in English and mathematics. If schools are to teach the new curriculum effectively across the full range of subject domains, there is an increased imperative for teacher subject knowledge to be further developed. At a time when subject associations have had their funding cut, and without centralised or localised CPD provision, there is an urgent need for schools to find ways of developing their staff.

A reductive, simplistic response to the accountability and standards agenda is to minimise and narrow the curriculum for children to ensure that more of the day can be spent learning what will be tested. The UCPS has been designed to include specialist teaching areas for subjects such as art and design, dance, environmental awareness, games and music. The entrance to the building offers windows looking into a large library area, and every classroom has access both to the learning street for collaborative mixed-age study and the outdoors. When planning the growth of the school, specific advice about the recruitment of specialist teachers for languages, music, computing, the arts, and science, mathematics and technology was included. The importance of enabling the primary sector to embrace the positive benefits of specialist teaching within subjects, therefore, is an area of system-wide development that can be supported and enhanced through a chance to observe this work in action at schools such as the UCPS. Teachers visiting the new school will be able to see for themselves that colleagues with high levels of pedagogical subject knowledge enable children to achieve more than many colleagues might think possible.

UTSs are ideally placed at the heart of universities to develop subject-specific expertise that can be shared beyond their own setting with schools in the locality. Opportunities to plan and record a curriculum offer that is informed by academics, learned societies and other experts should lie at the heart of each UTS. Where better, for example, to develop primary science, technology, mathematics and engineering skills than within the very heart of a university such as Cambridge?

A NEW COLLEGE OF TEACHING

At the time of writing, a fledgling College of Teaching is beginning to take shape (see chapter 10). If a future college is to achieve the impact that the profession requires, it will need to have reference points in institutions that offer an overarching model of excellence for pedagogy, research and professional learning. The opportunity for the college to form a close liaison with UTSs is potentially very fruitful. The aims of the college will be to enhance the quality of the profession through engagement with evidence and through seeking a membership of the highest quality. As UTSs develop and emerge as regional centres of inspiration, they could provide a physical regional presence for college activity. A vision for educational excellence in leadership means that we should 'be not afraid of greatness' (Shakespeare: *Twelfth Night*, II, v, 155). The UCPS is ideally placed to enact global influence by virtue of the opportunity to share practice. This is a position that cannot be squandered. All English primary schools stand to gain from the unique position that the UCPS holds and to learn alongside it.

SCHOOL IMPROVEMENT THROUGH EMPOWERMENT

The current government's policy approach towards school-to-school support is underpinned by grants allocated to Teaching Schools. This is another area of the self-improving system that is building expertise among a range of system leaders (as mentioned previously in note 1). These roles include National Leaders of Education (NLEs), Local Leaders of Education (LLEs) and Specialist Leaders of Education (SLEs).[14] The official intention is to move advisory work away from local authorities and into the hands of schools themselves. In this area, the new UTSs should be ideally placed to actively support school development work both via high-quality research-informed professional learning and through opportunities for participants to observe teaching. Ideally, UTS leaders will work across their regions alongside Teaching Schools, local authorities, Regional Schools Commissioners, a church diocese and others in a mission to empower improvement. Opportunities to develop accredited leadership courses or initiatives such as assessment qualifications or mastery qualifications should be at the heart of what may be offered through close university–school collaboration.

REGIONAL LEADERSHIP OF LEARNING

The Government's movement towards school autonomy has meant that many advisory structures that previously existed to support schools locally have changed or disappeared. In their place, it is becoming apparent that new regional leadership roles need to be developed to ensure that all schools are connected and supported effectively. I have argued elsewhere (Peacock, 2014) that new models of school inspection and peer review are needed. One such model would be for regions to form collaborative teams of professionals dedicated to linking excellence within schools as a means of encouraging quality. Regional Schools Commissioners would benefit from the opportunity to have greater knowledge about their areas and to understand where the hotspots of excellence exist in order to support school improvement. Local intelligence, willingness and a capacity to share ideas, linked with UTSs with the facilities, expertise and the vision to help others could provide a new model of collective school improvement. Commissioners could then lead tightly understood networks for improvement. Teaching Schools and their alliances would be well placed to liaise with UTSs to ensure that coverage of school support and innovation meant that all schools were connected within a community. Instead of the current inspection system that engenders fear, this proposal could create a means of recognising quality, by connecting excellence and building expertise.

STRONGER TOGETHER

The story of the UCPS cannot be the story of just one school and one headteacher. It needs to be one of collective ambition inspired by a pioneering model that, potentially, leads to university-school partnerships springing up all over the country. The greatest risk for the UCPS is that too much is likely to be expected from too few. Strength of ambition, optimism and informed university-school partnerships must emerge from an opportunity within a self-improving system for headteachers and academics to seize the initiative to form new kinds of collaboration that build on and extend the vision for UTSs outlined here.

THE IMPORTANCE OF ROLE MODELS AND ALTERNATIVE VOICES

Within the clamour of competing voices seeking attention for their own view of education, it is important for school leaders to take time to read, reflect and be inspired by colleagues who have chosen to devote their professional life to furthering knowledge about teaching and learning. When we were writing *Creating Learning without Limits* (Swann et al., 2012), I kept a leadership journal every week for 18 months. When I looked back at this journal, it became apparent to me that my professional courage was forti-fied time and time again by the knowledge that I had gained from reading studies by educational heroes such as Susan Isaacs (1930), Gordon Wells (2009), Black and Wiliam (2001), and many more. Alongside this reading, my own studies and engagement with research through further profes-sional study and writing provided me with another reference point for decision-making.

The strength of the English school system is only as good as the quality of its teaching and leadership. I am convinced that professional learning and connections made through educational debate and enquiry provide the keys to developing and building the calibre of the leaders that our schools need. Compliance and risk-averse leadership tends more towards management than towards the kind of leadership that the system needs if the intention is to achieve collective empowerment and ambition. The role of UTSs working alongside educational researchers, subject special-ists, Teaching Schools and other system leaders could be transformative if openness to new knowledge lies at the heart. This relies on leadership that resists old certainties and allows the art of the possible to emerge as a means to inspire collaborative innovation.

WHOSE VOICES ARE HEARD IN PRIMARY EDUCATION?

One of the key roles for the new UCPS will be to amplify the voice of pri-mary and early years practitioners. It will be important for the school to achieve high standards whilst retaining a broad curriculum that is expertly taught. Once this has been achieved, the UCPS will be ideally placed to work alongside other agencies such as the Regional Schools Commissioner, pro-fessional associations and the College of Teaching to ensure that the issues that are likely to impact upon primary-aged children and their teachers are fully understood.

The more that politicians and the inspectorate lead the debate and quieten voices that appear to counter the latest thinking from elsewhere, the more the system risks losing the very essence of excellence within the best teachers. The model of creating a working school at the heart of a university that prides itself on a tradition of excellence and freedom of thought, therefore, is a compelling one.

PRIMARY ASSESSMENT – A CASE IN POINT

English primary schools struggled to accept the abolition of a national system for assessing progress via levels of attainment. The National Curriculum levels were originally intended to provide broad descriptors of progression across primary and secondary education. However, over a period of years, at a time of increasing accountability and pressure on schools to provide evidence of progress and attainment, the levels morphed into increasingly complex and demanding measures of school performance. The government became persuaded that levels were beginning to set limits on expected outcomes from pupils and announced that they were no longer appropriate or relevant in relation to the revised National Curriculum.

When assessment levels were abolished by the government, this decision was met with disbelief by many people, and subsequently with anger and bewilderment by others. Although some schools began to collaborate to devise new systems for ensuring that progress could be recorded and valued, many others met the centralised invitation to innovate as irritating rather than liberating. Gradually, through this deliberately disruptive policy, the profession is beginning to join together to make sense of assessment and to recognise the importance of building expertise in this area. At the time of writing, despite confusion over assessment announcements from the government, there is a groundswell of professionals who have seized the moment to build new moderation strategies and the sharing of materials to support principled assessment practice. Optimism formed of enlightened empowerment backed by research evidence and expertise enables teachers to find a way through the national policy to achieve excellence. This is precisely the kind of territory that the new UCPS will be ideally placed to support at a system level in the future.

FREEDOM TO INNOVATE

From my point of view as a headteacher, the courage to determine my school ethos, engage with research and manage my own budget has been liberating, and has enabled me to put the needs of my children and staff first. The story of how Wroxham turned around from special measures to outstanding is well documented (Swann et al., 2012), and a large part of that school leadership innovation came from the freedom and capacity to respond to the needs of the school. Wroxham was one of the smallest schools designated as a Teaching School in the first round of applications in 2011. My response to the invitation from the then Secretary of State, Michael Gove, to engage in school improvement without a template provided from the centre was to feel liberated and excited. Not everyone, however, felt this way. At the induction conference for new Teaching School leaders, for example, there was an undercurrent from colleagues who were expecting and seeking leadership and guidance from the National College for Teaching & Leadership (NCTL).[15]

Although the NCTL had been established to build leadership expertise, the high-stakes accountability system in England had inadvertently contributed to passive, risk-averse leadership at a system level. As teachers we are used to identifying learned helplessness amongst pupils, but perhaps we are less likely to see this as a condition affecting ourselves and our peers as school leaders. In this regard, I recall coming down from my room on the second day of the Teaching Schools induction conference and bringing with me a copy of *How to Change 5 000 Schools* (Levin, 2008). I was intrigued by the success achieved by schools in Ontario, Canada, and wanted to read about this to understand how in a very small way my new alliance of schools at Wroxham might be able to learn it. Before the second day even began, however, two other primary headteachers joined my table at the conference, looked across at me and sneered: 'Oooooh! Reading books are we?'

For me, this incident sums up the absolute imperative to establish the new UCPS. For too long, it has been acceptable, almost expected, that engagement with research and professional study amongst primary colleagues is not something that should be anticipated. If teachers are not encouraged to believe that they should be constantly developing expertise, the profession is doomed to become moribund. In the final report of the *Cambridge Primary Review*, Robin Alexander calls for the following:

> We now need to move to a position where research-grounded teaching repertoires and principles are introduced through initial training and refined and extended through experience and CPD, and teachers acquire as much command of the evidence and principles which underpin the repertoires as they do of the skills needed in their use. The test of this alternative view of professionalism is that teachers should be able to give a coherent justification for their practices citing (i) evidence, (ii) pedagogical principle and (iii) educational aim, rather than offering the unsafe defence of compliance with what others expect. Anything less is educationally unsound. (Alexander, 2010, p. 496)

Some colleagues who have read this call to arms have wondered at the ambition of such an aspiration. In fact, it has become increasingly apparent to me that it is precisely through engagement with research and tussling with the big ideas and principles in education that we enable schools to become the places that we want and need them to be.

A VISION FOR UNIVERSITY TRAINING SCHOOLS

In summary, this chapter has considered the current educational landscape and has attempted to visualise the potential impact that UTSs could begin to have. This is not a vision that relies exclusively on money. UTSs would benefit from being purpose-built, but do not have to be. The vision for excellence through university–school partnership costs nothing, but has a great deal to offer. If the English education system is genuinely self-improving, members of the profession do not need to wait for permission. If they are convinced of the importance of collaboration as opposed to isolation, of the imperative of ideas as opposed to compliance and of the necessity of positivity as opposed to fear, they have a new model of school improvement to explore. The beautiful new school building in Cambridge can do much to inspire colleagues to make new partnerships but we must do more than stand back and watch. Educators need to get involved, take action and collectively celebrate the consequences for our children.

Notes

1 'System Leader' refers to the scope for influence and impact provided by high-profile individual school leaders in England. In addition, there is formal provision for appointment to a series of leadership roles designated by system level or specialism, details of which are found below in the section on school improvement.
2 'Teaching schools are outstanding schools who work with other schools to provide excellent support and training and development to both new and experienced school staff.' They form alliances with supported schools and strategic partners. The alliances focus on six areas: initial teacher training, CPD, school to school support, research and development, System Leaders in Education and succession planning, see *Teaching Schools: The School Perspective* (National College for Teaching & Leadership), October 2015, p. 3, https://www.gov.uk/government/publications/teaching-schools-the-school-perspective.
3 The Teaching Schools Council comprises headteachers of Teaching Schools elected by their peers. It is a national body that represents the interests of the national network of about 600 Teaching Schools, see http://tscouncil.org.uk/the-tsc/.

4   An educational charity with a mission to end educational inequality, see https://www. teachfirst.org.uk/what-we-do.

5   A CPD programme run by the Open Futures Trust, see http://www.openfutures.com/.

6   Eight Regional School Commissioners monitor the performance of free schools and academies for the Secretary of State for Education, with each Commissioner supported by a headteacher board, see https://www.gov.uk/government/organisations/ schools-commissioners-group/about/our-governance.

7   An "independent grant-making charity dedicated to breaking the link between family income and educational achievement", founded by the Sutton Trust, see https://educationendowmentfoundation.org.uk/.

8   The Sutton Trust is a charity that addresses educational inequality and is dedicated to social mobility through education, see http://www.suttontrust.com/.

9   See https://educationendowmentfoundation.org.uk/evidence/teaching-learning-toolkit.

10 A 'grass-roots, teacher-led organisation aimed at improving research literacy in the educational communities', see: http://www.workingoutwhatworks.com/en-GB/About.

11 Informal meetings for teachers, facilitated via the TeachMeet website, to 'share good practice, practical innovations and personal insights in teaching with technology', see https://en.wikipedia.org/wiki/TeachMeet.

12 A non-profit organisation that spreads ideas through web-accessed talks, see https:// www.ted.com/talks.

13 The acronym SCITT means school-centred initial teacher training.

14 NLEs: 'Outstanding headteachers who work with schools in challenging circumstances to support school improvement'; LLEs: 'experienced headteachers who coach or mentor new headteachers or headteachers whose schools are in challenging circumstances'; SLEs: 'experienced middle or senior leaders with a specialism (for example, maths, initial teacher training, behaviour)' who develop other leaders, see https://www.gov.uk/guidance/ system-leaders-who-they-are-and-what-they-do specialist-leaders-of-education-sles.

15 An executive agency within the DfE with the responsibility for improving the quality of schools and the teaching workforce, see https://www.gov.uk/government/ organisations/national-college-for-teaching-and-leadership/about.

References

Alexander, R. (ed.) (2010). *Children, Their World, Their Education: Final Report and Recommendations of the Cambridge Primary Review* (London: Routledge).

Black, P. & Wiliam, D. (2001). *Inside the Black Box: Raising Standards through Classroom Assessment* (Kings College, School of Education: BERA).

Central Advisory Council for Education (1967). *Children and Their Primary Schools: A Report of the Central Advisory Council for Education* (England) (London: HMSO).

Department for Education (2010). *The Importance of Teaching: The Schools White Paper 2010* (London: HMSO).

Department for Education (2013). *The National Curriculum in England: Framework for Key Stages 1 to 4*. see www.gov.uk.

Hart, S., Dixon, A., Drummond, M.J. & McIntyre, D. (2004). *Learning without Limits* (Maidenhead: Open University Press).

Isaacs, S. (1930). *Intellectual Growth in Young Children* (London: Routledge).

Levin, B. (2008). *How to change 5 000 schools* (Cambridge, Mass: Harvard Educational Publishing Group).

Peacock, A. (2014). Leadership without limits, in J. Hallgarten, L. Bamfield & K. McCarthy (eds) (2014). *Licensed to Create* (London: RSA), pp. 49–54.

Peacock, A. (2016). *Assessment for Learning without Limits* (Maidenhead: McGraw Hill).

Swann, M., Peacock, A., Hart, S. & Drummond, M.J. (2012). *Creating Learning without Limits* (Maidenhead: McGraw-Hill).

Wells, G. (2009). *The Meaning Makers* (Bristol: Multilingual Matters).

5   Releasing the imagination: Celebrating the art of the possible

James Biddulph

It is odd being a Headteacher without a school building, staff or children. Walking around the skeletal structure of our school, it is hard to imagine the conversations between adult and child, to see playtime through the round courtyard, to hear singing, the normal chatter of school life. It is hard to consider the practicalities. Our vision is compelling, I think, but how will we release it from the printed page? Where will the imagination fly? How will we celebrate? What is really possible in a high-stakes accountability educational context? How will we realise the potentials for every child, teacher and member of community? How do I lead the way?

(from my headteacher's journal, April, 2015)

Spaces waiting to be filled
High ceilings, limitless
Can't wait for the voices to fill these corridors
Can't wait for the learning to begin
Can't wait for the energy, the buzz
Can't wait to fill the void.

(reflection from Suzi Bray, assistant headteacher
following her first visit to school, July 2015)

In this chapter I explore our vision and ethos and consider the challenges and opportunities of beginning a new school, in a new community, within a new educational landscape. There are two parts: the first relates to the educational theoretical positions that informed our vision; the second to the practical ways in which we gathered a team to realise the possibilities presented in the vision statement. I build on chapter 1, which described the need for our school in a new community development in the North West Cambridge project. Likewise in chapter 2, Peter Gronn explained the purpose of the free school movement in English education, considering what a University Training School (UTS) could be. Together with Alison Peacock's contribution, the authors of these chapters hint at the potential of the school and consider the nature of the risks.

Leading a school, whether new or established, is as much about developing systems and considering the practicalities as it is about the vision and ethos. But the vision is the route map and the ethos the spirit that guides the way; without these there are only buildings and practicalities. In my journal reflection above I raised questions about the challenge of articulating a school vision and the vital role of leadership that is about communicating and orchestrating a compelling vision (Novak et al., 2014, pp. 3–16), and developing a rich context to lead *educational lives* for us all.

So, as the metal structure wound its way out from the fields that were once the university's farm, our vision circled in our minds and conversations, discussed between governors and our new staff, rehearsed and evolving as we attempted to understand how we could *Release the Imagination* and *Celebrate the Art of the Possible.* How did we arrive at this strap-line? How did we form our approach? What principles guided our decisions?

THEORISING OUR VISION: FINDING A LANGUAGE

During our inaugural year (2015–16), the House of Commons Education Committee launched an inquiry into education in England. It asked a number of questions about the purpose of education in England, the ways in which schools evaluate the quality of education and whether they currently meet these measured standards. Only five years before this, a significant and comprehensive review of primary education was undertaken, asking similar questions, the *Cambridge Primary Review* (Alexander, 2010). The ongoing attempt to define a good education remains a contested area within which we collide with political habits, mindsets and vocabularies. Furthermore, with the market-force propagation of free schools and academies, and decentralisation of education away from local authorities, school communities are required to define the characters, qualities and purposes of *their own* educational offer. In a world of 'super-diversity' (Cantle, 2012, p. 4), the added challenge and promise of intercultural interaction poses more diverse responses to the questions about education, its purpose and the experience that families and society want for their children. It is an opportunity to relish.

As well as defining what an effective education could be, questions about individual responsibility and the democratic values of tolerance and fairness, respect and rule of law are increasingly emphasised in government policy. The notion of 'British values' became prevalent, for example, leading to a requirement for schools to encourage and develop such attitudes within their communities. Finding the language to express our vision for the new school, in a politically divergent lexicon, was both challenging and necessary. Philosophers John Dewey and Ludwig Wittgenstein understood the centrality of language *as practice* – that it is something we do and live by. Over the last two decades the language of education has transformed into a language of learning (e.g. learner-centred, assessment for learning, children described as learners rather than pupils). This change involves a repositioning of the relationship between teacher and child, and raises questions about authority, knowledge, curriculum and voice. Whose knowledge? Which knowledge is valued? By whom? And how does a school construct relationships that are rooted in values that help to create a learning environment in which everyone achieves? Furthermore, the language has even moved beyond learning, with educators grappling with the possibilities and challenges of developing 'democratic education for a human future' (Biesta, 2006, pp. 138–9), which suggests an apocalyptic sense that children deserve an education fit for a complex world future of uncertainty.

As expressed in chapters 1–3, the University of Cambridge Primary School (UCPS) has three distinctive aspirations: to be a brilliant primary school, to support ITE (or training) and to become a beacon of research-informed and research-generating professional learning. This was unprecedented territory, as Peacock explained (chapter 4). Our school was to be the first of its kind. Thus, the distinctive character of the UCPS as a UTS urged us to answer questions to define who we are, our core purpose and our relevance in a UK (and world) context. The connection between an 800-year old world-class university and a brand new primary school wedded the vision for our school that built relationships between theory and practice, not as polarities in the educational discourse but rather as a symbiotic relationship: it was about *theorising practice* and *practising theory* (Burnard et al., 2015). The relationship also linked our purpose with that of the university's mission, namely, 'to contribute to society through the pursuit of education, learning and research at the highest international levels of excellence',[1] the encouragement of a questioning spirit, and the provision of an education that enhances the ability of students to learn throughout life. What would this mean for a primary school? How would it be realised in the classrooms? How would teachers enable children and spark a questioning spirit?

As with the *Cambridge Primary Review* (Alexander, 2010), *Learning without Limits* (Hart et al., 2004), and *Creating Learning without Limits* (Swann et al., 2012), we wanted our school vision to be grounded in empirical research with a humanistic and democratic notion of education at its core. We wanted an educational experience that was about developing a 'shared, hopeful vision that pays attention to the diversity of perspectives in the human community' (Novak et al., 2014, p. 5), and which challenged traditional notions of children's ability as fixed to versions of transformability. The idea was to develop a school community of people 'living educationally' (Novak et al., 2014, p. 4): reflective, aspirational and actively engaged educators, and equally, children who were central to the principles and were co-constructors of *their* educational experience. Moreover, we did not perceive education in terms of global capitalisation. Rather, we saw 'our educational responsibility as a responsibility for the humanity of the human being' (Biesta, 2006, p. 106) – that there was a higher purpose, as well as the important logistics and practicalities of teaching the basics of reading, writing and mathematics.

The task of synthesising the diverse responses to such questions and understanding differing stakeholders' views was a key part of my role as headteacher. The literature about school leadership emphasised the importance of knowing one's core moral purpose and centred on the personal passions of being an educator (Day, 2004). I started the synthesis of these two ideas by reflecting on myself, my own vision and core purpose. I needed to speak the language as a practice, as my own practice, so that it would be authentic.

THEORISING MY PRACTICE: PERSONALISING THE VISION

My own experiences of learning as an educator, most memorably being in Nepal where I lived and taught for a year, guided my thinking. I remember one moment of realisation. On a bus from Nepal to India, I read a book that I had picked up in a small bookshop near a Kathmandu bus station. I felt inspired by the words, which looked to the possibilities in education and offered a perspective that guided my thinking:

> Life is a well of deep waters. One can come to it with small buckets and draw only a little water, or one can come with large vessels, drawing plentiful waters that nourish and sustain ... the school should help its young people discover their vocations and responsibilities. (Krishnamurthi, 1981, p. 44)

The sense of education as a vital opportunity to connect, and to integrate thought and feeling, was present in the text. I learnt that 'without deep integration of thought and feelings, our lives are incomplete' (Krishnamurthi, 1981, p. 11). In questioning the purpose of education, Krishnamurthi challenges what he sees as conventional orthodoxies based on fear, power and control, which are systemic, and propagated in the interactions between pupil and teacher, and he urges us to revolt by 'keep[ing] [our] intelligence highly awakened' (Krishnamurthi, 1981, p. 11). I was keen to develop my theoretical language in order to be able to articulate what my practice and experiences were revealing. From reading Krishnamurthi's theory I became interested in the power dynamics within schools, between teacher and child, and the systems that sustain such assumptions and structures.

I learnt to be a teacher at the Faculty of Education, University of Cambridge. Inspiring, challenging and enriching, the PGCE course set me on a trajectory that emphasised the need for reflection beyond examining my practice, and instead to 'find ways of looking at the learning experience from different perspectives, engaging in the messy frustrating and rewarding "clay" of learning' (Barth, 1990, p. 49). I subsequently completed two Master's degrees with the intention of challenging my own thinking, and to help me consider what my core moral purpose was (and what it could become). The 'dance', as it were, between the theoretical positioning inspired by the degree courses and my own practice, built in me an emerging choreography that defined my view of learning, the principles that guided each professional movement and the educational performance that I thought valuable to rehearse. From this personal positioning, the governors, Faculty academics and I evolved our hopes and aspirations for the new school.

Our vision emanated from educational theorists who attempted to answer the questions about the purpose of a democratic education. It grew organically from discussions, presentations and related to research. Maxine Greene's work resonated especially, bringing to light the responsibility of educators to find ways to *re-position perspectives* through an active engagement with open-space-making. *Releasing the Imagination* (Greene, 2000) most closely resonated with my thinking. In this book, Greene advocates that teachers model the provocation to learners to pose their own questions and 'name their worlds' (Greene, 2000, p. 58). Her words were about inclusion, asking big questions, considering alternatives, developing a mindset to release the possibilities inherent in the human imagination – to improve each child's opportunities to enjoy a happy, connected, choice-rich and contributing human life. Her emancipatory vision of education related to and informed our focus on pupil voice, diverse life experiences and the influence of school structures on children's educational experiences. This thinking related closely to the academic work from the Faculty of Education, especially Rudduck and McIntyre (2007) on pupil voice and agency, and the various contributors to the *Cambridge Primary Review*. Greene's (2000, p. 58) call for 'teachers themselves to maintain an open and interpretative approach', and for reality to be understood as *interpreted* experience, with multiple perspectives and interpretations within a given context, validated my concerns and sense of purpose to find different ways through for children.

Our final vision statement expresses our commitment to exemplary teaching and learning for children. We aim to be creative, bold, free-thinking and rigorous. Our decisions are underpinned by a commitment to the values of excellence, equity and learner empowerment. All this is linked with the theories of Maxine Greene, Paulo Friere and John Dewey, who emphasised equality and humanistic educational approaches that considered a holistic experience as a key principle of a good education. We explained to UCPS parents our intention to put into practice what matters to children, within an innovative professional learning community for teachers. In seeking to provide outstanding education for the children, the school would always engage and partner with neighbouring primary schools, in the spirit of collaboration and community.

We defined our aims founded on three pillars of *ambition, innovation* and *inclusion*:

Ambition: everyone will be encouraged and enabled to achieve and attain highly;

Innovation: the learning community will benefit from belonging to a research and teacher education community both within the school itself and as part of wider university and school partnerships;

Inclusion: diversity will be welcomed in a caring environment where everybody will be valued.

Our school logo demonstrated the three pillars as a tangible expression of the vision. The use of the university lion (from the university emblem) represented ambition; the shield design linked with the North West Cambridge Development (NWCD) brand, thereby suggesting innovation, sustainability and contemporary design; and the colourful palette referred to inclusion and diversity. As one of the first adaptations of the university emblem, we felt proud about what our new logo would mean for the children and their families in our new community.

Figure 1: The new UCPS logo

Essentially, within a democratic education, we want to teach children that learning is not a competition. Instead, we want to inspire everyone to strive and learn from mistakes. We intend to foster our three principles of ambition, innovation and inclusion through a culture in which empathy, respect, trust, courage and gratitude are explicitly and implicitly taught within a democratic community. We want every voice to be valued and everyone empowered to be the best that he or she can be. Our view of democracy translates into the importance of collaboration – together, everyone achieves more. Beneath our three aims, we developed five virtues or values that would guide our policies and approach to teaching and learning, behaviour management and various other practical matters. We considered our values as vital to ensure that learning and limitless possibilities become a truth for our children and teachers. Within a culture of developing ideas, we identified the following values, unpacking each with more detail:

Empathy: listening carefully to others, learning together for the benefit of all;

Respect: treating everyone with dignity;

Trust: building relationships with a shared vision;

Courage: developing resilience, determination and releasing the imagination to develop possibility-thinking attitudes;

Gratitude: acknowledging one another with good manners, with thoughtfulness and consideration for each member of our community, and the contribution they make.

Central to all this is our commitment to listening to children, encouraging dialogue and debate, and finding opportunities for every voice to be heard.

PRACTISING OUR VISION: SPEAKING OUR LANGUAGE

In this section, I share the ways in which we tried to articulate the vision in tangible ways that began making it a reality. I commence with a note from my journal that identifies the challenges I perceived in living the vision with the new team that was for the first time coming together:

> Day One: at my kitchen table – woke up early. Our new team arrives. I've called the professional development day a 'Meeting of Minds'. The slides ask what our hopes are for the children in our school (even though we haven't yet met them!). How do we create a brilliant primary school together? The vision is written. I've spoken it numerous times to parents who will be bringing their children to our school. How it is 'lived' depends on the meeting of our minds today and I leave for school in a few minutes with some apprehension and creative anxiety. Today we enjoy the process of extending the vision from paper, to breath, to action, to voice to song ... (Reflection from my headteacher's journal, September, 2015)

Figure 2 sets the agenda for our visioning day. It was our *practising of the theory* that underpinned the vision and ethos of the school. How would we construct a staff professional development session that would model the principles described within our vision statement? How would we translate them to form a new shared language? The aims of the session were presented as:

- To establish and explore our ethos and vision; to define and share an ambitious, inclusive and innovative attitude to our work;

- To build a positive and trusting team; establishing relationships;

- To begin our journey to excellence with a memorable and stimulating creative, challenging and connecting professional learning opportunity.

Figure 2: An Agenda for the 'Meeting of Minds'.

Agenda of the first day of visioning	Purpose
'Open to being alive in learning' – Building community (1) Line Games Line up in alphabetical order of surname Line up in reverse alphabetical order of most recent country visited Line up in alphabetical order, without talking, according to hobby (miming) Organising Games Get into groups of favourite animal (without talking) Get into groups of favourite food Circle Game (Names, actions, memorised dance) 'Release your voice' Vocal warm up – echo vocalisations, sirening/conversation in pairs, parachute 'leader' game Quick song – 'I don't know what you came to do' – turn-taking	Welcome; share aims; a day full of creativity, challenge and opportunities to connect.
Reflective Moment (1) Talk with partner about what just happened. How does it relate to our thinking about education? What does it mean for you? How would we document this to show evidence of progress, mastery of thinking, learning? Write a reflective note to self in your research journal.	Building a sense of the value of reflection; resilience; open-mindedness;, developing relationships; expressing ideas.
'Open to being alive in learning' – Building community (2) What is community? Decide what attributes of a community allow it to function effectively? Focus on positives. Define these and share back to wider group (write on flip chart/post-it notes) Who is in our community? Roles: floor cards. In pairs – find a floor card that has quotes and inspiring educational theoretical text – which makes you both think. Discuss what the floor card means for you in relation to the roles and responsibilities that people have in our school. Move two or three times to different cards. In larger groups, look at the roles in school and discuss what is expected from each person's role. Write three or four expectations on post-it notes and add to the role 'people cutouts' on the walls. Roles: Headteacher, Senior Leader, Teacher, Teaching Assistant, Admin Assistant, Site Manager Reflective moment (2) What evidence is there that people have been thinking, learning from one another, mastery of skills/thinking differently, etc?	Building a shared understanding; co-constructing the vision; demonstrating democratic notions of education; understanding roles and responsibilities as interconnected. Co-construct the meaning of the vision statement.

Continued over page

'Open to being alive in learning' – Building community (3) Meditation and Mindful Breathing Read aloud 'Basic Lists of Feelings and Needs' (taken from Non Violent Communication by Marshall Rosenberg, https://www.cnvc.org) Have we all experienced the feelings and expressed/understood the needs? Feelings tell us about our needs, so we can make achievable requests to make things better. Feelings and Needs Blues: Jane teaches chorus, then in groups, complete a verse each on song handout. All share and sing each other's verses. Everyone involved in writing and being involved – how is every voice heard?	Developing a mindful approach to problem solving; feeling the challenge of learning out of one's comfort zone; connecting and building community through the arts.
'Open to being alive in learning' – Building community (4) Song Writing How do we demonstrate the 'release of imagination'? How will teachers and other staff respond to the risks of singing and creative song writing (possibly the first time for many?)	Connecting and building community through the arts; Provide challenging learning experience for all staff.
Evaluation and reflective moment feedback (James to create form) How do we encourage reflexivity in our practice?	

We began with the normal ice-breaking games that gave an opportunity for colleagues to meet, ask questions, find out about one another and laugh. We asked questions about our aspirations for our children: what would a UCPS child be like when they leave us? Figure 3 documents our initial thoughts; it was a useful exercise to bring to view the centrality of children in our decision-making.

Figure 3: A vision for our children

Creative	Open-minded	Reflective
Happy	Tolerant and interested in other ways of living and thinking	Resilient
Polite and respectful		Community-driven
Kind and supportive	Hard working	Reaching their potential
Independent	Friendship makers	Inspired by the world around them
Questioning	Contributors	Determined
Learning about effort	Mastering concepts	Innovative
Excited	Asking for more	Problem-solvers
With good knowledge that can be applied	Self-regulators	Solution-focused people

The vision for our children would guide us as we came to the practicalities of running the school. Looking at the list of expectations, we asked: How would we design learning experiences so that we would also develop their open-mindedness or sense of community? How would our interactions with our children and their families evidence our solution-focused attitude, and signal that we too were excited about learning? How else would children believe that these aspects were important and valued? How would children describe what they would be like as they prepared to leave for secondary school?

Each staff member was given a journal, and was invited to record and document their journey during our school's first year (for the purpose of journals, see Gray & Malins, 2004; Etherington, 2004). We hoped that this would start a process of reflexivity, build discussion of our experiences and acknowledge the importance that we placed on being mindful, the development of the resilient attitudes that are so necessary in starting a school – and in being creative. I asked each staff member to write a letter from their future self (a year on) to their current self, giving advice and offering suggestions about the process of realising our vision for children at the UCPS. One of our teachers wrote the following:

August 2016 (one year since I started at UCPS)

Dear Past Luke,

It's been a year. Wow! What a journey?! The school represents an opportunity to re-think school norms and through this lead others in doing so. We need to build on what is positive from our previous experiences, collective school cultures and knowledge, and transform what might be improved on.

A key question: have we made a learning situation that would deeply inspire others and is significantly different to the status quo? If not, perhaps an opportunity is being missed; how do we evolve and reconstruct without unnecessary judgment? Our core purpose and evaluation must be concerned with children – always at the centre of our practice. Whilst other influences may need to be attended to, our efforts have to lead to a direct and positive impact on the children under our roof and this will lead to our collective success. In the process of this, we must remember the 'right drivers' for system building and show in practice to others how these can work.

Yours with kindness,

Future Luke

(Letter to self, written by Luke Rolls, class teacher and member of leadership team)

In this example, Luke talks of the 'collective' and of community, the need for systems, our responsibility to direct positive impact and the deep inspiration needed from teachers to be able to inspire the children in their care. In this letter, he identifies the kind of teacher whom he wants to be, and how this would contribute to the realisation of our vision for our children and essentially also for our teachers and staff members. The circular building and architectural principles of the school grounded the vision in a physical space, but Luke's words bring to view the centrality of relationships that were bound by a vision (or route map), and committed to overcoming the challenges together.

Suzi Bray and I built other opportunities to be creative, working in unusual ways with a new team and using the arts as a valuable approach to interconnect and communicate. We also planned the session to include opportunities for the whole team, administrators, site manager, finance personnel, teaching assistants and teachers, to try to experience the type of learning described in the vision for the children. We believed that everyone in our community had a part to play in the educational experience of the children and that to live the vision we had to explore together and define ourselves *in relation to* the vision. It had to be co-constructed.

A professional colleague of mine who shared our passion, Jane Wheeler, co-led the day with us. She is an outstanding internationally renowned music leader.[2] On reflection, this was a key decision because in having an external workshop leader, our assistant headteacher and I were able to be fully involved as co-participators: an essential repositioning of ourselves as learners with the new team with whom we were co-creating. This approach related to Maxine Greene's (2000, p. 58) invitation for educators to collectively 'name their worlds' – we were naming our vision together.

In terms of our democratic view of education, by joining in and also being out of our comfort zones we too were demonstrating the risks, challenges, potentials and opportunities for learning. During the course of the day, the whole staff team wrote a song to bring together our ideas and creatively articulate our vision that was increasingly shared, and now sung! Figure 4 presents our co-written lyrics:

Figure 4: *Release the Imagination*, co-written by the inaugural staff team of UCPS

RELEASE THE IMAGINATION

VERSE 1

Every child has a voice

Every bird has a song

Everyone has a choice to help someone belong

Fly like a skylark reaching for the sky,

Here there are no limits, we are learning how to fly.

CHORUS

Release the imagination

It's time to have some fun,

Engage with everyone.

Release the imagination

Don't let the world pass us by,

Spread our wings and fly.

VERSE 2

Celebrate creativity

Celebrate the things we learn

Celebrate community

Free to work as one.

Fierce like a phoenix rising from the fire,

Ignite the spark within us,

And we can travel far.

CHORUS

MIDDLE 8

Communicate – with each other.

Collaborate – all together

Celebrate – our life together.

Challenge yourself, challenge others, challenge the world.

Most of the staff had never been involved in such a creative music-making experience. Their feedback expressed the hopes, anxieties and potentials of the professional journey on which they had embarked:

> I think from today, I understand the vision as: everyone having a voice, being respected and valued, sharing the same goals ... I realised that this is the very beginning of my own learning journey with the school and how lucky I am. Being creative as we were today is essential to find ways through for every child.

> ... the most valuable part of the day was the way James and Jane created a space where we could come together and feel comfortable. We all want so much from this school. It has to be about the children – whatever has to show them ways through.

> I think writing the song together made us all feel extremely valuable for it gave us a chance to work together – equal, not the headteacher telling us, but together – we are all in it as responsible as the next person in our team.
>
> (Three extracts from three teaching assistants
> following our professional learning day.)

Remembering the view that our *language is our practice*, in these examples we begin to hear the vision re-articulated. As individuals grappled with their own definitions, in relation to their own personal and professional journeying, the shifts, adaptations and the changes needed in their own practice were considered and reflected upon. 'Finding ways through for every child' was a sentence that became a leitmotif for our staffroom discussions. Was this a naïve idea? What was our purpose for education? What were our hopes for our children? For all our children? For all our staff? For all our community?

DEVELOPING PROFESSIONAL TRUST: THEORISING PRACTICE, PRACTISING THEORY ... IN PRACTICE

What we also hoped for in the first few days was to empower our staff team with professional trust. During one conversation with the staff, I explained a moment during the ground-breaking ceremony when the Vice Chancellor dug the first hole on our school site. In his speech, he reiterated the university's commitment to excellence, turning to me and saying, 'Mr Biddulph, that is what we expect from our primary school, a place of excellence'. I joked with staff how I went pale and clammy at the realisation of these high expectations for our (and the university's) new school – and me as its headteacher. Whilst the pressure is ever-present, I felt (and remain) committed to developing my own leadership so that the expectations of the outstanding university also become our expectations for our youngest scholars. As Alison Peacock explained in chapter 4, the challenge for all schools is to meet the expectations of high-stakes accountability frameworks (such as Ofsted Inspections and standardised assessment tests / SATs), and yet hold onto the sense of innovation and autonomy given to schools through the decentralisation of the education system. How would we develop systems and a culture of ideas so that everyone was trusted to be brilliant? How would staff know that my challenge and support, a key aspect of my role and responsibilities, was about raising the quality for all children and staff? How would monitoring of the school's work be conducted with professional trust at its core?

We started by working collaboratively with all staff to give ownership and responsibility for evolving the vision into the principled practice that we expected. My own Master's and Doctoral studies looked to the co-construction of meaning. My own teaching practice intended to bring children on a journey of discovery with me, with creativity and knowledge acquisition as commensurate and not opposite. I resisted defining everything that we would do in the school. I worked with the teachers in developing the curriculum, but saw my role as to question and mirror what they were designing and saying rather than giving ideas. I delegated responsibility to other staff to create processes and documents to facilitate the smooth functioning of the school. My assistant headteacher, Suzi Bray, problematised the tricky balance of being a school leader:

> It's the first day of school today and although tired, I'm excited and hopeful for the day. I can hear the teachers in their classrooms and need to stop checking in on them! If I do, perhaps they will think I am 'checking up on them'. I want to be there to support them, to find ways to help, but helping too much suggests that they need it. That I don't trust in their ability to find their own solutions. (Reflections from Suzi Bray, assistant headteacher after the first week of opening)

Where I focused my attention was on defining and redefining, articulating and re-articulating the principles upon which all our decisions ought to be made. For example, in writing the UCPS's teaching and learning policy, we suggested that effective learning would relate to our values and express our view of high quality teaching. A section of the policy reads:

Characteristics of Effective Learning, as related to our Values, are:

Empathic: Everyone thinks about the learning experience of everyone else in the school community;

Respectful: Pupils demonstrate a respect for the acquisition of new knowledge, developing understanding or practising skills. They respect the role of the adults and others in teaching them and supporting their learning. All adults respect the voice of the children in our care;

Trusting: Children acknowledge to the teacher and peers when learning is a challenge or struggle and seek support/guidance. Staff create a trusting culture conducive to learning. Everyone will show commitment to learn – children are encouraged to always try their best, expect a lot from themselves and strive to improve the quality of their outcomes;

Courageous: Responding to challenge with resilience, creativity and courage;

Grateful: Listen carefully, demonstrate good manners and think about others.

High-quality teaching is based on:

- Knowing every child well and understanding their needs;
- Encouraging every child to contribute and empowering children to lead their own learning (e.g. through a self-regulating environment);
- Irresistible planned learning with excellent subject/skills knowledge; made meaningful through cross-curricular links;
- Teaching of oracy through dialogue & questioning;
- Exciting learning tasks that engage positive behavior;
- Focused and meaningful evaluation and assessment;
- A culture where everyone is expected to learn more, learn better and are ambitious for themselves and everyone else in the school community.

(Extract from the UCPS Teaching and Learning Policy, 2015)

This was one way to enact our vision. However, the question arose again and again: How we would live by our vision and values? It was through our dialogue that we captured the essence and evolved our understanding through a co-constructed process. I wanted to emphasise the 'co-' aspect in defining what we wanted. I tried to tell stories to express my version of the vision. In the following example, told to me by a Hindu Monk, I described the interconnected nature of our work – to show how everyone's role was essential in inspiring the very best learning for all our children. It was our collective responsibility:

There was once a young man walking in the countryside. As he walked he came across a quarry where three people were sitting, hard at work.

'Excuse me sir,' said the young man, 'can you explain what it is you are doing here on this sunny day?'

'Can you not see BOY!? It is obvious. I am cracking large stones into smaller stones and it is very hard and I have no time to speak with you ... be gone!'

The young man did not dither and moved to the next person.

'Excuse me madam, but why are you so hot and tired? What is it that you are doing?' he asked cautiously.

'Don't waste my time you lazy young man. I am too busy bashing rocks. I will bash your head if you don't leave me be,' she shouted, red-faced and dusty.

In the far corner there was a very old wizened man. The young man walked to see him.

'And you sir, what are you doing?'

'Argh ... can you not see?' spoke the man with a gleeful smile on his wrinkled face.

'You are bashing rocks? You are cracking stones?' the young man answered.

'Argh, foolish boy. My hands may be red and raw, but I am not bashing rocks. Can you not see that every stone and rock that I craft from the larger stones and rocks are much more than what you can see? I am building a cathedral, can you not see?'

And the young man saw at once that with every tired crack and weakened blow, the man smiled longer and wider for he knew that he was contributing to something more wonderful than he could at first see ... he was building a cathedral.

(Retold from a story told to me by Sacinandana Swami, 2013)

And we were building a school. The vision was becoming a shared one. In the dark moments during the dark month of January, I hoped that our story-telling would guide us to see the cathedral that we were trying to craft! There are so many schools that want something similar for their children and staff. We believed in our potential to become one of the contributors to a self-improving system, like Dame Alison Peacock, who has led an outstanding primary school with principles anchoring her team's practice to the core. We were in the exciting position, however, of starting with a blank canvas.

RELEASING THE IMAGINATION: CELEBRATING THE ART OF THE POSSIBLE

To close this chapter, I return again to Maxine Greene. Her work represents my own personal and professional sojourn in the realms of theory. This so-journ was not ivory-tower theorising but always something rooted in my own experiences. As the headteacher of our school, I hope to demonstrate the relationship that exists between theory and practice – that our school would be a place of practising theory and, with the Faculty of Education, theorising practice. In many ways, reading Greene's work and the theories of Dewey (1934), Freire (1996) and Krishnamurthi (1981) was a process of releasing my own imagination. My professional experiences have been ac-companied by a personal compulsion and desire to find out, enquire and build my own understanding of my and our practice. Our school hopes to reposition teachers as teacher-researchers; to wed the relationship between research, theory, ethics and practice; to bind this way of thinking about the processes of teaching and learning through an understanding of what we do, why we do it and how we improve our work; to foreground assumptions about education, being educated and living educational lives.

What does this strapline, *Releasing the Imagination: Celebrating the Art of the Possible*, really mean? In nine words it attempts to capture an aspir-ational vision for education. My own interest in understanding children's perspectives and their lived situations and experiences related to a view that teaching and learning 'are matters of breaking through barriers – of expectation, of boredom, of predefinition' (Greene, 2000, p. 14). Like Dewey and Greene, I saw that there were no guarantees in education but instead numerous openings and possibilities. The 'releasing' was as much about teachers' professionalism and learning as it was about children's, and in relation to 'imagination': 'to learn and to teach, one must have aware-ness of leaving something behind while reaching toward something new, and this kind of awareness must be linked to imagination' (Greene, 2000, p. 20). The potentials of opening a new school required, in our view, deep reflection about the purpose of education and the language that we use to develop it for and with the children in our care. It required imaginative teachers, because 'teachers incapable of thinking imaginatively … are unable to communicate to the young what the use of imagination signifies' (Greene, 2000, p. 36) – a sense of awe and wonder, values, relationships, spiritual growth, community and learning to name one's world and one's individual contribution to it.

Releasing the Imagination is about openings and possibilities. We want our researching teachers to be inspired, to live educational lives, to be imaginative, innovative and courageous. We trust in their professionalism. We trust that they will galvanise their children to become brilliant learners, who themselves are imaginative, innovative and courageous. *Celebrating the Art of the Possible* is much more complex to define, except that we will celebrate the ideas that collectively and individually arise; we will craft the way that we teach and learn in partnership with children and families; we will capture how our staff make it possible for each child. In the end our vision is about commitment to the betterment of society; it holds a naïve and yet powerful view that education, the business of teaching and learning, can change the world. We aspire to this, knowing that the journey is long, arduous, terrifying and risky … and worth every step for every child who walks through our wide-open doors.

Thanks are extended to Suzi Bray (assistant headteacher) and Luke Rolls (class teacher and member of leadership team) for allowing inclusion of their personal reflections. Thanks also to the whole inaugural staff team who created our wonderful song; their words are shared with permission. Thanks to Jane Wheeler, who inspired us to release our voices.

Notes

1 See chapter 1, note 5.
2 Jane Wheeler is the director of Living Song; http://www.livingsong.co.uk.

References

Alexander, R. (ed.) (2010). *Children, Their World, Their Education: Final Report and Recommendations of the Cambridge Primary Review* (London: Routledge).

Barth, R.S. (1990). *Improving Schools from Within: Teachers, Parents and Principals can make a Difference* (San Francisco: Jossey-Bass).

Biesta, L (2006). *Beyond Learning: Democratic Education for a Human Future* (Colorado: Paradigm).

Burnard, P., Apelgren, B. & Cabaroglu (eds) (2015). *Transformative Teacher Research: Theory and Practice for the C21st* (Rotterdam: Sense Publishers).

Cantle, T. (2012). *Interculturalism: The New Era of Cohesion and Diversity* (Hampshire: Palgrave Macmillan).

Day, C. (2004). *A Passion for Teaching* (Oxford: RoutledgeFalmer).

Dewey, J. (1934). *Art as Experience* (New York: Penguin).

Etherington, K. (2004). *Becoming a Reflexive Researcher* (London: Jessica Kingsley).

Freire, P. (1996). *Pedagogy of the Oppressed* (Harmondsworth: Penguin).

Gray, C. & Malins, J. (2004). *Visualising Research: A guide to the Research Process in Art and Design* (London: Ashgate).

Greene, M. (2000). *Releasing the Imagination: Essays on Education, the Arts and Social Change* (San Francisco: Jossey-Bass).

Hart, S., Drummond, M.J., Dixon, A. & McIntyre, D. (2004). *Learning without Limits* (Maidenhead: Open University Press).

Krishnamurthi, J. (1981). *Education and the Significance of Life* (New York: Harper One).

Novak, J., Armstrong, D. & Browne, B. (2014). *Leading for Educational Lives: Inviting and Sustaining Imaginative Acts of Hope in a Connected World* (Rotterdam: Sense Publishers).

Rudduck, J. & McIntyre, D. (2007). *Improving Learning through Consulting Pupils* (Oxford: Routledge).

Swann, M., Peacock, A., Hart, S. & Drummond, M.J. (2012). *Creating Learning without Limits* (Maidenhead: McGraw-Hill International).

6 Ensuring developmentally appropriate practice in the early years of primary schooling

David Whitebread and Penny Coltman

Part of the core provision of the University of Cambridge Primary School (UCPS) will be a 78-place nursery, catering for three- to four-year olds, and three reception classes for four- to five-year olds. Currently in the UK these two years are designated as the Early Years Foundation Stage (EYFS), while the first two years of compulsory schooling, Year 1 and Year 2, are designated as Key Stage 1. A seamless integration of the EYFS and Key Stage 1 is desirable for a number of evidence-based developmental reasons, and was the case in the recent past, but this is not the norm at the present time in English education. In particular in current English provision there is a clear disjunction between pedagogical approaches in these two phases. While much EYFS provision is appropriately play-based, the norm in Year 1 provision is a diet of much more formal, seat-based instruction.

In contrast, within the UCPS, a play-based pedagogical approach will be extended into Key Stage 1. This approach was central to the original bid for the school to the Department for Education (DfE) and is being adopted in light of overwhelming evidence, both from the UK and from international studies, of the benefits of an extended period of play-based experience for young children. Studies have demonstrated significant positive outcomes in relation to both academic achievement and emotional well-being. In this respect, the UCPS expects to be at the leading edge of international best practice. But as ever, in a climate of high-stakes accountability (see chapters 4 and 5), the school leaders will need to balance their own courage with the realities and practicalities of external diktat and scrutiny.

This chapter reviews the evidence from developmental and longitudinal studies concerning the long-term benefits of high-quality early years provision and the critical role of playful learning approaches within that. It begins with a review of the move towards high-quality early childhood education (ECE) internationally, and the evidence that is driving this. This is followed by a review of the growing evidence of the relationships between early play experiences and aspects of development which are established predictors of enhanced achievement and well-being, and of the environmental contexts that support these aspects of high-quality ECE provision. Within the chapter, contributions of the UCPS staff are presented, together with some early examples of projects and aspects of practice illustrating fundamental principles embodied in their vision.

EARLY CHILDHOOD EDUCATION: GLOBAL PERSPECTIVES

The provision of ECE across the world is currently in a period of rapid growth and development. The combination of historical, educational, economic and political forces playing into the dynamics of this situation is complex and needs to be understood in order to be clear as to where English practice is located in the development of ECE provision globally, and in which direction we believe it needs to be headed.

Historically, ECE provision has been deeply influenced by a range of nineteenth- and early twentieth-century European thinkers and educationalists, including the Austrian Rudolph Steiner, the Italian Maria Montessori and the Briton Susan Isaacs to name only a few. Their influence is present today across the world. While their approaches appear superficially to have quite different emphases, there are certain common elements which underpin their success and ongoing influence. These include the role of early education in supporting children's natural development rather than in providing instruction, an emphasis on play, which Isaacs described as the 'child's work', and an essentially child-centred approach emphasising careful observation of children to guide appropriate provision. Both Steiner and Isaacs also took the view that over-formal schooling before the age of seven would be damaging.

Most fundamentally, these thinkers were driven by the belief that a child's early experiences have a profound influence on their development and later life, and this belief has been supported by recent educational research, which has formed the second major influence on the current situation. Following on from the original Perry Preschool Project (Schweinhart, 1993), there have been numerous further studies in the US (Campbell et al.,

2002) and many other countries which have shown that high-quality ECE programs contribute to long-term academic, emotional and social benefits, particularly for children from low socio-economic backgrounds. A key finding here, however, is that the quality of ECE provision is crucial, with low-quality provision being demonstrably associated with language, social and developmental problems (OECD, 2001, 2006). Research by economists has further supported this position by demonstrating the many long-term economic benefits of investment in ECE (Heckman, 2006, 2011; Heckman et al., 2013).

At the level of public policy and political discourse, however, the picture has been much more mixed, particularly in recent decades. On the one hand, alongside the developing educational and economic research demonstrating the impact of high quality ECE, the United Nations has worked to establish internationally agreed-upon goals for the provision of high-quality ECE, and numerous reports have attempted to delineate the essential ingredients that define 'high quality' (OECD, 2012; Whitebread et al., 2015b). During the same period, however, within a number of developed countries, including the UK, Australia and the USA, many of these essential tenets have been increasingly challenged, and formal, direct instruction has been introduced into the curriculum for increasingly younger children.

KEY ELEMENTS IN EARLY LEARNING AND DEVELOPMENT: PLAY, ORAL LANGUAGE AND SELF-REGULATION

These current 'earlier is better' policies, which are advocated and adopted in the face of the evidence to the contrary by many governments, make it particularly important to restate the growing evidential base supporting informal, play-based approaches in ECE up to the age of seven years (i.e., up to the end of Key Stage 1 in UK primary schools). It also makes it particularly important that the UCPS demonstrates how this might be achieved practically, and that it is demonstrably more effective in terms of child outcomes.

In the context of this primary school the recommendations of the *Cambridge Primary Review* (Alexander, 2010), the most comprehensive independent enquiry into the condition and future of primary education in England for over 40 years, have underpinned many of the central tenets of the UCPS. The *Review* was emphatic in its support of the extension of play-based pedagogical practices of the EYFS at least until the age of six.

Although in terms of national policy this endorsement has regrettably not been adopted, within the UCPS there is a determination to extend active play-based learning throughout Key Stage 1 and indeed to retain many elements of this throughout the primary age range.

In relation to the advocacy of a later start to formal instruction as the dominant mode of educational provision, there are two interrelated issues corresponding to two bodies of evidence which inform this debate. These are concerned with the contribution of playful experiences to children's development as learners, and the consequences of starting formal learning at ages four to five. As regards the first, there are several strands of evidence that all point towards the importance of play in young children's development, and the value of an extended period of playful learning before the start of formal schooling. These arise from anthropological, psychological, neuroscientific and educational studies. A range of anthropological studies of children's play in extant hunter-gatherer societies (Gray, 2009) and evolutionary psychology studies of play in the young of other mammalian species (Smith, 2006) have identified play as an adaptation strategy which evolved in early human social groups and enabled humans to become powerful learners and problem-solvers. Neuroscientific studies have supported this view of play as a central mechanism in learning. Pellis and Pellis (2009), for example, have reviewed many studies showing that playful activity leads to synaptic growth, particularly in the frontal cortex, that part of the brain responsible for all the uniquely human higher mental functions. A range of experimental psychology studies has also consistently demonstrated the superior learning and motivation arising from playful as opposed to instructional approaches to learning in children (Sylva et al., 1976; Pellegrino & Gustafson, 2005; Whitebread & Jameson, 2010). Within educational research, a longitudinal study by Marcon (2002) demonstrated that, by the end of their sixth year in school, children whose pre-school model had been academically-directed achieved significantly lower marks in comparison to children who had attended child-initiated, play-based pre-school programmes.

Work in developmental psychology has identified two crucial processes which underpin this relationship and which give clear guidance to ECE professionals as to the outcomes from children's play that they can beneficially support. Playful activity has been shown to support children's early development of symbolic representational skills fundamental to the range of semiotic systems through which humans represent meaning. Christie and Roskos (2006), for example, have reviewed evidence that a playful approach to language learning, as opposed to formal instruction, offers the most powerful support for the early development of phonological and literacy skills.

To effectively embed a playful approach to learning at the UCPS, there is a commitment amongst staff to model playfulness themselves. Headteacher James Biddulph comments:

> I model playfulness with staff. We dress up and become involved in engaging children in the memorable laughable moments. I model that I don't know all things but am excited to playfully find out. I try to excite teachers to find playfulness in their own professional learning.

Play is seen as an essential priority in providing contexts for learning in the foundation stage, with children spending the greater part of each day directing their own lines of enquiry and exploration. An overarching topic or theme is introduced each term, but the aim is for children's playful learning experiences to encompass a wide variety of lines of development. The key phrase is that 'anything is possible'. The structure of the Reception class day is designed to embrace engagement with this activity by both teachers and teaching assistants. Children's ideas for playful learning are first discussed with them to access ideas about what they would like to do and achieve during their play. PLODs (activities to facilitate 'possible lines of development') are constructed from the children's interests and ideas so that learning experiences are more purposeful, relevant and motivational. Focused learning times are minimal, comprising a short reading session first thing in the morning, a mid-morning group activity which encourages children to work collaboratively, and a brief mathematics session after lunch. Snack time is a free-flow event so that children's immersion in their play is uninterrupted.

Early years principles of play evolve as children progress through the school. The search for age-appropriate play experiences to enhance learning continues to be a learning curve. Allowing children to plan their learning and lead their play has opened doors for teacher creativity and child engagement. Indoor opportunities for children to extend their learning through self-directed play in Key Stage 1 are largely accommodated within the spacious 'learning street', an open area shared between the classes. As children progress through the year groups, some playful activities become more active, experiential learning opportunities, which may be structured or may, for example, involve carousels of activities or the accommodation of children in pursuing specific aspects of learning in their own playful ways. An example of this is the incorporation of free-style mathematics in which children explore the manipulation of numbers. In the illustration shown in Figure 1, it can be seen that children have explored number facts and patterns, representing their ideas through both numeric and iconic symbols. In this instance, children are taking ownership of their learning in an essentially playful manner, setting their own goals and targets as they enjoy exploring mathematical ideas.

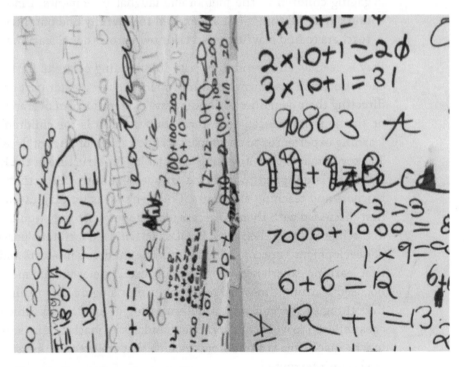

Figure 1: Free-style mathematics Year 2

Within the context of literacy, the school has been working in collaboration with the Faculty of Education's Play, Learning and Narrative Skills (PLaNS) project, which has developed and evaluated an innovative approach to teaching narrative and writing skills in primary education through guided play. This approach gives children control over their learning process in a fun, hands-on and engaging way, while providing the necessary instructional support through the design of activities and explicit learning objectives. This project, directed by Dr David Whitebread (Principal Investigator) with Dr Marisol Basilio (Research Associate), was funded by the LEGO foundation (Whitebread, et al., 2015a).

Figure 2: Collaboratively building a scene with LEGO™, which will later be used to support writing

A strong feature of playful learning in Years 1 and 2 is roleplay. In Year 1 a roleplay shop is a longstanding feature of the learning street and offers children opportunities for playful experience of handling money in 'real' interactions. Year 2 teacher Luke Rolls here describes a roleplay activity which emerged from a class discussion about zoos:

> Children have an input over the direction of learning within a topic. There is an effort to co-construct with the class what might happen next as a way to move forward. In recent learning about zoos, after having explored some different arguments for and against, the class decided they would like to stage a protest where some were animal rights campaigners, some were police and some were zookeepers. All parties were given time and challenged through dialogue to develop their materials and be prepared for the protest. The next day, police officers had bought in some costumes, hats and badges, the campaigners had produced protest signs and banners and the zookeepers had rehearsed their arguments for why their environment was actually a great place for the animals. It was then time for the protest to occur and children acted completely in role and spoke passionately for their purpose.

Figure 3: Children in role as they explore aspects of animal rights

Through all kinds of physical, constructional and social play, children develop their skills of intellectual and emotional self-regulation; that is, they learn to be aware of and control their own physical, mental and behavioural activity (Whitebread et al., 2005, 2007; Whitebread, 2010). A growing number of empirical educational studies suggest that early play experiences enhance young children's self-regulation (Ponitz et al., 2009; Hyson et al., 2006), and that educational interventions supporting children's self-regulation are the most effective in supporting children's development as learners (Wang et al., 1990; Hattie, 2009).

The second strand of evidence concerns studies directly addressing the length of time that children spend in pre-school, play-based educational settings, and the age at which they start formal schooling. Three exemplar studies illustrate the findings of this body of research. First, a longitudinal study of 3 000 children funded by the DfE itself, Sylva et al. (2004) showed that an extended period of high-quality, play-based pre-school education made a significant difference to academic learning and wellbeing throughout the primary school years.

Second, studies by Suggate and colleagues (Suggate, 2007; Suggate et al., 2012) have compared groups of children in New Zealand who started formal literacy lessons at ages five and seven. Their results show that the early introduction of formal learning approaches to literacy does not improve children's reading development and may be damaging. By the age of 11 there was no difference in the level of reading ability between the two groups, but the children who started at five developed less positive attitudes to reading and showed poorer text comprehension than those children who had started later. Third, in a separate study of the relative reading achievement of 15-year old students across 55 countries (Suggate, 2009), analysed as a function of school entry age, no significant association between reading achievement and school entry age was found.

This evidence, directly addressing the consequences of the introduction of early formal schooling, combined with the evidence on the positive impact of extended playful experiences, raises important and serious questions concerning the direction of travel of Early Childhood Education (ECE) policy currently in the UK and elsewhere. There is an equally substantial body of evidence, which there is not space to address here, concerning the worrying increase in stress and mental health problems among children in England and other countries where ECE is being 'schoolified' (Gray, 2011), and which suggests strong links with the loss of playful experiences and increased achievement pressures.

ENVIRONMENTAL CONTEXTS THAT SUPPORT HIGH-QUALITY EARLY CHILDHOOD EDUCATION PROVISION

There is also a range of evidence investigating the environmental contexts that support the development of children's playfulness, oral language and other representational abilities, and their development as self-regulating learners. Broadly, this research indicates the importance of an emotionally warm and positive social climate in the classroom, of high expectations and challenge, of support for children's sense of autonomy and competence, and of opportunities for metacognitive talk when emotional and cognitive mental processes are articulated and discussed.

Some studies have focused on specific areas of the classroom environment and others have examined the interplay of a variety of factors. In studies specifically examining the role of emotional warmth, for example, this factor has been found to be generally associated with children's persistence and positive emotional response to challenging tasks (Pino-Pasternak et al., 2010; Suchodoletz et al., 2011). Howe (2010) has provided an authoritative review of research on emotional and social aspects of learning, and has shown that children's social experiences in classrooms, particularly in relation to their experiences of friendships, have a very powerful effect on a range of academic and emotional outcomes. The evidence that she presents endorses the importance of teachers' support of the friendship skills of individuals, for example, particularly with overly aggressive or shy and anxious children. The other very clear message from this review is the crucial significance of structures and procedures within classrooms. The poor outcomes for social competencies and friendships arising in classrooms in which individual performance is emphasised, and in which children are grouped by ability, are contrasted with the positive social outcomes in classrooms where co-operation is emphasised and working on tasks collaboratively in mixed ability groups is a more common feature.

In a separate body of research, mostly focused on parenting, but equally applicable to the teacher–child relationship, styles of interaction have been investigated. This work has shown that 'authoritative' parenting, as opposed to 'authoritarian', 'permissive' or 'uninvolved' styles, leads to the most positive outcomes for the child (Baumrind, 1967; Maccoby & Martin, 1983). Authoritative parents are the most emotionally warm and affectionate towards their children. In addition, however, they also set clear and consistent standards for their children's behaviour and convey high expectations of their performance. At the same time they demonstrate clear respect for the child's developing need for autonomy and independence, and support the child's adherence to the standards and rules established through discussion and negotiation, explaining their reasoning rather than simply asserting their authority. This style has been shown to support children's developing self-efficacy and self-regulation and, hence, their success as learners. Authoritative parenting has also been found to be associated with a range of positive outcomes in relation to children's social competence. As children, they most easily make relationships with other children and adults, and are generally the most popular amongst their peers.

Support for autonomy has also attracted a considerable body of classroom-based research. Over-controlling interactions between parents and children have consistently been related to poor self-regulatory development (Stevenson & Crnic, 2012), while parental support for their children's autonomy has emerged in a number of studies as a key predictor of self-regulation and academic achievement (Mattanah et al., 2005; Pomerantz & Eaton, 2001). In research reporting successful interventions supporting self-regulation in the primary classroom, there is a strong emphasis on practices which promote a positive emotional climate, and support children's sense of autonomy and competence. For example, giving children opportunities for decision-making, setting their own challenges, assessing their own work, encouraging positive feelings towards challenging tasks, emphasising personal progress rather than social comparisons, and responding to and training children's helpless beliefs, have all been shown to be characteristic practices in classrooms promoting high levels of self-regulated learning (Meyer & Turner, 2002; Perry, 1998; Nolen, 2007). Implementing classroom activities in small groups has also been shown to encourage greater autonomy (Eurydice, 2009; Laevers, 2003). In line with this general pedagogical direction, consultation with children to elicit their perspectives and their active input in decision-making has been shown to increase their self-esteem and foster social competence (Broström, 2010; Clark et al., 2003; Sommer et al., 2010).

The examples of child-directed play given above illustrate an important aspect of the opportunities planned to allow children to make their own choices and decisions, but this is just one facet of an approach which respects children and encourages them to be active participants in their learning and members of their school community. Children are encouraged to become independent in all aspects of their school life: as thinkers, as learners, and in their daily routines. The UCPS values of empathy, respect, trust, courage and gratitude are at the heart of practice, and are considered to be a key part of developing key skills for self-regulation.

In the UCPS Reception class, the development of social and emotional aspects of self-regulation is a priority. Teacher Ashleigh Tutchener illustrates how she promotes this:

> I help my class to develop social and emotional self-regulation through modelling strategies and through questioning children in such a way that they resolve issues themselves. A lot of the time we also detach emotions from the children and imprint them onto a puppet or a toy. I have found this makes the children feel less intimidated and more motivated as they are discussing how something else is feeling rather than themselves. In response to the children's verbal contributions the puppet then portrays different feelings. The language used by the puppet then feeds into the children's vocabulary and supports their ability to express their emotions to others.

Year 1 teacher Charlotte Brereton describes her focus on the value of trust:

> I teach children that we can't see trust, or touch it, but it can increase or disappear due to our actions. For example, when the children were exploring aspects of measure they were trusted to go beyond the classroom to measure in the learning street or in the outdoor learning space, working independently.

In Year 2, approaches to motivational self-regulation continue to be developed. With the class, teacher Luke Rolls discusses protocols for 'What to do when you don't know what to do'. These prompts might include: 'Look at the board' (e.g. success criteria), or 'Talk to your learning buddy or use resources to help you'. In this way, children are enabled to develop as autonomous independent learners who are empowered to seek solutions without automatic recourse to an adult.

Finally, the role of metacognitive talk in enhancing children's self-regulatory abilities cannot be over-emphasised. This can be brought about in two main ways. The first is by requiring children to work together to solve problems in collaborative groups. Quite a body of work has now shown that, even with very young children, collaborative forms of learning, including groupwork and peer-tutoring, can enhance self-regulation in classroom situations (Brown 1997; Whitebread et al., 2007). The key ingredients here appear to be that the children are obliged to express their ideas, give reasons to support their opinions, attempt to come to an agreed approach, and reflect on the performance of the group in attempting the task. In this way the processes of learning are made visible (Whitebread et al., 2015c).

The second is metacognitive talk in teacher–child discourses. A series of studies within educational contexts reported by Ornstein et al. (2010) demonstrated that the amount of contingent metacognitive talk by teachers is a strong predictor of academic outcomes. Children taught by first-grade mathematics teachers who regularly made suggestions of memory strategies that the children could use, and asked metacognitive questions aimed at eliciting strategy knowledge from the children (such as: 'How could you help yourself to remember this?'), showed significantly improved strategy use and ability to remember relevant mathematical facts. These differences were not only present at the end of the first grade, but were still present at statistically significant levels three years later.

Setting the tone for the promotion of meaningful talk within the school, James Biddulph comments:

I try and develop opportunities for children to talk with me as their headteacher. I want to have a relationship through which children know they will be listened to deeply. They need to know that what they say has relevance and meaning for me as their headteacher, and realise that talk is about connection and community.

This view of the centrality of talk within a community dovetails together the importance of communication with the school's expressed values of respect and empathy, and establishes a rich context for the development of spoken language.

In the Reception class, children are empowered to voice opinions and to contribute meaningfully to decision-making wherever possible. Such contexts range from choosing activities and resources to deciding what to share and celebrate with their parents at an assembly. These are vital examples of developing agency in which even very young children are making real decisions about their learning.

In Year 1, children further develop the use of talk partners to share ideas and in turn develop questioning. Teacher Charlotte Brereton uses a number of 'talk for writing' techniques, blending the development of talk with aspects of literacy as well as cross-curricular themes such as personal and social education:

I like to use drama ideas such as 'conscience alley'. A character from a story known to the children wrestles with a difficult dilemma, perhaps a moral choice. What should be done? The rest of the class form a double line; a corridor along which the character must travel and at the end of which a decision must be taken. All through the journey along the alleyway the children in line whisper advice or warnings based on their knowledge of the story. An activity like this reveals a great deal about the children's understandings and interpretations of the narrative, involves a great deal of celebration of questioning and offers rich opportunities for modelling talk.

Systematic approaches across the curriculum continue to be adopted in Year 2 for the development of oracy. Luke Rolls explains:

In maths, dialogue is used as a fundamental tool for understanding, conjecturing, debating ideas and generalising. Number talks invite children to share their 'way' of seeing the maths and we compare different ideas and representations. In 'thinking lessons' children are first given a problem to solve in pairs without any lead/hints from the teacher.

They come back together as a class to share multiple solutions and representations. With some orchestration from the teacher, children are given the platform to debate their solutions between themselves. The elicited 'cognitive conflict' produces a lot of discussion and learning skills are developed alongside this. Subsequently children reflect on how well they cooperated together and the extent to which they were open-minded to others' views. We have just started to develop a time for free-style maths [see earlier example], where a number talk leads to children gathering and explaining their ideas and ways of knowing. I have found the idea of 'speaking frames' helpful. As children will work with their learning buddy they are encouraged to ask, for example, 'Do you agree that … ?'

LUNCHTIME AT THE UNIVERSITY OF CAMBRIDGE PRIMARY SCHOOL

A component of the school's day that brings many of these elements together is lunchtime. Unusually, no children bring packed lunches at the UCPS. This is in part facilitated by the government's funding of school meals up to the end of Year 2, but the intention is to continue this tradition as the school extends beyond these years.

The dining hall is furnished with large round tables, each of which comfortably seats eight children. Table plans are produced each term, which seat a mix of year groups at each table. Individual personalities are taken into account. In some cases, friends and siblings sit together, and in others children are actively encouraged to make new relationships. This arrangement encourages children throughout the school to become acquainted with each other, to learn names and to develop an awareness of, and take responsibility for, the needs of others. Even the youngest children are thus viewed by all as an integral and valued part of the school community. The success of this mixing of children has been welcomed by staff and the intention is to continue this model as the school grows.

Meals are served on china crockery to emulate familiar eating routines. As in any large and diverse community of children, there are a number with individual dietary requirements and so, in the interests of both safety and respect, adults serve the prime component of the main course to the children. Vegetables or other accompaniments are placed in dishes in the centre of the tables.

At this point the children take responsibility for their lunch. Older children help younger children to access or cut up their food, supported by adults who either sit with the children to eat or are at hand circulating around the dining room. Originally it was anticipated that the older children would take care of the younger ones, but over time a greater balance has emerged, with younger children helping to serve their older fellow diners and assisting each other in managing cutlery. Visitors to the school rarely need encouragement to stay to eat as the conversation with children is increasingly confident, courteous and enjoyable.

Figure 4: Lunchtime at the UCPS

As the main course finishes, children are responsible for taking their own plates to the serving hatch where they methodically deposit cutlery and food remains, and collect dessert. This part of the day is a favourite for many as it embodies the school as a cohesive family. James Biddulph comments:

Seeing children 'living' their lunch experience is great. They help one another. They check that they are leaving their space clean, to respect themselves and others. They show that they are learning about our values and trying to live them in their daily lives.

YOUNG CHILDREN LEARNING OUTDOORS AT THE UNIVERSITY OF CAMBRIDGE PRIMARY SCHOOL

More about the design of the outdoor environment integral to the school is reported elsewhere in this book. However, it was established at a very early stage in the planning of the school that the outdoor learning and teaching environment should be a seamless continuation of the indoor space in order to maximise the opportunities for children to engage in playful tasks that involve problem solving and creativity, thus supporting the development of self-regulation and metacognitive processes (Parker, 2015).

The aspiration for the outdoor environment is that it should invite exploration and evolution through the agency of children. Its construction is diverse, with features including undulations, small waterways, wooded areas, open spaces and shelters, and there is variety in the materials used for ground coverings and pathways. Thus, through time, an accommodating landscape will evolve within which children can integrate their own ideas for the creation of small spaces.

Equipment provided in the outdoor environment will be flexible, offering the maximum potential for children to take ownership of its nature, purpose and potential. In this spirit, provision to date includes planks, guttering, wooden blocks and large boxes. Real tools are provided for digging in muddy ground or gardening in raised beds, and, in view of the vagaries of British weather, priority considerations are the provision of shelter, shade and storage for waterproof clothes and boots. Small sheds contain regularly used items to support learning across the curriculum. Skills of early mark-making, and later emerging and purposeful writing development, for example, are assisted through roleplay supports such as chalks with writing logs, slates or shaped boards, brushes and water, or sticks and sand.

It is anticipated that the UCPS's expressed intention of *Releasing the Imagination* will be strongly facilitated by the outdoors as children explore and respond to their discoveries through talk, two- and three-dimensional art, writing, music and dramatic play in a plurality of representations. James Biddulph describes a vision of cohesive learning throughout the school environments:

> Children will become engaged in project making of their own design, with an outdoor area that gives meaningful opportunities for them to pursue their own interests. The outside should be dovetailed with the inside, making sense so that if a child is learning about unicorns, which was the

case recently, they are designing unicorn habitats outside, creating story boards on big boards, marking out the routes of the story on the ground using chalk, drawing the characters that their friends can be, exploring where other creatures live, writing a guide book about how to look after unicorns, understanding what 'uni' means (perhaps making links with other words that have 'uni' in them), singing and dancing as unicorns in a wonderful cornucopia of engaged, active, smiling children who are learning to communicate, collaborate and construct. Children loving learning.

FUTURE PLANS

Nursery provision within the UCPS is not yet in place. Part of the additional distinctiveness of the school's learning community, however, will be the location of the nursery classes within the same suite of spaces as the rest of the EYFS. This will help to afford a pattern of progression through the EYFS and the remainder of the school, which is continuous and consistent, avoiding the potential disruption to early learning of the transition between surroundings and pedagogical approaches. Additional nursery provision, which will form a part of the overall North West Cambridge Development (NWCD), will not be a part of the UCPS, but its close proximity will allow for the development of a close relationship with the school, with the effect that very young children will be enabled to settle quickly and confidently into the school, with the benefit of continuity in learning provision.

Among broader, structural elements that are vital to ensuring high quality in early childhood education, close relations with the school's wider community is widely recognised as an essential component (Whitebread et al., 2015b). As the NWCD is still under construction at the time of writing, there is no established catchment area. This is not to say that the school has yet to develop a sense of community. A thriving parents' association is firmly established and is supported by frequent newsletters, social activities and other events. Indeed, before the school opened, children and their families met during the summer to allow children to forge early friendships and to become familiar with key school staff. As the houses of the development are built, the catchment of the school will evolve and may develop elements of transience as 2000 of the proposed homes are for postgraduate students of the university.

Figure 5: An expert enriches thinking and learning

The community to which this school belongs extends well beyond the families of the children. The school is a member of the wider community of the university, rendering facilities such as museums, galleries and the Botanic Garden accessible as partners and resources. The University of Cambridge community also offers access to a wealth of expertise. The UCPS's role as a research school is explored elsewhere in this book but, beyond the domain of research, events have already taken place that have benefited even the youngest of learners as the school has tapped into this unique resource. Early in its first year the school hosted a mathematics day, which was supported by two professors of mathematics (see Figure 5), and NRich, the university-based mathematics project which aims to enrich the mathematical experiences of all learners.

It is very early days for the school, as it is still in year one of what is clearly an enormously exciting project. However, it is already evident that its staff have a profound commitment to developing evidence-based practice, and to developing themselves as teacher-researchers who are constantly reflective about their practice. All of those involved with the school recognise that, through the opening of the UCPS, we have been given an opportunity to provide a school that genuinely places the welfare and learning of the children at the heart of every decision, and allows the children to take responsibility for their own learning and their own school. In this way, we aspire to create a school that authentically engages in *Releasing the Imagination* and *Celebrating the Art of the Possible*.

Acknowledgements

Special thanks are due to Suzi Bray (assistant headteacher) for her generous, insightful and multiple contributions to this chapter. Thanks also to all those members of the school community whose words are shared with permission.

References

Alexander, R. (ed.) (2010). *Children, Their World, Their Education: Final Report and Recommendations of the Cambridge Primary Review* (London: Routledge).

Baumrind, D. (1967). Child care practices anteceding three patterns of preschool behaviour, *Genetic Psychology Monographs*, 75: 43–88.

Broström, S. (2010). A voice in decision making young children in Denmark, in M. Clark & S. Tucker (eds), *Early Childhoods in a Changing World* (Stoke-on-Trent: Trentham Publications), pp. 155–64.

Brown, A.L. (1997). Transforming schools into communities of thinking and learning about serious matters, *American Psychologist*, 4: 399–413.

Campbell, F.A., Ramey, C.T., Pungello, E., Sparling, J. & Miller-Johnson, S. (2002). Early childhood education: Young adult outcomes from the Abecedarian Project, *Applied Developmental Science*, 6(1): 42–57.

Christie, J.F. & Roskos, K.A. (2006). Standards, science, and the role of play in early literacy education, in D.G. Singer, R.M. Golinkoff & K. Hirsh-Pasek (eds), *Play=Learning* (Oxford: Oxford University Press), pp. 57–73.

Clark, A.S., McQuail, S. & Moss, P. (2003). *Exploring the Field of Listening to and Consulting with Young Children*, Research Report No. 445 (London: Thomas Coram Research Unit, University of London).

Eurydice, (2009). *Early Childhood Education and Care in Europe: Tackling Social and Cultural Inequalities* (Brussels: Eurydice).

Gray, P. (2009). Play as a foundation for hunter-gatherer social existence, *American Journal of Play*, 1(4): 476–522.

Gray, P. (2011). The decline of play and the rise of psychopathology, *American Journal of Play*, 3(4): 443–63.

Hattie, J. (2009). *Visible Learning: A Synthesis of over 800 Meta-Analyses Relating to Achievement* (London: Routledge).

Heckman, J. (2006). Skill formation and the economics of investing in disadvantaged children, *Science*, 312(5782): 1900–1902.

Heckman, J. (2011). The economics of inequality: The value of early childhood education, *American Educator*, 35(1): 31–47.

Heckman, J., Pinto, R. & Savelyev, P. (2013). Understanding the mechanisms through which an influential early childhood program boosted adult outcomes, *American Economic Review*, 103(6): 2052–86.

Howe, C. (2010). *Peer Groups and Children's Development*, (Chichester: Wiley-Blackwell).

Hyson, M., Copple, C. & Jones, J. (2006). Early childhood development and education, in K.A. Renninger & I. Sigel (eds), *Handbook of Child Psychology*, 4 (New York: Wiley), pp. 3–47.

Laevers, F. (2000). Forward to basics! Deep-level-learning and the experiential approach, *Early Years*, 20(2): 20–29.

Maccoby, E.E. & Martin, J.A. (1983). Socialisation in the context of the family: Parent-child interaction, in E.M. Hetherington (ed.), *Handbook of Child Psychology*, 4 (New York: Wiley), pp. 1–101.

Marcon, R.A (2002). Moving up the grades: Relationship between pre-school model and later school success, *Early Childhood Research and Practice*, 4(1): 517–30.

Mattanah, J.F., Pratt, M.W., Cowan, P.A. & Cowan, C.P. (2005). Authoritative parenting, parental scaffolding of long-division mathematics, and children's academic competence in fourth grade, *Journal of Applied Developmental Psychology*, 26(1): 85–106.

Meyer, D. & Turner, J.C. (2002). Using instructional discourse analysis to study scaffolding of student self-regulation, *Educational Psychologist*, 37: 17–25.

Nolen, S.B. (2007). The development of motivation to read and write in young children: Development in social contexts, *Cognition and Instruction*, 25: 219–70.

OECD (2001). *Starting Strong I* (Paris: OECD Publishing).

OECD (2006). *Starting Strong II* (Paris: OECD Publishing).

OECD (2012). *Starting Strong III: A Quality Toolbox for Early Childhood Education and Care* (Paris: OECD Publishing).

Ornstein, P.A., Grammer, J.K. & Coffman, J.L. (2010). Teachers' 'mnemonic style' and the development of skilled memory, in H.S. Waters & W. Schneider (eds), *Metacognition, Strategy Use & Instruction* (New York: Guilford Press), pp. 23–53.

Parker, C. (2015). 'This is the best day of my life! And I'm not leaving here until it's time to go home!': The outdoor learning environment, in D. Whitebread & P. Coltman (eds), *Teaching and Learning in the Early Years*, fourth edition (London: Routledge), pp. 93–118.

Pellegrini, A.D. & Gustafson, K. (2005). Boys' and girls' uses of objects for exploration, play and tools in early childhood, in A.D. Pellegrini & P.K. Smith (eds), *The Nature of Play: Great Apes & Humans* (New York: Guilford Press), pp. 113–35.

Pellis, S. & Pellis, V. (2009). *The Playful Brain: Venturing to the Limits of Neuroscience* (Oxford: Oneworld Publications).

Perry, N. (1998). Young children's self-regulated learning and contexts that support it, *Journal of Educational Psychology*, 90(4): 715–29.

Pino-Pasternak, D., Whitebread, D. & Tolmie, A. (2010). A multi-dimensional analysis of parent-child interactions during academic tasks and their impact on children's self-regulated learning, *Cognition & Instruction*, 28(3): 219–72.

Pomerantz, E.M. & Eaton, M.M. (2001). Maternal intrusive support in the academic context: Transactional socialization processes, *Developmental Psychology*, 37(2): 174–86.

Ponitz, C.C., McClelland, M.M., Matthews, J.S. & Morrison, F.J. (2009). A structured observation of behavioral self-regulation and its contribution to kindergarten outcomes, *Developmental Psychology*, 45(3): 605–19.

Schweinhart, L.J. (1993). Significant benefits: The highscope Perry Preschool Study through age 27, *Monographs of the HighScope Educational Research Foundation*, 10 (Ypsilanti, MI: HighScope Educational Research Foundation).

Smith, P.K. (2006). Evolutionary foundations and functions of play: An overview, in A. Göncü & S. Gaskins (eds), *Play & Development: Evolutionary, Sociocultural and Functional Perspectives* (Mahwah, NJ: Lawrence Erlbaum), pp. 21–49.

Sommer, P.D., Pramling Samuelsson, I. & Hundeide, K. (2010). *Child Perspectives and Children's Perspectives in Theory and Practice* (New York: Springer).

Stevenson, M. & Crnic, K. (2012). Intrusive fathering, children's self-regulation and social skills: A mediation analysis, *Journal of Intellectual Disability Research*, 57(6), 500–12.

Suchodoletz, A.V., Trommsdorff, G. & Heikamp, T. (2011). Linking maternal warmth and responsiveness to children's self-regulation, *Social Development* 20(3): 486–503.

Suggate, S.P. (2007). Research into early reading instruction and luke effects in the development of reading, *Journal for Waldorf/R. Steiner Education*, 11(2): 17.

Suggate, S.P. (2009). School entry age and reading achievement in the 2006 Programme for International Student Assessment (PISA), *International Journal of Educational Research*, 48: 151–61.

Suggate, S.P., Schaughency, E.A. & Reese, E. (2012). Children learning to read later catch up to children reading earlier, *Early Childhood Research Quarterly*, 28(1), 33–48.

Sylva, K., Bruner, J.S. & Genova, P. (1976). The role of play in the problem-solving of children 3-5 years old, in J.S. Bruner, A. Jolly & K. Sylva (eds), *Play: Its Role in Development and Evolution* (Harmondsworth: Penguin), pp. 55–67.

Sylva, K., Melhuish, E.C., Sammons, P., Siraj-Blatchford, I. & Taggart, B. (2004). *The Effective Provision of Pre-School Education (EPPE) Project*, Technical Paper 12 (London: DfES/Institute of Education, University of London).

Wang, M.C., Haertel, G.D. & Walberg, H.J. (1990). What influences learning? A content analysis of review literature, *Journal of Educational Research*, 84: 30–43.

Whitebread, D. (2010). Play, metacognition and self-regulation, in P. Broadhead, J. Howard & E. Wood (eds), *Play and Learning in the Early Years* (London: Sage), pp. 161–76.

Whitebread, D. & Jameson, H. (2010). Play beyond the foundation stage: Story-telling, creative writing and self-regulation in able 6 to 7-year olds, in J. Moyles (Ed.). *The Excellence of Play*, third edition (Maidenhead: Open University Press), pp. 95–107.

Whitebread, D., Jameson, H. & Basilio, M. (2015a). Play beyond the foundation stage: Play, self-regulation and narrative skills, in J. Moyles (ed.), *The Excellence of Play*, fourth edition (Maidenhead: Open University Press), pp. 84–93.

Whitebread, D., Kuvalja, M. & O'Connor, A. (2015b). *Quality in Early Childhood Education – An International Review and Guide for Policy Makers*, report for the World Innovation Summit for Education (Dohar: WISE).

Whitebread, D., Pino-Pasternak, D. & Coltman, P. (2015c). Making learning visible: the role of language in the development of metacognition and self-regulation in young children, in S. Robson & S. Quinn (eds), *The Routledge International Handbook of Young Children's Thinking and Understanding* (London: Routledge), pp. 199–214.

Whitebread, D., Bingham, S., Grau, V., Pino-Pasternak, D. & Sangster, C. (2007). Development of metacognition and self-regulated learning in young children: The role of collaborative and peer-assisted learning, *Journal of Cognitive Education and Psychology*, 3: 433–55.

Whitebread, D., Anderson, H., Coltman, P., Page, C., Pino-Pasternak, D. & Mehta, S (2005). Developing independent learning in the early years, *Education 3–13*, 33: 40–50.

7 Teacher education and University Training Schools: What lessons can be learned from Finland?

Riikka Hofmann and Hannele Niemi

(HOW) CAN WE LEARN FROM OTHER COUNTRIES' TEACHER EDUCATION SYSTEMS?

The Finnish education system has received attention all over the world because of the repeated high learning outcomes of Finnish 15-year olds in the OECD's PISA surveys.[1] Finnish students' knowledge and skills in problem-solving, scientific, mathematical and reading literacy are at or near the highest level of international standards, with only a few students in the lowest PISA categories. Likewise, differences of learning outcomes between Finnish schools are small. A commitment to equity in the Finnish education system and the high quality of the teachers are widely considered to be central explanatory factors (Niemi, 2012b; Sahlberg, 2011; Darling-Hammond, 2010).

In 2010 in England, the Schools White Paper, *The Importance of Teaching*, claimed that '[t]he only way we can ... have the world-class schools our children deserve, is by learning the lessons of other countries' success' (Department for Education, 2010, p. 3), and suggested specifically the Finnish teacher education system and its university teacher training schools as models from which England should learn. In the wake of the White Paper, the first author of this chapter was asked by the then Head of the Faculty of Education at Cambridge to organise and facilitate a study tour to Finland for the Faculty's leadership team and the then head of strategy for Initial Teacher Training (ITT) at the Training and Development Agency (TDA), Michele Marr (see chapter 2). We undertook this trip in March 2011. We visited the Departments for Teacher Education and Behavioural Sciences at the University of Helsinki, the University of Helsinki Teacher Training

Schools, one of Finland's PISA research groups, as well as the Finnish National Board of Education. As a Professor of Education at the University of Helsinki, the second author has written extensively on Finnish education and teacher education. She was also one of the Helsinki hosts for the Cambridge Faculty delegation. This chapter is one outcome of the conversations resulting from that visit.

There has been a debate in the UK in recent years regarding how the Finnish education system should be described to British audiences, and what lessons can be drawn from it. Critics have suggested that people in other countries have tended to look at Finland through their own lens (Alexander, 2012; Oates, 2015). Yet these same authors have arrived at little agreement over the different interpretations. This lack of agreement illustrates the difficulty of describing an entire education system, including the history, culture and social structures within which it is embedded (see Niemi, 2012b; Sahlberg, 2011; Simola, 2005). Nevertheless, it is important that we are able to learn from the challenges that others have faced in creating systems of teacher education and university-linked training schools, and the solutions that have been found (see Alexander, 2012; Sahlberg, 2011).

The question arises, then, not only of *what*, but *how*, lessons can be learned from another system. Alexander (2012) emphasises that the study of, and reflection on, other national education systems should contribute to national analysis, not replace it. Rather than looking at the case of another country through an external lens, we propose looking at *one's own* system, using another system as a lens that enables us to come to see aspects of it that are taken for granted. A local historically developed common sense strongly shapes what aspects of a local education system are perceived as inevitable, rather than historically and culturally contingent, and malleable (Rainio & Hofmann, 2015). Dominant ways of thinking and talking about education have been shown to infiltrate our perceptions such that attempts to develop and implement new ideas are not necessarily seen by participants within the system (Hofmann, 2016b; 2008). Without making those local established ways of thinking visible, it is difficult to change the practice that they conceptualise.

In this chapter we discuss analytically the Finnish case and the kind of interpretative lens that it might offer for considering English teacher education and University Training Schools (UTSs). As background, we briefly outline the current Finnish teacher education system and policy.

Finnish education and the teacher education system

To understand the context of Finnish teachers' work we describe briefly the central characteristics of the Finnish education system. Finnish teacher education serves the nine-year comprehensive schools attended by all students between the ages of seven and 16, as well as post-compulsory upper secondary education (leading to the nationwide matriculation examination) and alternative post-compulsory vocational education. Both routes provide access to higher education. All these stages of education are taxation-funded and free of charge to students. Class teachers usually teach comprehensive classes 1 to 6 (primary) and subject teachers classes 7 to 9 (lower secondary). (For more details of the Finnish education system, see Jakku-Sihvonen & Niemi, 2006a).

While Finnish teachers commonly use classroom-based tests to evaluate students' progress, there are no standardised nationwide evaluations of learning outcomes during the nine-year comprehensive school. Since school inspections were discontinued in 1991, quality assurance takes place through self-evaluations of schools, along with sample-based national assessments, most commonly in the last year of comprehensive schooling. Mathematics and the mother tongues (Finnish and Swedish) are evaluated regularly and other subjects in alternate years. The results are used to enhance or improve the system but are not published. Curricula are developed locally by the local education authorities and by each school, within the loose national curriculum framework set by the Finnish National Board of Education (Kumpulainen & Lankinen, 2012).

Teacher education for comprehensive schools and upper secondary schools, as well as for general subjects in further education, is provided by the university teacher education departments. All candidates have to obtain a five-year Master's degree to become a qualified teacher (see section 2 below). Teacher education is a very popular degree and only a small proportion of applicants is accepted (Niemi & Jakku-Sihvonen, 2011).

Teacher education degrees consist of the academic disciplines of education and relevant subject studies (30–40 per cent), research studies comprising research methods and Bachelor's and Master's theses (about 20 per cent), pedagogical studies, including teaching practice (about 20 per cent), as well as studies in communication, ICT, career planning and option modules. Teaching practice is organised in university teacher training schools and local partner field schools, and is supervised by university teachers, university training school teachers or local school mentors depending on the phase of practice (Jyrhämä, 2006). Teacher training schools play an important role in the Finnish teacher education system. All teacher education departments have a training school. These schools are part of universities and are specialised to support the student teachers' learning and development. Training schools also have a commitment to develop teaching and learning by creating and trialling new methods. For example, the University of Jyväskylä Teacher Training School has its own publication series. This series includes reports from research and development projects implemented in the school (Niemi, 2016).

We start our discussion of the Finnish teacher education system and the potential lessons to which it may give rise by first considering the development of Finnish university teacher training schools. As was suggested earlier, we cannot simply introduce policies from one cultural-historical location to another and assume that these will work the same way. It might be useful to think about how our reform efforts may be shaped by the assumptions and practices of those who worked in the field before us (see Hamilton, 1989). We ask whether there are features that we consider inevitable – or innovative – because previous generations of teachers, teacher educators and policy-makers in Finland have (or have not) emphasised them.

GAINING AN AUTONOMOUS VOICE: TEACHER EDUCATION AS AN INDEPENDENT FIELD INSTEAD OF TOP-UP TRAINING

Tracing central ideas back in time

Teaching, originally undertaken by the clergy, has enjoyed an important place for centuries in Finnish culture. Due to the influence of the Bishop of Turku, Mikael Agricola, in the sixteenth century, education and literacy came to be seen as the right and duty of everyone. The ability to read was noted in church documents and became the condition for being able to marry, and helped give rise to an (internationally early) idea of mass education (Kuikka, 2010; Niemi, 2012b).

As teaching gradually moved from provision by the clergy to a separate teaching profession, various forms of teacher education developed from the nineteenth century onward. These served a tripartite education system during the shift from Swedish to Russian rule and the declaration of independence, and the devastations of the 1918 civil war, and World War II and its aftermath (see Kuikka, 2010; Sahlberg, 2011). Early forms of teacher education were varied and very different from today. There were separate streams for teachers of secondary (or grammar) schools and elementary (or folk) schools. Elementary school teachers were educated, in seminars, in teacher training colleges first founded in 1863. Secondary school teachers studied their subjects in the respective university subject departments while attending lectures on teaching methods. The first chair for a professor of teaching and teacher education was established at the University of Helsinki in 1852, and the professor was tasked with developing teacher education and lecturing on teaching methods (Kansanen, 2012; Niemi, 2012b).

Upon graduation, student teachers undertook year-long practical training. To organise this practical training, a teacher training school was established in Helsinki in 1864. Training school teachers became responsible for the practical training of student teachers, with more training schools established around the country. These training schools, however, were independent of the universities and, like other publicly maintained schools, were under the auspices of the Schools Inspectorate. Their connections with universities were very limited and a professor of teacher education had little influence over them (Niemi, 2016).

Some of the core principles of Finland's current teacher education policy are traceable back to the nineteenth century and especially the work of Uno Cygnaeus. Cygnaeus was a Finnish elementary school developer, chief inspector and education visionary who studied in central Europe and introduced many of the core ideas still recognisable today in Finnish education, and teacher education policy and discourse. These involve the notion of teaching as a vocation, characterised by a love of the common people and a strong professional ethic of care; an emphasis on a strong and equal presence of academic subjects, the arts and practical skills for all children; and a focus on educating girls and enabling an independent life and career for women (see Kauranne, 2010; Sahlberg, 2011).

These ideas are so well grounded in the Finnish national discourse about, and structures of, teaching and schooling that they are rarely questioned. For example, from an English perspective, it may seem surprising that in Finland the government sets the minimum mandatory number of weekly teaching hours for all subjects, including music, art, crafts and design, and home economics for all schools. The legislation has actually recently increased the minimum mandatory teaching hours for arts, craft and practical skills subjects for all pupils, while the teaching hours for mathematics have remained unchanged (Ministry of Education and Culture, 2012).

Elsewhere, the first author of this chapter described such a shared cultural common sense as a lived ideology. A lived ideology does not mean that the people in a particular setting necessarily share a permanent set of beliefs. Rather, it means that 'they recognise and use the same ways of conceptualising and understanding their professional practice and the contradictions it involves' (Rainio & Hofmann, 2015, p. 1817, and see Billig et al., 1988). We do not suggest that England should simply adopt the specific fundamental notions behind Finnish teacher education, such as the emphasis on the arts. We offer these ideas underlying much Finnish teacher education discourse as a tool with which to probe historically developed ideas about teaching and learning that are taken for granted, and hence potentially invisible, in England.

The radical reform:
The emergence of Finnish teacher education as an independent and autonomous academic field

The more well-known developments in Finnish teacher education emerged in the 1960s and 1970s. The heavily debated decision by the Finnish Parliament in 1968 to radically reform the education system into a nine-year comprehensive school for all children involved a great change in the organisation of teacher education. In 1971 all Finnish teacher education moved to universities (including elementary teacher training, previously offered by the colleges) (Kuikka, 2010; Niemi, 2000, 2012b; Sahlberg, 2011). However, Kansanen (2012) emphasises that teacher education cannot be considered academic simply because it is carried out in a higher education institution. He suggests that the way in which Finnish teacher education has been organised is fairly exceptional.

In this reform, primary (class) teacher education was provided by a university degree. As with other subjects at the time, this was a research Master's degree that included undergraduate and Master's-level studies as part of a five-year programme that required a research dissertation. Since 2005, when Finnish higher education aligned its degrees with the Bologna agreement,[2] teacher qualifications have required both Bachelor's and Master's studies (three years Bachelor's or 180 ECTS, and two years Master's or 120 ECTS[3]), in which pedagogical studies are included. While this form of first degree was common for most subjects across much of Europe prior to the Bologna agreement for the harmonisation of higher education (Jakku-Sihvonen & Niemi, 2006b), it was exceptional in international comparisons to place primary school teacher education in the same category. Interestingly, Kansanen (2012) suggests that serendipity may have played a part here. All other university degrees were being reorganised in this manner, and teacher education, having just entered the university sector, became organised in the same way.

This way of organising teacher education has significant consequences that are worth considering. Firstly, a Master's-level teacher education degree offered primary and secondary teachers full eligibility to undertake subsequent doctoral studies if desired (Niemi, 2016). Secondly, it meant that teacher educators were required to have PhDs as well as a degree in teacher education and experience of classroom teaching. More importantly, a chair of teacher education was created to lead each teacher education department, and chair-holders are expected to have a research track record, as well as practical experience, in teaching and teacher education. The organisation of teacher education around a professorial chair of teacher education concretely links teacher education to ongoing research, rather than simply locating it in a university context (Kansanen, 2012). This model also means that teacher educators belong to a shared research community (see Niemi, 2016). There is an interesting implication here for UTSs in England, not only because of the role that research plays in learning to teach, but because the Finnish model highlights the importance of a shared research community. It invites us to ask whether and how teacher educators and student teachers in England can form a shared research community, as well as who leads and facilitates the intellectual work of this community.

The path to the highly autonomous education and teacher education systems that Finland is known for today were developed through a very centralised system immediately post-reform (Niemi, 2012b; Sahlberg, 2011). In the 1970s and 1980s, a fairly strict core curriculum was set for teacher education – and the education system – by the Ministry of Education. The aim was to standardise quality and unify the developing programmes. Since 1995, the new decrees have provided only a loose framework for universities to plan their teacher education programmes (Niemi, 2000). As a consequence, teacher education in Finland enjoys much greater autonomy from regulatory control than in other countries (Moon, 2003; Kansanen, 2012). In England, by comparison, there is an ongoing debate about who should decide about teacher education. In Finland, such decisions lie clearly with the academic departments of teacher education – including their teacher training schools – led by a professor. This raises an interesting question for England with its trend towards school-based teacher education: How might the new University of Cambridge Primary School (UCPS) become a serious (research-based, yet practical) voice in the wider policy conversations about teacher education?

TEACHERS AS LEARNING PROFESSIONALS: FACILITATING TEACHER LEADERSHIP

In this section we refer to two key characteristics of current education policy discussions. Firstly, these discussions of teaching and learning in schools emphasise the need to support students' critical and analytical thinking besides their learning of facts and skills (Binkley et al., 2012; Ruthven et al., 2016). Inevitably, this point means that scholars need to ask how teachers become able to support the development of such skills in their students. How, for example, do teachers themselves learn analytical and critical inquiry skills (Niemi & Nevgi, 2014)? Finnish teacher educators argue that it is not sufficient to leave this learning to CPD. Instead, research and inquiry form a central part of Finnish initial teacher education from the start (Niemi & Jakku-Sihvonen, 2011; Sahlberg, 2011).

Secondly, a central policy focus in education internationally, and in particular in England, emphasises the need for evidence-based practice in teaching and learning (Goldacre, 2013; Hofmann, 2016b). If so, then teachers need to be able to read and evaluate evidence, and reflect on how it could be implemented in their particular settings. And yet Niemi and Nevgi (2014, citing Levin, 2004) remark how educational institutions often lack the research knowledge and background to engage in research partnerships or make use of research findings in their work. How, then, do teachers draw on research evidence in their practice if they have not gained the skills of evaluating research (Krokfors et al., 2011)? The Finnish case is one example of the ways of integrating a research and inquiry perspective and skills into teacher education. It provides an opportunity to consider what role research-based teacher education may play in teaching and teachers' work.

With regard to international comparisons, the research element in Finnish teacher education is substantial. Finnish research suggests that a strong research component may support the development of teachers' professional competences and learning. Finnish student teachers' sense of professional competence and professional learning were found to be associated with their self-evaluated research skills and understandings (Niemi & Nevgi, 2014). This was particularly the case where the research component had been taught using active learning methods. At the same time, this study also suggested that simply adding or encouraging such elements is unlikely to be sufficient. The quality of the teaching and supervision of the research elements of the teacher education degree were found to be core challenges. Scalability of a research-intensive teacher education model may be a challenge internationally. It would be important to investigate more closely the kinds of research elements – and the kinds of teaching methods with which these are taught – that are particularly useful for practising teachers in England. The UCPS might play a central role here through its close connection with a research-intensive university with strong research methods training in its PGCE, MEd and EdD courses.

We are not suggesting that a research-based approach in Finland means that teachers in general are necessarily conducting their own research (although some do, see below). However, research on teachers', mentors' and student teachers' understandings of, and feedback on, research studies suggests that through such studies, teachers learn alternative ways of working, reflecting, dialoguing and gaining feedback for their work. These carry over into an analytical and reflexive approach to their teaching practice (Jyrhämä & Maaranen, 2012).

The notion of teachers as learning professionals in the title of this section, then, carries a two-fold meaning. With it we refer to the idea of teachers as research-based experts in children's learning, and also to teachers as professionals who continuously develop their own work. This kind of approach to teaching and teacher professionalism might be thought of as teacher leadership, as described by Lieberman (1992) and Hilti (2011). Niemi (2015) has discussed how Finnish teacher education aims to develop the leadership of teachers who have a vision and understanding of high-quality teaching and school development, who are also responsible for a school-based local curriculum, and who are able to draw on research knowledge and work collaboratively to enhance teaching and learning in their schools. This approach resonates with the notions of teacher leadership developed at the Cambridge Faculty of Education, where this idea is understood as being about purposefully seeking to draw on knowledge and collaborations to enhance pupils' learning – and is also about teachers' own professional learning (Alexandrou & Swaffield, 2012; Frost, 2012).

We are not suggesting simply a repeat of the Finnish system, because that also has its challenges. There are reports, for example, of a disconnection in Finnish teacher education between theory and research methods, and teaching practice. This disconnect has in the past also applied to relationships between university departments and the previously autonomous teacher training schools (Kosunen & Mikkola, 2002; Niemi, 2016; Westbury et al., 2005). The interesting question here, therefore, is: how might the UCPS – in collaboration with Faculty researchers – come to an understanding of developing and facilitating (the conditions for) teacher leadership in English schools? As a new school established in collaboration with the Faculty of Education, the UCPS is in an excellent position to contribute to developing teacher leadership in its own right, through the facilitation of collaborations between university-based research and teacher education, and school-based research-informed practice. Moreover, the UCPS should be encouraged to document these developments for the benefit of other such schools and systems.

INTER-PROFESSIONAL COLLABORATION IN EDUCATION AND TEACHER EDUCATION

We argue that inter-professional collaborations informed by mutual learning are a central defining characteristic of current Finnish teaching and teacher education. These collaborations are to be understood both structurally and personally. They entail collaborations between university departments of teacher education, university teacher training schools and teacher training partnership schools (and increasingly other institutions: see Niemi et al., 2012). And they also involve collaborations between university-based researchers, teachers and teacher researchers, as well as other professionals. It is important, however, to note that the processes of developing such collaborations in Finland have been far from smooth and easy. Practices are not only historically cumulative and knowledge-laden, but are also emotionally freighted and given direction by what is valued by those who implement them (Edwards, 2010). We suggest that it may be helpful for an English audience to consider some of the bottlenecks that the Finnish system has faced in developing such collaborations.

Bringing together teacher education departments and training schools

As we have mentioned, part of the Finnish education and teacher education reform of the 1970s entailed that teacher training schools became part of the newly established university departments of teacher education. These training schools have catchment areas like other schools (and the local authority pays for the education of the children who attend them). They are, however, formally part of a university, and independent of local authorities and the state. A proportion of all their teaching is undertaken by student teachers, who are supervised and mentored by the senior teaching staff of the training school.

Developing collaborations between the different institutional actors in teacher education has entailed the overcoming of many barriers. Training schools in Finland had a history of being relatively independent institutions with their own work and communication cultures. They had developed their own models of leadership, often around strong individual leaders. They were not used to having to collaborate closely with other institutions or to distribute the leadership of their activities. This initially created friction within the new model of teacher education in which teacher education departments, university subject departments and training schools had to share the leadership of educating student teachers.

While it was still suggested fairly recently that there are gaps in communication between these different institutional actors (Kosunen & Mikkola, 2002), through systematic efforts at developing collaboration and communication, new ways of working together have also been found (Niemi, 2016). These have involved creating joint forums for discussion, strategic planning for collaboration and the undertaking of joint research projects (Niemi, 2016, 2012a; Meisalo, 2007). The Finnish experience highlights how genuine collaborative approaches to teacher education that cross institutional boundaries do not emerge by themselves. Lack of cooperation and continuity between teacher education and regular schools can mean that the potential effects of teacher education are not realised once teachers start working in schools (Niemi, 2000). UTSs, however, should lead the development and modelling of such cooperation and continuity.

Drawing on the Finnish case, we propose the approach developed by Edwards (2011, 2012) and her colleagues in their research on inter-agency work as a useful framework for such development work between the Faculty and the UCPS. Edwards suggests that to be able to work at, and across, inter-professional boundaries, all institutional partners need purposefully to develop common knowledge. Such common knowledge is not just about the transfer (or sharing), or even translation (or clarification), of knowledge and practices from one institution to the other (Edwards, 2011, citing Carlile, 2004). Effectively collaborating across such institutional cultures and boundaries is likely to require the shared creation of new knowledge and understanding. This may also represent a potential research focus for the UCPS. To be able to produce common knowledge that can mediate responsive professional action requires engagement with the knowledge and motives of the others. Such engagement needs to be relational: it needs to pay serious attention to what matters for the other contributing experts in the collaboration (Edwards, 2011).

Energising teachers through inter-professional collaborations

Similar challenges exist in collaborations between different professionals. While Finnish teachers spend a long time studying in departments of education, with a substantial proportion of their studies focusing on research, collaborations between teachers and university-based researchers do not necessarily run smoothly, as noted by Hakkarainen et al. (2008). These authors point to gaps in university-based researchers' understandings of teachers' everyday practice. Besides, while newly-qualified Finnish teachers' competences in teaching, critical reflection, ethical engagement and planning have been evaluated as good (Niemi, 2011), their readiness for relational work and expertise has been found to be in need of improvement (Niemi, 2000, 2011). At the same time, the Finnish experiences suggest that when they are successful, such inter-professional collaborations are a huge source of learning for all parties.

Recent work in Finland has focused on this challenge: professional and inter-professional networking and collaboration have emerged as central mediating dimensions for sustainable educational development (Niemi et al., 2012; Hofmann, 2016a). Educational research studies in Finland now typically involve close collaborations between full-time researchers and practicing teachers, and are characterised as processes of trust-building, developing shared worlds and mutual learning. These studies pay close attention to the teachers' experiences and views of implementing and trialling new innovations (Aarnio et al., 2014; Kankaanranta & Vahtivuori-Hänninen, 2014; Korhonen et al., 2014; Hofmann, 2016a). There are opportunities for student teachers during their studies to participate in such research projects (Westbury et al., 2005). Innovations in these studies are described as something that cannot simply be offered and received. The implementation of research-based innovations requires that all parties learn and change.

While the emphasis in England is increasingly on the production of large-scale evidence of what works (Goldacre, 2013; Haynes et al., 2012), successful implementation in schools of findings from such research requires an understanding of change in teaching practice. It also necessitates a reciprocal relationship between the teaching profession and university-based researchers. Our research suggests that such a reciprocal relationship requires a conscious effort to understand and align with what matters most to the other partners in their work (Hofmann & Mercer, 2015; Hofmann, 2016b). Some such reciprocal work has been taking place in Finland (Niemi et al., 2012). At the same time, due to the relative scarcity of large-scale and evaluation studies in Finland, knowledge about the scalability of such efforts is lacking. Moreover, such models need to reflect local school and wider cultures. The UCPS may provide a platform for developing models of reciprocal research and development work for England. The outcomes of such work could also inform the design and impact of large-scale trials. Beside the production of evidence, the Finnish experience suggests that successful reciprocal research-practice collaborations can be a source of energy for maintaining a thriving educational ecosystem (Niemi et al., 2012).

RENEWABLE SOURCES OF ENERGY FOR THE EDUCATIONAL ECOSYSTEM

Teacher retention is of central concern to education systems internationally. Overall, teachers in Finland have been very committed to, and satisfied with, their profession (Simola, 2002 and Santavirta et al., 2001, cited in Simola, 2005; Niemi, 2012a). Attrition from teacher education programmes and declining teacher retention have not been major problems. Teacher education up until the university reform of the 1970s was understood as educating teachers for a 40-year career (Kuikka, 2010). Even more recently, studies have suggested that young Finnish teachers see theirs as a positive long-term profession (Niemi, 2000). Many economic, social and cultural explanations for the commitment and satisfaction of Finnish teachers can be considered. One interesting perspective offered recently by Finnish authors and commentators is that educational collaborations might be thought of as occurring in ecosystems and that these require renewable sources of energy (Niemi et al., 2014b; Hofmann, 2016a). So, what might function as renewable sources of energy in teaching and teacher education? The autonomy that Finnish teachers maintain is commonly suggested in Finnish studies as a central attractive feature of the teaching profession (Webb et al., 2004; Rasku & Kinnunen, 1999, cited in Webb et al., 2004). It has been suggested that the opportunity and support required to engage in innovations that one is inspired about, and to take risks, is a source that keeps energising Finnish teachers to remain, and thrive, in their jobs

(Niemi et al., 2014a; Hofmann, 2016a). As discussed above, teacher education in Finland reflects this autonomous future role.

Another issue (perhaps an unusual one from an English perspective) that
gets raised in these discussions takes us back in history. We have already
discussed in section 2 how academic subjects and the arts, and subjects ori-
ented towards practical skills (such as woodwork and textiles) all enjoyed
a central position in early Finnish teacher education. Kuikka (2010, p. 16)
suggests that this was seen as significant not only for the children, but
for the enjoyment of their teachers who faced 'working in classroom for
many decades'. The position enjoyed by the arts and skills subjects remains
strong in Finland today; they are perceived as a source of job satisfaction
and enjoyment, and even fun, by Finnish teachers (Webb et al., 2004).

The Finnish education system is ambitious and much of its teaching is
often described as fairly traditional (Krzywacki et al., 2012; Lavonen &
Juuti, 2012; Toom & Husu, 2012). At the same time the Finnish education
system is quite practical. The enjoyment of the teachers in their work is a
central focus in Finnish research and policy (see Niemi et al., 2014a). This
emphasis invites the question of what might be the central sources of enjoyment and energy for teachers in English schools that have the potential
to balance the pressures created by high-stakes testing, leagues tables and
school inspections.

A ROLE FOR UTSs IN TEACHER EDUCATION – A PLACE FOR UNIVERSITIES?

This chapter has discussed the role that universities and a research-based
approach play in the development of future teachers in Finland, a focus
of a recent Schools White Paper in England (Department for Education,
2010, p. 24). Finnish research suggests that research studies are associated with a sense of professional competence and professional learning.
In this sense they propose that research-based teacher education lays a
foundation not only for supporting students' critical and analytical skills,
but for evidence-based practice in education. Moreover, research training
is seen as important for teachers to be able to take the role of autonomous
ethical professionals who can gain a voice as public intellectuals in discussions about education (Niemi, 2000). We suggested that UTSs in England
might be in a good position to investigate the extent to, and ways in, which
research elements in teacher education are useful in teacher education.
Linked with this, we also asked whether the UCPS could take the lead in

developing teacher leadership in the England, and research and document this development.

In the context of these discussions we have posed the following questions for English teacher education and the newly established UTSs. Firstly, we posed some potential problems in the formation of a shared research community across a university faculty and a UTS, and the intellectual leadership of such a community. Secondly, we queried how a UTS could become a (research- and practice-based) voice in the discourse of English teacher education. Thirdly, we queried what the sources of energy might be for English teachers currently and into the future, in UTSs and more widely.

At the same time we acknowledged that, if there is discontinuity in thinking and practice between university teacher education departments and the schools in which qualified teachers work, then research-based teacher education may lose its potential impact. We drew on cultural-historical theorising to suggest that in order for teacher education to enable teachers to draw on these multiple ways of knowing, the different institutions involved in teacher education must come to understand what matters to their collaborators (Edwards, 2010; Hofmann, 2016b). They must develop common knowledge that accounts for differences in perspectives, as well as creating links that facilitate relational expertise (Edwards, 2011). We suggested that the new UTSs are in a unique position to be developing, facilitating and theorising such boundary collaborations.

The Finnish experience also suggests that besides learning skills and theories, a strength of university-based teacher education is the opportunity to experience the process of teacher education not only as an apprentice teacher but as a learner. The Finnish research that we cited suggested that a core mediating factor for the benefit of research-based studies was students' experiences of being taught through active teaching methods in university settings. Those experiences were seen to mediate student teachers' capabilities of supporting such learning experiences in their students in school (Niemi & Nevgi, 2014). UTSs may then provide a further mediating layer that can enable students to try out such strategies in an environment of a real school, albeit one that embraces the forms of learning familiar from university settings. In this way it can act as a bridge to research-based teaching in (those many) schools that have not got a close connection with a university.

As the Finnish example illustrates, teacher education reforms take time and commitment (Sahlberg, 2011). Christensen and Lægreid (2007) emphasise that all public sector reforms require patience. They require changes in organisational culture and the building of mutual trust, all of which is time-consuming. They suggest that the role of a successful reform agent in such situations is to operate more as a gardener than as an architect or an engineer (see also Edwards, 2010). We close by asking if the UCPS is thought of as a garden, whether it might be considered as the annual garden show for the hosting university department of education, a kind of model site, a (or perhaps the) place 'to see cutting-edge garden design, new plants and find ideas to take home' (RHS Chelsea Flower Show, 2016). Drawing on our discussion of the Finnish experience, we suggest thinking about it instead as the botanic garden. University botanic gardens are places that are reasonably permanent, whose work has an underlying scientific basis and is systematically documented. They are also places that are open to the public to learn from, which communicate with other similar institutions to offer information, and undertake scientific or technical research (Botanic Gardens Conservation International, 2016). What makes such institutions different from publicly maintained parks (or, in our case, schools) is that they are institutions that document their activities 'for the purposes of scientific research, conservation, display and education' (Botanic Gardens Conservation International, 2016). Might not this be a goal for the UCPS?

Notes

1 PISA refers to the Programme for International Student Assessment, a triennial international survey which tests the skills and knowledge of 15-year olds in reading, science and mathematics, see http://www.oecd.org/pisa/home/.
2 The Bologna agreement is a reform process aimed at creating comparability in the standard and quality of higher education qualifications across Europe. The degree cycle is based on a two-cycle model, as was already in use in the UK. The first cycle ends in a Bachelor-level degree, the second in a Master's degree, see http://www.ehea.info/.
3 ECTS is the European Credit Transfer System which is used in the Bologna process as a tool for achieving comparability across degrees and countries. Each ECTS point is equivalent to approximately 28 hours of students' work (covering all study activities, including taught sessions and independent work) and can be used to express the workload involved in segments of degrees and whole degrees, see http://ec.europa.eu/education/ects/ects_en.htm.

References

Aarnio, A., Lipponen, L., Vahtivuori-Hänninen, S. & Mylläri, J. (2014). Schools and companies in a co-configurative collaboration, in H. Niemi, J. Multisilta, L. Lipponen, & M. Vivitsou (eds),

Finnish Innovations and Technologies in Schools: A Guide Towards New Ecosystems of Learning (Rotterdam: Sense Publishers), pp. 155–63.

Alexander, R. (2012). Entitlement, freedom, minimalism and essential knowledge: Can the curriculum circle be squared?, in *CPPS Westminster seminar*, 23. http://www.robinalexander.org.uk/wp-content/uploads/2012/04/CPPS-text-Alexander-120423.pdf.

Alexandrou, A. & Swaffield, S. (2012). Teacher leadership and professional development: perspectives, connections and prospects, *Professional Development in Education*, 38(2): 159–67.

Botanic Gardens Conservation International (2016). Botanic Gardens Conservation International website. Retrieved from https://www.bgci.org/resources/1528/.

Billig, M., Condor, S., Edwards, D., Gane, M., Middleton, D. & Radley, A. (1988). *Ideological Dilemmas: A Social Psychology of Everyday Thinking* (London: Sage).

Binkley, M., Erstad, O., Herman, J., Raizen, S., Ripley, M., Miller-Ricci, M. & Rumble, M. (2012). Defining twenty-first century skills, in P. Griffin, B. McGaw & E. Care (eds), *Assessment and Teaching of 21st Century Skills* (Dordrecht: Springer), pp. 17–66.

Christensen, T. & Lægreid, P. (2007). The whole-of-government approach to public sector reform, *Public Administration Review*, 67(6): 1059–66.

Darling-Hammond, L. (2010). Steady work: How Finland is building a strong teaching and learning system, in L. Darling-Hammond, *The Flat World and Education: How America's Commitment to Equity Will Determine Our Future* (New York: Teachers College Press), pp. 15–25.

Department for Education (2010). *The Importance of Teaching: The Schools White Paper 2010* (London: HMSO).

Edwards, A. (2010). *Being an Expert Professional Practitioner: The Relational Turn in Expertise*, vol. 3 (Dordrecht: Springer Science & Business Media).

Edwards, A. (2011). Building common knowledge at the boundaries between professional practices: Relational agency and relational expertise in systems of distributed expertise, *International Journal of Educational Research*, 50(1): 33–39.

Edwards, A. (2012). The role of common knowledge in achieving collaboration across practices, *Learning, Culture and Social Interaction*, 1(1): 22–32.

Frost, D. (2012). From professional development to system change: Teacher leadership and innovation, *Professional Development in Education*, 38(2): 205–27.

Goldacre, B. (2013). Building evidence into education. Report for the *Department for Education, UK*. See http://media.education.gov.uk/assets/files/pdf/b/ben%20goldacre%20paper.pdf.

Hakkarainen, K., Bollström-Huttunen, M. & Hofmann, R. (2008). Teacher-researcher dialogue and expansive transformation of pedagogical practices, *Nordic Journal of Digital Literacy*, 3: 157–78.

Hamilton, D. (1989). *Towards a Theory of Schooling* (London: Falmer).

Haynes, L., Service, O., Goldacre, B. & Torgerson, D. (2012). Test, learn, adapt: developing public policy with randomised controlled trials, *Cabinet Office-Behavioural Insights Team*. See https://www.gov.uk/government/uploads/system/uploads/attachment_data/file/62529/TLA-1906126.pdf.

Hilti, E.B. (2011). *Teacher Leadership: The 'New' Foundations of Teacher Education – A Reader* (New York: Peter Lang).

Hofmann, R. (2008). *Ownership in Learning: A Sociocultural Perspective on Pupil Engagement, Collaboration and Agency in the Classroom* (Unpublished PhD thesis, University of Cambridge).

Hofmann, R. (2016a). Review of H. Niemi, J. Multisilta, L. Lipponen & M. Vivitsou (eds), (2014). *Finnish Innovations and Technologies in Schools: A Guide Towards New Ecosystems of Learning, Teacher Development*, 20(2): 434–36.

Hofmann, R. (2016b). Leading professional change through research(ing): Conceptual tools for professional practice, in P. Burnard, T. Dragovic, J. Flutter & J. Alderton (eds), *Transformative Professional Doctoral Research Practice* (Rotterdam: Sense Publishers), pp. 141–54.

Hofmann, R. & Mercer, N. (2015). Teacher interventions in small group work in secondary mathematics and science lessons, *Language and Education*, online: 1–17.

Jakku-Sihvonen, R. & Niemi, H. (2006a). Introduction to the Finnish education system and teachers' work, in R. Jakku-Sihvonen & H. Niemi (eds), *Research-Based Teacher Education in Finland: Reflections by Finnish Teacher Educators* (Turku: Finnish Educational Research Association), pp. 7–16.

Jakku-Sihvonen, R. & Niemi, H. (2006b). The Bologna process and its implementation in teacher education, in R. Jakku-Sihvonen & H. Niemi (eds), *Research-Based Teacher Education in Finland: Reflections by Finnish Teacher Educators* (Turku: Finnish Educational Research Association), pp. 18–29.

Jyrhämä, R. (2006). The function of practical studies in teacher education, in R. Jakku-Sihvonen & H. Niemi (eds), *Research-Based Teacher Education in Finland: Reflections by Finnish Teacher Educators* (Turku: Finnish Educational Research Association), pp. 51–70.

Jyrhämä, R. & Maaranen, K. (2012). Research-orientation in a teacher's work, in H. Niemi, A. Toom & A. Kallioniemi (eds), *Miracle of Education* (Rotterdam: Sense Publishers), pp. 97–112.

Kankaanranta, M. & Vahtivuori-Hänninen, S. (2014). Building an ecosystem for developing educational use of technology in Finnish schools, in H. Niemi, J. Multisilta, L. Lipponen & M. Vivitsou (eds), *Finnish Innovations and Technologies in Schools: A Guide Towards New Ecosystems of Learning* (Rotterdam: Sense Publishers), pp. 115–28.

Kansanen, P. (2012). Mikä tekee opettajankoulutuksesta akateemisen? *Kasvatus & Aika*, 6(2): 37–42.

Kauranne, J. (ed.) (2010). *Ajankohtainen Uno Cygnaeus* Suomen kouluhistoriallinen seura.

Korhonen, T., Lavonen, J., Kukkonen, M., Sormunen, K. & Juuti, K. (2014). The innovative school as an environment for the design of educational innovations, in H. Niemi, J. Multisilta, L. Lipponen & M. Vivitsou (eds), *Finnish Innovations and Technologies in Schools: A Guide Towards New Ecosystems of Learning* (Rotterdam: Sense Publishers), pp. 99–113.

Kosunen, T. & Mikkola, A. (2002). Building a science of teaching: How objectives and reality meet in Finnish teacher education, *European Journal of Teacher Education*, 25(2–3): 135–50.

Krokfors, L., Kynäslahti, H., Stenberg, K., Toom, A., Maaranen, K., Jyrhämä, R. & Kansanen, P. (2011). Investigating Finnish teacher educators' views on research-based teacher education, *Teaching Education*, 22(1): 1–13.

Krzywacki, H., Pehkonen, L. & Laine, A. (2012). Promoting mathematical thinking, in H. Niemi, A. Toom & A. Kallioniemi (eds), *Miracle of Education* (Rotterdam: Sense Publishers), pp. 115–30.

Kuikka, M. (2010). Opettajankoulutus eilen, tänään ja huomenna. Teoksessa Ajankohtainen Uno Cygnaeus. Suomen Kouluhistoriallisen Seuran Vuosikirja, 1–18.

Kumpulainen, K. & Lankinen, T. (2012). Striving for educational equity and excellence, in H. Niemi, A. Toom & A. Kallioniemi (eds), *Miracle of Education* (Rotterdam: Sense Publishers), pp. 69–81.

Lavonen, J. & Juuti, K. (2012). Science at Finnish compulsory school, in H. Niemi, A. Toom & A. Kallioniemi (eds), *Miracle of Education* (Rotterdam: Sense Publishers), pp. 131–47.

Lieberman, A. (1992). Teacher leadership: What are we learning? in C. Livingston (ed.) *Teachers as Leaders: Evolving Roles* (Washington: National Education Association), pp. 159–65.

Meisalo, V. (2007). Subject teacher education in Finland: A research-based approach – The role of subject didactics and networking in teacher education, in R. Jakku-Sihvonen & H. Niemi (eds), *Education as Societal Contributor* (Frankfurt am Main: Peter Lang), pp. 161–80.

Ministry of Education and Culture (2012). Basic Education of the Future: National Objectives and Distribution of Lesson Hours (Tulevaisuuden perusopetus—valtakunnalliset tavoitteet ja tuntijako; the document in Finnish, abstract in English) Report 6. http://www.minedu.fi/export/sites/default/OPM/Julkaisut/2012/liitteet/tr06.pdf?lang=fi.

Moon, B. (2003). A retrospective view of the national case studies on institutional approaches to teacher education, in B. Moon, L. Vlasceanu & C. Barrows Leland (eds), *Institutional Approaches to Teacher Education within Higher Education in Europe: Current Models and New Developments* (Bucharest: Unesco – Cepes), pp. 321–37.

Niemi, H. (2000). Teacher education in Finland: current trends and future scenarios, in *Teacher Education Policies in the European Union*, Proceedings of the Conference of Teacher Education policies in the European Union and Quality of Lifelong Learning, Loule, 22, pp. 843–55.

Niemi, H. (2011). Educating student teachers to become high quality professionals: A Finnish case, *CEPS Journal*, 1(1): 43–66.

Niemi, H. (2012a). Teacher education for high quality professionals: An analysis from the Finnish perspective, in O.-S. Tan (ed.), *Teacher Education Frontiers 2020* (Singapore: National Institute of Education), pp. 43–70.

Niemi, H. (2012b). The societal factors contributing to education and schooling in Finland, in H. Niemi, A. Toom & A. Kallioniemi (eds), *Miracle of Education* (Rotterdam: Sense Publishers), pp. 19–38.

Niemi, H. (2015). Teacher professional development in Finland: Towards a more holistic approach, *Psychology, Society & Education*, 7(3): 279–94.

Niemi, H. (2016). Academic and practical: Research-based teacher education in Finland, in B. Moon, B. (ed.) (2016). *Do Universities Have a Role in the Education and Training of Teachers? An International Analysis of Policy and Practice* (Cambridge: Cambridge University Press).

Niemi, H. & Jakku-Sihvonen, R. (2011). Teacher education in Finland, in M. Valenĉiĉ Zuljan & J. Vogrinc (eds), *European Dimensions of Teacher Education: Similarities and Differences* (Ljubljana: Faculty of Education, University of Ljubljana and the National School of Leadership and Education, Kranj), pp. 33–51.

Niemi, H. & Nevgi, A. (2014). Research studies and active learning promoting professional competences in Finnish teacher education, *Teaching and Teacher Education*, 43: 131–42.

Niemi, H., Toom, A. & Kallioniemi, A. (2012). *Miracle of Education* (Rotterdam: Sense Publishers).

Niemi, H., Multisilta, J., Lipponen, L. & Vivitsou, M. (2014a). *Finnish Innovations and Technologies in Schools: A Guide Towards New Ecosystems of Learning* (Rotterdam: Sense Publishers).

Niemi, H., Multisilta, J., Lipponen, L. & Vivitsou, M. (2014b). Prologue: Towards a global ecosystem, in H. Niemi, J. Multisilta, L. Lipponen, & M. Vivitsou (eds), *Finnish Innovations and Technologies in Schools: A Guide Towards New Ecosystems of Learning* (Rotterdam: Sense Publishers), pp. ix–xii.

Oates, T. (2015). Finnish fairy stories, http://www.cambridgeassessment.org.uk/Images/207376-finnish-fairy-stories-tim-oates.pdf

Rainio, A.P. & Hofmann, R. (2015). Transformations in teachers' discourse about their students during a school-led pedagogic intervention, *European Journal of Social and Behavioural Sciences*, 13(2): 1815–29.

Royal Horticultural Society (2016). https://www.rhs.org.uk/shows-events/rhs-chelsea-flower-show/about-the-rhs-chelsea-flower-show.

Ruthven, K., Mercer, N., Taber, K.S., Guardia, P., Hofmann, R., Ilie, S. & Riga, F. (2016). A research-informed dialogic-teaching approach to early secondary school mathematics and science: The pedagogical design and field trial of the epiSTEMe intervention, *Research Papers in Education*, online: 1–23.

Sahlberg, P. (2011). *Finnish Lessons: What Can the World Learn from Educational Change in Finland?* (New York: Teachers College Press).

Simola, H. (2005). The Finnish miracle of PISA: Historical and sociological remarks on teaching and teacher education, *Comparative Education*, 41(4): 455–70.

Toom, A. & Husu, J. (2012). Finnish teachers as 'makers of the many', in H. Niemi, A. Toom & A. Kallioniemi (eds), *Miracle of Education* (Rotterdam: Sense Publishers), pp. 39–54.

Webb, R., Vulliamy, G., Hämäläinen, S., Sarja, A., Kimonen, E. & Nevalainen, R. (2004). Pressures, rewards and teacher retention: A comparative study of primary teaching in England and Finland, *Scandinavian Journal of Educational Research*, 48(2): 169–88.

Westbury, I., Hansén, S.-E., Kansanen, P. & Björkvist, O. (2005). Teacher education for research-based practice in expanded roles: Finland's experience, *Scandinavian Journal of Educational Research*, 49(5): 475–85.

8   The contribution of University Training Schools to developing research-informed professional knowledge in teaching: Ideas from the Cambridge Faculty of Education

Kenneth Ruthven

INTRODUCTION

A range of ideas developed in the University of Cambridge Faculty of Education suggest ways in which a university training school might make a distinctive contribution to the development of a research-informed knowledge base for teaching: specifically ideas of the *knowledge-creating school* (Hargreaves,[1] 1999), of *warranting practice* (Ruthven, 1999, 2005) and of *practical theorising* (McIntyre,[2] 1995).

THE KNOWLEDGE-CREATING SCHOOL

In proposing the notion of the *knowledge-creating school*, Hargreaves (1999) speculated that the development of professional knowledge about teaching would benefit from approaches to knowledge creation and management that were attracting attention in other knowledge-based industries at the time. More recently, emphasising the interdependence of schools in such efforts, he has embedded this notion within the broader one of a *self-improving school system* (Hargreaves, 2010). Viewing schools as necessarily the primary sites for the cultivation of new professional knowledge, Hargreaves envisages them becoming institutions that do so more purposefully and collectively.

Activity supporting the creation of professional knowledge

In developing his argument, Hargreaves identified four particular forms of activity supporting the creation of professional knowledge: professional tinkering by teachers; school-based teacher education; school-based research by teachers; and knowledge brokering by intermediaries.

Professional tinkering by teachers

The fundamental type of knowledge-creating activity that Hargreaves singles out is the professional tinkering which teachers undertake in the course of their work, developing and improving their practice through informal experimentation. Such experimentation may arise from teachers' dissatisfaction with some aspect of current practice, from their motivation to try out some new idea, or indeed from a combination of these. This tinkering necessarily calls for some modification of existing systems of practical action, sometimes accompanied by a corresponding change in ways of thinking (and talking) about this practice. The cycles of trial, reflection and improvement that such tinkering involves play a key part not just in the development and refinement of innovative practice and the professional knowledge associated with it, but in the appropriation of these by a wider audience.

In the knowledge-creating school, then, knowledge-creating activity would capitalise on the reservoir of new practices resulting from this informal professional tinkering, but would become more institutionally managed. From this reservoir, new practices would be chosen for more systematic exploration and examination on the basis of promising results from the initial trialling that they had already undergone, and of their being particularly relevant to current institutional priorities. Then a larger group of teachers, working in a wider range of contexts, would examine a promising practice, developing and testing it further, and investigating its transferability between persons and its transposability between places. One key characteristic, then, of a knowledge-creating school is the development of professional tinkering beyond a stage of informal individual activity into a stage of formal institutional activity involving more collective and systematic examination of promising practice through a managed process of experimentation.

School-based teacher education

The cultivation of professional knowledge is also supported by deep involvement in school-based teacher education, whether that be initial teacher education (ITE) or continuing professional development (CPD). (While Hargreaves emphasises the former, many of his observations appear equally relevant to the latter.) Here, following Nonaka and Takeuchi (1995), Hargreaves distinguishes between knowledge that is tacit (and typically operational in form) and knowledge that is explicit (and typically propositional in form). Equally, he endorses Nonaka and Takeuchi's suggestion that the creation of professional knowledge is primarily concerned with the mobilisation and conversion of tacit knowledge. Different types of shift involving these two types of knowledge define four types of 'knowledge conversion'. First there is 'socialisation': relaying tacit knowledge of professional practice between persons through joint activity and shared experience, notably through forms of apprenticeship. Second there is 'externalisation': articulating tacit knowledge so as to create counterpart explicit knowledge, notably through analytic dialogue. Third, there is 'internalisation': activating explicit (typically propositional) knowledge within professional practice so as to create some counterpart tacit (normally operational) knowledge (i.e. skill), typically through tinkering aimed at realising this activation. Finally, there is 'combination': synthesising elements from different bodies of explicit knowledge with a view to developing professional practice, often through interaction in which differing types of expertise are brought to bear in joint pursuit of a common goal.

In particular, these processes support knowledge growth on the part of mentors as well as trainees. While trainees are the obvious direct beneficiaries of socialisation and internalisation, in the process of supporting trainees, mentors are frequently obliged to engage in some form of externalisation, precipitating corresponding development in their professional knowledge. Equally, supervisory discussions are likely to expose mentors to ideas differing from those familiar to them that trainees have encountered elsewhere, creating opportunities for combination. Hargreaves argues, then, that:

> On-the-job training leads to on-the-job learning, which in turn leads both mentor and trainee to engage in additional tinkering. Yet it is no longer individualised tinkering, but a version that springs out of a form of knowledge creation that uses all four modes of knowledge conversion. All the elements of ... knowledge creation are in place, simply waiting to be managed more actively. (Hargreaves, 1999, p. 132)

School-based research by teachers

A further line of activity supporting professional knowledge creation is school-based research by teachers, typically aimed at improving some aspect of practice. Often following an action research model, such research creates productive conditions for developing new professional approaches, clarifying their rationale and method, and activating, testing and refining them through tinkering. Equally, pursued more collectively, such research provides opportunities for knowledge conversion through working in a team with other colleagues on a joint project, networking with teachers in other schools pursuing similar projects, and interacting with external research supervisors. Again, such activity clearly has the potential to contribute to a more explicitly managed programme of knowledge creation within a school.

Knowledge brokering by intermediaries

The coordinated development of professional knowledge across a school can be supported by the presence of staff capable of acting as effective intermediaries between classroom teachers, and between them as a group and those responsible for the governance of a school. (Recognising that, in smaller schools, notably primary schools, tiers of management may not be so well developed and strongly defined, I have introduced here a less managerial terminology than that used by Hargreaves.) These intermediaries need to understand differing perspectives and priorities within these groups, and to be able to bridge successfully between them in negotiating suitable programmes of knowledge creation, exchange and development for a school.

Phases of managed knowledge creation

The discussion above of forms of activity supporting knowledge creation has already signalled the shift that Hargreaves envisages towards establishing schools in which processes of knowledge creation are more actively managed and productively coordinated. He discusses institutional custodianship of this process in terms of four specific aspects: auditing the professional knowledge available, managing the creation of new knowledge, and validating, then disseminating, the knowledge created.

Auditing professional knowledge

Relevant knowledge about professional issues is likely to be spread across a school community. For the school to make organised and well-informed progress in tackling an issue, sources of useful knowledge need to be identified and appropriate contributions elicited. Equally, any significant gaps in collective knowledge need be identified so that they can be addressed. In due course, too, the results of auditing professional knowledge across the school can inform the targeted provision of appropriate professional development. Nevertheless, an important obstacle to effective knowledge audit is that much professional knowledge takes the form of practical know-how that is neither easily articulated nor already codified. In this light, Hargreaves suggests that knowledge audit is most easily conducted in a collaborative school culture that encourages the externalisation associated with frequent and high levels of professional talk and sharing among teachers. Equally, he points to the need to devise innovative approaches to mapping professional knowledge of this type.

Managing knowledge creation

Central to the notion of a knowledge-creating school is the idea that:

> professional knowledge creation [be] not seen as a random, undirected activity of the minority of individual teachers with a creative talent, but as a whole-school process that has to be managed – with the allocation of material and temporal resources, co-ordination of people and activities, regular monitoring and support. (Hargreaves, 1999, p. 126)

Beyond these issues of prioritisation and resourcing, Hargreaves identifies clusters of wider school characteristics likely to support development of organised knowledge-creation. A prerequisite is an institution focused on improvement and open to change. Equally, creative and innovative professional thinking calls for a culture in which diversity is valued and alternative viewpoints respected; one that encourages experimentation and treats mistakes as opportunities for learning. Institutional planning needs to be sufficiently coherent to establish shared goals and agreed approaches, but flexible enough to allow for contingency in responding to emergent events and particular circumstances. This, Hargreaves suggests, is best achieved through strong decentralisation, flexible organisation and flat hierarchies, marked by devolution of responsibility to staff respected for their task-relevant expertise (rather than for their organisational status), formation of temporary developmental structures (rather than reliance on established bureaucratic structures), and by an informality of professional relationships, which encourages intensity of collegial discussion. Finally, to operate effectively, a knowledge-creating school must be sensitive to its various stakeholders and have strong awareness of the wider professional environment. In particular, it needs to access and exploit external knowledge, and be ready to engage in external collaboration to advance knowledge creation.

Validating professional knowledge

Hargreaves regards professional knowledge as validated only once it has been translated into practice that works demonstrably and repeatedly. He notes that there are varying bases, with differing degrees of credibility, for making such judgements about 'what works'. One base is the individual ('ipsative') or collective ('social') professional judgement of the teachers concerned, supported perhaps by comparison with their previous practice or the parallel practice of others. A second base is the ('independent') judgement of external experts, familiar with a wide range of professional practice and skilled in its assessment. A third base involves more explicit methods of assessment, following established procedures of a more 'judicial' or 'scientific' character, built on systematic collection and analysis of relevant evidence. Hargreaves (1999, pp. 128–9) notes that it is possible – and indeed desirable – to appeal to all three types of base, and suggests that: 'The knowledge-creating school will apply demanding forms of knowledge validation to supply evidence for the effectiveness of its new practices'. However, he notes that rigorous validation of the third type is not well developed in schools.

Disseminating professional knowledge

The development of knowledge-creating schools would strengthen the capacity to disseminate professional knowledge through the stronger possibilities that apprenticeship and tinkering offer to convey, and perhaps to externalise tacit knowledge as well as to contextualise explicit knowledge. Where tacit knowledge is concerned, while it is possible (and not unusual) for professional development in other settings to seek to acknowledge and address such knowledge, the emphasis tends to be more on explicit knowledge. Equally, the methods employed at alternative sites for professional development remain at an important remove from authentic practice in a school setting. While exercises such as reviewing or designing professional resources, examining records of professional practice or simulating such practice have developmental value, they typically fall short of supporting fully functional development of the requisite tacit professional knowledge in use under authentic teaching conditions. Equally, however, in a school setting, the capacity to disseminate tacit knowledge is enhanced by a degree of externalisation. In particular, training for the performance of complex tasks through apprenticeship strategies such as modelling and coaching benefits from the availability of means of representing and conceptualising task performance in terms of components that can usefully be distinguished but also need to be coordinated.

Hargreaves recognises that it will be difficult for individual schools to establish adequate capacity to realise such a model. Accordingly, he emphasises the formation of what he refers to as 'tinkering networks' of schools. Such associations of schools would not just capitalise on the forms of activity already described, but ensure that they reach across institutions (assisted in particular by new technologies) to create high levels of inter-school communication and collaboration. In this model, Hargreaves sees dissemination between schools as being fostered not just through interaction between participating teachers from different schools, but through their movement between schools. What part, then, might a University Training School (UTS), and the University of Cambridge Primary School in particular, play in such networks?

UNIVERSITY TRAINING SCHOOLS

Government policy in England in recent years has fostered the growth of autonomous school networks, based on Teaching Schools and academy chains, aspiring to the kind of knowledge-creating and self-improving model advanced by Hargreaves. Equally, government policy has increasingly marginalised the place of universities in ITE and the CPD of teachers. Accordingly, the activity – and thus the capacity – of many university education departments, particularly those in research-intensive universities, has shifted away from these professional areas as resources for them have diminished and they have become increasingly problematic to manage and sustain.

Under these circumstances, certain limitations which Hargreaves highlighted have only become more pronounced as education departments in research-intensive universities have shifted their emphasis away from supporting the creation of professional knowledge and towards the application of disciplinary social science:

[W]here the focus of professional knowledge creation is teaching and learning, or the management of schools and classrooms, the knowledge gap between researcher and practitioner is sufficiently great to make the researcher-led creation of usable or actionable knowledge especially hazardous. If knowledge creation is primarily concerned ... with the mobilisation and conversion of tacit knowledge, then many research-ers simply do not share the tacit knowledge of teachers, because either they have never been schoolteachers or it is some years since they were. (Hargreaves, 1999, p. 135)

The distinctive position of University Training Schools

From this viewpoint, the arrival of UTSs creates a new niche in which universities might retain, perhaps even enhance, expertise directly relevant to the creation and dissemination of professional knowledge for school teaching; expertise that university departments of education are finding increasingly difficult to sustain in the face of government policy changes. Essentially, a UTS combines the functions of an ordinary school with strong involvement in research-informed approaches to ITE and continuing teacher education, and to professional knowledge creation – exactly the distinguishing characteristics of Hargreaves' knowledge-creating school. These additional functions are supported by the close association of a UTS with its university's department of education and other relevant sources of expertise within the wider university. Equally, such a school is well placed to sit at the interface between schools and its university in the creation of professional knowledge, by virtue of the continuing direct involvement of its staff in school teaching. As such, then, a UTS has the potential to become a crucial node within a larger network of knowledge-creating schools; a network either based on existing teacher education partnerships (and the associated university department of education), or on other types of emerging multi-school structures.

Fundamental questions facing University Training Schools

In pursuing such a role, a first task, not just for the UTS concerned but for the wider network of schools, would be to flesh out Hargreaves' account of the knowledge-creating school into one or more operational models. Indeed, a key area of research for the network would be to develop viable and effective models of knowledge creation and the professional knowledge to support their implementation. There would be useful scope here for the involvement of staff from the university education department (or business school), specifically those interested in issues of organisational management and development, particularly as they relate to professional knowledge. Amongst the questions that need to be addressed are the following:

- What are viable and effective approaches to organising projects aiming to create, validate and disseminate professional knowledge, both within a single school, and across several schools?

- What are viable and effective approaches to auditing available professional knowledge relevant to an issue, aiming to identify both existing capacity within a school and developmental needs across it?

- What are viable forms of infrastructure capable of providing effective support for knowledge brokering and project planning within and between schools and other institutions (such as university departments)?

One imagines that such questions would be addressed in an iterative manner through the progressive refinement (in a tinkering manner) and articulation of one or more models. This would then enable implementations of such models to be examined more systematically by analysing their effectiveness in fostering the desired processes of knowledge auditing, brokering, creation, validation and dissemination.

Experience from an existing network of knowledge-creating schools

The Cambridge Faculty of Education and some of the regional schools with which it works already have relevant experience to draw on from a university-schools partnership for educational research (SUPER),[3] which has now been running for many years (McLaughlin et al., 2006). Reviewing this partnership, McIntyre & Black-Hawkins (2006) noted that the university had indeed made the kinds of contribution anticipated by Hargreaves in his discussion of knowledge-creating schools. In particular, the university had played a crucial role in acting as the hub of the partnership network, providing its infrastructure and organising maintenance activities, training and supporting teachers and students in developing and using research skills, and supporting the externalisation of professional craft knowledge and its combination with other types of knowledge. McIntyre and Black-Hawkins (2006, p. 188) also comment on how, 'Instead of a symmetric partnership in which each partner helps the other to pursue its own distinctive goals, this is an asymmetric partnership, with the school partners in the front-line role and the university faculty in a crucial support role'. This is an important asymmetry which the introduction of a UTS into such a network might serve to mitigate, and which might permit some redistribution of the university effort and contribution.

Resourcing the knowledge-creation activities of University Training Schools

Nevertheless, however reconfigured, such a network would still face the challenge of adequately resourcing its activities, which SUPER has encountered – as discussed at greater length by McIntyre and Black-Hawkins. This means that, in seeking to answer the research questions posed above, it would be particularly important to pay close attention to the levels of resourcing and types of staffing required to support different models of knowledge auditing, brokering, creation, validation and dissemination, and to have regard to the sustainability of these models as well as their effectiveness. If knowledge-creating schools in general – and UTSs in particular – are to take on more wide-ranging and demanding functions than ordinary schools, then they need to be adequately resourced to carry out these additional functions. Sustainability will not be achievable on the basis of voluntary efforts from staff already discharging demanding professional duties or of the diversion of limited resources intended for other purposes.

WARRANTING PRACTICE

Over recent years, schools and teachers in England have been subject to an accountability regime driven by evaluation of student outcomes against mandated targets and inspection of professional practice against imposed models. This has promoted strategic compliance across the system, rather than fostering professional engagement and critical thinking. Although government policy now espouses the granting of greater autonomy to schools and teachers (as discussed by Alison Peacock in chapter 4), with a corresponding reduction in centralised prescription, the cumulative influence of this continuing accountability regime has been inimical to many of the aspects of school culture on which the development of effective knowledge-creation depends – as sketched in the earlier section on managing knowledge creation. To break out of this straitjacket, what is required is a school-based approach to accountability, capable of fostering the development of professional practice and the creation of associated professional knowledge, and sufficiently rigorous to represent a compelling alternative to the current approach.

Principles for warranting practice

The idea of creating 'warranted practice' (Ruthven, 1999, 2005) represents one attempt to articulate such an approach. Very simply, it suggests that schools and teachers should take responsibility for developing and assuring the quality of their own professional practice. The qualifier 'warranted' for a professional practice carries two important senses. The first is of providing reasoned grounds for the practice as intended. The second is of assuring that the practice as implemented does indeed realise its claims. Thus, warranting of a professional practice calls for:

- articulation of a clear operational model for the practice, explicitly indicating the ends to be sought and the means to be employed;

- provision of a coherent rationale for that model, showing how its intended operation is well grounded in wider professional knowledge and takes account of evidence from its implementation;

- monitoring of practice, based on principles of triangulation: of implementation against intention; between different types of relevant evidence; across internal participants and against external standards;

- continuing analysis and revaluation of the operational model in light of evidence from monitoring practice, and of developments in professional knowledge.

It is important to emphasise that the warrant derives not from the particular content of practice, but from the forms of scrutiny to which it has been successfully subjected. Indeed, it is precisely to centre attention on this continuing process of scrutiny that it may be better to talk of an ongoing 'warranting of practice' rather than of a once-and-for-all 'warranted practice'.

Previous experience of warranting practice

The development of this notion provides an illustration of progression through professional tinkering. Much of the idea of warranting practice was implicit in Ruthven's approach to articulating and validating his own innovative practice as a teacher of advanced mathematics (Ruthven, 1989).

Subsequent experience as a teacher and teacher-educator motivated him to refine the idea and develop a more explicit articulation of it (Ruthven, 1999). He then sought to operationalise the notion in a wider range of professional contexts through a collaborative research project conducted within the SUPER project initiated by the Cambridge Faculty of Education. The *Developing Warranted Practice in the Use of Information and Communication Technology* project involved around 20 teachers in five secondary schools in teacher research to investigate promising innovative *Technology Integrated Pedagogical Strategies* for supporting subject teaching and learning across the secondary curriculum. Supported by Faculty staff, the participating teachers worked individually or in pairs, meeting collectively to report and review the progress of their research and to discuss emergent issues. The common framework for research design involved each case being investigated with a view to developing warranted practice by articulating and refining the practical theory guiding the pedagogical strategy, and by analysing and evaluating the teaching and learning processes central to the strategy in operation, including their impact on relevant aspects of student attitude and attainment.[4] In turn, the participating Faculty researchers conducted further analyses across all the cases (e.g., Deaney et al., 2006; Hennessy et al., 2003; Ruthven et al., 2005).

Reviewing the evolution of the SUPER partnership, Black-Hawkins and McIntyre judged this work on warranted practice as being:

> [t]he partnership project that was generally the most successful ... [It] achieved significant success in relation to both academic and practitioner criteria. Through the articulation of not only good practices but also rationales for these practices, and the sharing of these within and between subject departments, the schools found the project to be highly productive in terms of the professional development of staff. At the same time, useful research-based conclusions were derived and reported in academic papers. (Black-Hawkins & McIntyre, 2006, p. 151)

Nevertheless, Ruthven reported that the research process was treated and valued by schools and teachers primarily as a local mechanism for developing the person-embodied and setting-embedded expertise that they required. While a follow-up study (Deaney & Hennessy, 2007) found that almost all of the participating teachers had subsequently disseminated their practice further within their own school, often embedding it within the scheme of work for their department, little wider dissemination had taken place, even to other schools within the partnership itself.

Networking the warranting of practice

The context in which *Technology Integrated Pedagogical Strategies* took place, of course, was one in which most of the within-school forms of joint activity through which further dissemination to colleagues took place were not available to support wider dissemination beyond the originating school, given the organisational circumstances in which teachers were working. Thus, while the extant examples of the warranting of practice suggest that it holds promise as a mechanism for the local creation, validation and dissemination of innovative professional practice and knowledge, there would need to be provision for such joint activity to be fostered across sites for this approach to make its full contribution to the work of a network of knowledge-creating and self-improving schools. One way in which this could be achieved would be for a UTS itself to become a demonstration/participation site both for innovative warranted practices and for the general approach of warranting practice. Teachers from other schools could be placed for appropriate periods in the UTS in a supernumerary capacity to enable them to participate in such joint activity, returning to their own school to lead development and warranting of the innovative practice there. Equally, building on an approach already employed by Teaching Schools, a teacher knowledgeable about an innovative practice that has already been warranted within the UTS could spend part of their time in other schools in the network in order to foster joint activity to develop that practice and the local warranting of it. Alternatively, of course, a more distributed model could be adopted, with demonstration/participation sites for particular practices and reservoirs of relevant expertise spread across the network, but still dependent on opportunities for some teachers to participate in joint activity in schools other than their own. Thus, all of these approaches would depend on there being sufficient capacity and flexibility available in school staffing to make these kinds of cross-school joint activity possible.

PRACTICAL THEORISING

There is an expectation that the new UTSs will act as sites for research involving a wide range of university departments. Equally, they are expected to play an important part both in the translation of the resulting theorised scientific knowledge into practical professional knowledge through the processes of 'combination' and 'internalisation' (as sketched earlier in this chapter) and in the dissemination of such knowledge through ITE and CPD.

The question of how best to approach the translation and activation of theorised scientific knowledge for practical professional purposes is one that has long exercised teacher educators. The Cambridge Faculty of Education has adopted a 'practical theorising' approach (McIntyre, 1995), which seeks to develop an informed and critical professionalism. Elucidating this approach within ITE, McIntyre wrote that:

> [T]he theoretical knowledge which we offer student teachers should be treated by them as tentative, inadequate and constantly to be questioned and, where appropriate, falsified; but it should also be knowledge which we offer them because we believe it to be of practical value to them as teachers. Our commitment to the process of experimentation and falsification should be equalled by our commitment to making available to our students theoretical knowledge which they will mostly, with refinement, be able usefully to assimilate to their professional thinking. (McIntyre, 1995, p. 366)

McIntyre sketches the main grounds for adopting such an approach as against one in which particular bodies of theoretical knowledge are given a more privileged status. First, he argues that student teachers enter teacher education with many preconceptions about teaching which provide starting points from which they build a personal practical theory of teaching over the course of their training. Implicitly or explicitly, the development of teachers' professional reasoning calls for them to reconcile existing ideas with new ones, or to reorganise them. Teacher educators would do best to acknowledge this process and to work with it. Equally, academic educational theories introduce selective frames of reference and rest on assumptions which are often value-laden. An intellectually honest teacher education should acknowledge this and help teachers to examine how such selections and assumptions relate to practical decisions and actions. Given these circumstances, a practical theorising approach enables teachers to develop coherent and defensible practices, a key characteristic of professionalism. Moreover, McIntyre points out that the forms of knowledge and argument which teacher education is ultimately concerned to develop differ from those of disciplinary research:

> The logic of knowledge use is to be found in *practical arguments* of which the conclusions are not truth claims but patterns of action; and it is the notion of 'practical arguments' that is useful for us in guiding our work as teacher educators and in making the task of theorising realistic for

our students. It is in the quality of our student-teachers' practical arguments, and the way in which we facilitate the development of these arguments, that the academic quality of our theory and theorising must be found. (McIntyre, 1995, p. 378, original emphasis)

This practical theorising approach infuses the strongly school-based courses of ITE offered in the Cambridge Faculty of Education. Particular examples of the approach in operation have been documented in a number of research publications (e.g., Counsell et al., 2000; Ruthven, 2001). Arguably, such an approach is equally applicable to courses of CPD, and it influences many of the higher degree courses which the Cambridge Faculty of Education offers for educational professionals. Although experienced teachers have more developed personal practical theories, the basic grounds for pursuing this type of dialogue between theoretical ideas and practical arguments continue to be operative.

As UTSs are likely to receive many more external requests for research involvement than they are able to accommodate, they will have to establish criteria and priorities for becoming involved in such activity. Arguably, here too, priority should be given to research shown to have the clear potential to contribute to developing practical arguments about teaching and thus to the creation of professional knowledge. Arguably too, priority should be given to research projects in which the relationship between external researchers and school professionals is one of clinical partnership through dialogue in a spirit of practical theorising, rather than one simply of data extraction by the researchers.

CONCLUSION

The recent establishment of UTSs introduces a new type of intermediary institution into the English schooling system, capable of occupying a unique position within a network of knowledge-creating schools by virtue of its close affiliation with a university department of education and its potential to become associated with research involving a wide range of other university departments. However, in order to make a distinctive contribution to the development of a research-informed knowledge base for teaching, such institutions will need to find a *modus operandi* which successfully exploits their unique position. Building on a cluster of ideas developed in the Cambridge Faculty of Education, a promising strategy for doing so would be to develop each UTS as the hub of a wider network of knowledge-creating schools, employing approaches to knowledge creation underpinned by the ideas of practical theorising and warranting practice.

Notes

1 David H. Hargreaves was Professor of Education in the Cambridge Faculty, 1988 to 2000.
2 The late Donald McIntyre was Professor of Education in the Cambridge Faculty, 1996 to 2004.
3 SUPER is the Schools University Partnership for Educational Research, see http://www.educ.cam.ac.uk/research/projects/super/.
4 More information about the project, including reports from the individual teacher enquiries can be accessed at http://www.educ.cam.ac.uk/research/projects/tips/. The degree to which the teacher reports were in a position to articulate the warrants that they established for the practices concerned was constrained by the particular reporting specifications set by the Best Practice Research Scholarship (BPRS) scheme through which their participation was funded.

References

Black-Hawkins, K. & McIntyre, D. (2006). The SUPER partnership: A case study, in C. McLaughlin, K. Black-Hawkins, S. Brindley, D. McIntyre & K. Taber (eds), *Researching Schools: Stories from a Schools-University Partnership for Educational Research* (London: Routledge), pp. 147–64.

Counsell, C., Evans, M., McIntyre, D. & Raffan, J. (2000). The usefulness of educational research for trainee teachers' learning, *Oxford Review of Education*, 26(3–4): 467–82.

Deaney, R. & Hennessy, S. (2007). Sustainability, evolution and dissemination of information and communication technology-supported classroom practice, *Research Papers in Education*, 22(1): 65–94.

Deaney, R., Ruthven, K. & Hennessy, S. (2006). Teachers' developing 'practical theories' of the contribution of information and communication technologies to subject teaching and learning: An analysis of cases from English secondary schools, *British Educational Research Journal*, 32(3): 459–80.

Hargreaves, D.H. (1999). The knowledge-creating school, *British Journal of Educational Studies*, 47(2): 122–44.

Hargreaves, D.H. (2010). *Creating a Self-Improving School System* (Nottingham: National College for School Leadership).

Hennessy, S., Ruthven, K. & Deaney, R. (2003). *Pedagogic Strategies for using ICT to support Subject Teaching and Learning: An Analysis across 15 Case Studies* (University of Cambridge, Faculty of Education). Retrieved from http://www.educ.cam.ac.uk/research/projects/istl/.

McIntyre, D. (1995). Initial teacher education as practical theorising: A response to Paul Hirst, *British Journal of Educational Studies*, 43(4): 365–83.

McIntyre, D. & Black-Hawkins, K. (2006). Reflections on schools-university research partnerships, in C. McLaughlin, K. Black-Hawkins, S. Brindley, D. McIntyre & K. Taber (eds), *Researching Schools: Stories from a Schools-University Partnership for Educational Research* (London: Routledge), pp. 182–98.

McLaughlin, C., Black-Hawkins, K., Brindley, S., McIntyre, D. & Taber, K. (2006). *Researching Schools: Stories from a Schools-University Partnership for Educational Research* (London: Routledge).

Nonaka, I. & Takeuchi, H. (1995). *The Knowledge-Creating Company* (Oxford: Oxford University Press).

Ruthven, K. (1989). An exploratory approach to advanced mathematics, *Educational Studies in Mathematics*, 20(4): 449–67.

Ruthven, K. (1999). Reconstructing professional judgement in mathematics education: From good practice to warranted practice, in C. Hoyles, C. Morgan & G. Woodhouse (eds), *Rethinking the Mathematics Curriculum* (London: Falmer), pp. 203–16.

Ruthven, K. (2001). Mathematics teaching, teacher education and educational research: Developing 'practical theorising' in initial teacher education, in F.-L. Lin & T. Cooney (eds), *Making Sense of Mathematics Teacher Education* (Dordrecht: Kluwer), pp. 165–83.

Ruthven, K. (2005). Improving the development and warranting of good practice in teaching, *Cambridge Journal of Education*, 35(3): 407–26.

Ruthven, K., Hennessy, S. & Deaney, R. (2005). Incorporating Internet resources into classroom practice: Pedagogical perspectives and strategies of secondary-school subject teachers, *Computers & Education*, 44(1): 1–34.

9   The possibility of evidence-informed primary schooling

Anna Vignoles, Jan Vermunt and Sonia Ilie

INTRODUCTION

Currently there is considerable discussion in educational circles of the concept of an evidence base to inform and shape the work of teachers, school leaders and policy-makers. In respect of two of the three pillars of quality envisaged for the University of Cambridge Primary School (UCPS), it is anticipated that the school will play a lead role in contributing to the research foundations for classroom learning, school improvement and teachers' professional learning. The path from research to policy and practice, however, is not linear and is often quite tortuous. Ideally, a problem in the real world, such as the low achievement of children from socio-economically disadvantaged backgrounds, should inform the research questions that researchers and practitioners, in collaboration with one another, address. The research then needs to generate knowledge and understanding that can inform practitioners' understanding and practice, and indeed policymaking. Often, elements of this cycle are missing, leading to lost opportunities for education research to inform what we do in schools and the wider education system. In this chapter, we provide an historical overview of the problems with generating and acting upon research that is suitable to inform practice. We then discuss the challenges and possibilities of what it means for education practice to be 'evidence-informed' or 'evidence-based'. In respect of the 'chaining' of knowledge, we describe possible pathways from research design through to the implementation of findings. We focus particularly on the chain of evidence from teacher learning and professional development, teaching practices and student learning processes to student learning outcomes. Finally, we conclude by discussing the role of the UCPS in creating a national dividend in research, including how the school will be contributing to the research itself and in collaboration with other schools and practitioners, and the transfer and translation of outputs into working teacher knowledge.

We start by first considering the rather turbulent history of evidence-based policy-making in education in the UK, an important detour that is needed to put the significance of the research relationship between the UCPS and the Faculty of Education into context and to provide some insight into the challenges that we, as part of the wider education community, will face when trying to build the research evidence base upon which primary school practitioners and policy-makers can draw. It is also important to highlight the fact that the UCPS and its relationship with the Faculty of Education at Cambridge is just one part of a wider movement within the education sector that is trying to empower practitioners by providing the kinds of research and evidence that can be used effectively in the classroom and drawn upon to inform practice. We hope the Faculty of Education and UCPS will play an important part in this wider endeavour.

EVIDENCE-BASED POLICY AND PRACTICE IN THE UK EDUCATION SYSTEM

An important purpose of education research, clearly, is to inform policy and practice. Hence the use that governments, practitioners and other stakeholders make of education research is critically important. Yet in the UK the relationship between the education research community and policy-makers has long been an uneasy one, with much criticism on both sides. At the heart of this rather bad-tempered debate are some fundamental issues about the aims of education, the purpose of education research and what kinds of research are needed to inform policy and practice.

We start with a conundrum which has long been recognised, namely whether educational researchers should allow their work to be guided and heavily influenced by the needs of the government of the day (Whitty, 2006). Certainly there is a place for research that challenges the status quo and questions the very legitimacy of any government's policies and questions (Gale & Densmore, 2003; Whitty, 2006). That does not imply, however, that research that specifically aims to influence practitioners or indeed policy-makers is inherently compromised. Nonetheless, in parts of the research community, such questions give rise to an uneasy view of research that is predominantly aimed at addressing policy questions which, in the words of Professor Stephen Ball, 'is always in some degree both reactive and parasitic' (Ball, 1997, p. 258). The extent to which this point might also apply to research that is predominantly focused on addressing questions facing practitioners is not clear and, arguably, the needs and motivations of policy-makers and practitioners are quite distinct. There are, according to some, also more fundamental problems with the notion of evidence-informed policy which are rooted in the fact that while governments seek concrete answers to policy problems, much of the research 'about education or schooling is not "about" policy at all' (Ball, 2005, p. 16). Even research that is aimed at influencing policy may also fail to have traction since, while governments appear sometimes to respond to research that is explicitly intended to influence policy and address a specific policy problem, they are much less responsive to broader research that may have major policy significance but that does not emerge from a specific government-defined policy problem.

As was pointed out in chapter 8, the Faculty of Education at Cambridge has a long standing tradition of engagement with the needs of practitioners and undertaking research that can be of great value to policy-makers. The path from research to policy influence has not always run smoothly though. Indeed, as Robin Alexander notes in relation to the findings of the *Cambridge Primary Review*, the study's critical engagement with the core tenets of the government's approaches to primary education (i.e. achievement standards, assessment procedures, and so on) struggled to gain traction with key government actors precisely because it was so challenging, even while practitioners themselves welcomed the results and recommendations of the *Review* (Alexander, 2010; 2011).

So, given the significant challenge of influencing education policy in a sustained and meaningful way through research, is there a place for a different approach to education research, or at least space for some scholars in the field to undertake more focused and directed research that is explicitly addressing key challenges faced by both practitioners and the wider system? If we take it as a given that governments like clear guidance as to which approach works better than another, does this suggest the need for a particular kind of pragmatic research? Or, as Professor David Hargreaves, writing in the late 1990s, and implicitly criticising previous approaches to policy-making and indeed many types of education research, put it:

> [T]here is another element in the new [Labour] government's approach which gives rise to optimism, namely its pragmatic approach to 'what

works' and to the rapid dissemination of 'good practice' throughout the education service. This is highly compatible with an evidence-based approach to professional practice in education, to parallel what is happening in medicine.

And:

Meeting the demands will entail more experimental studies and ideally a series of randomised controlled trials ... (Hargreaves, 1999, pp. 245–7)

Hargreaves' (1997, 1999) endorsement of a pragmatic approach to evidence-based policy-making and his plea for more robust evidence could have been written today; so too his implicit criticism of the types of research generated by education researchers and, indeed, the methods that were being used at that time. We discuss both issues in turn.

UK policy-makers continue to stress many of the same issues that Hargreaves highlighted: the desire of the government to have evidence of 'what works', the parallels drawn with medicine and the plea for robust causal evidence of the impact of education policy and practice. Implicit in this critique of the relationship between education research and practice is a view that much of the research produced by the research community fails to be sufficiently relevant to inform either policy or practice. Or, as Ben Goldacre, in his recent review of the use of education research in policy-making, explained:

I think there is a huge prize waiting to be claimed by teachers. By collecting better evidence about what works best, and establishing a culture where this evidence is used as a matter of routine, we can improve outcomes for children, and increase professional independence. (Goldacre, 2013, p. 4)

In the UK, in response to this long-standing plea from within and without the scholarly community for education research that can inform policy and practice (Rudduck, 1998; Saunders, 2010; Tooley & Darby, 1998), the government has invested in numerous research programmes and so-called 'What Works' centres. These endeavours are generally designed to produce research that can directly inform what schools do – instrumental research, in other words. For example, the previous Coalition government established the EEF[1] to commission large-scale trials to investigate the impact of school and teacher practices. The EEF has the express aim of reducing the socio-economic gap in pupils' achievement and, whilst it commissions research from academics, it has also played a major role in steering the education research community to produce more of this particular kind of research evidence on the effectiveness of different practices.

Whether one agrees with this direction of travel or not, there is no doubt that the funding made available by the EEF has prompted the education research community to engage in a large number of trials which have produced evidence on the impact of different practices. From a critical perspective, this may have led to an 'instrumental separation of aims and means in the conduct of research' (Oancea, 2016, p. 109), particularly as the EEF funding stream has also arguably increased both the inclination and the capacity within universities' departments of education to carry out this kind of research. Before dismissing this activity as entirely instrumental, however, it is important to reflect on the way in which the EEF has commissioned this research. By involving the academic community and even more crucially the practitioner community in the research process, the scrutiny that both academic and non-academic actors place upon research carried out within the EEF's remit requires that these studies have intrinsic academic value, and are more than simple instruments in the attainment of particular policy-related goals (Oancea, 2016).

In addition to the top-down approach to generating evidence to inform education policy and practice, there has been an independent and parallel movement amongst practitioners. Specifically, there appears to be a growing view amongst many practitioners that research needs to better inform practice, as manifest by organisations such as researchEd (2016).[2] Initiated by teachers in 2013, researchEd is a now global movement that aims to bring together practitioners and academics to improve both the quality and relevance of the research base and the impact that it has on practice by increasing teachers' research literacy, and creating an online space for collaboration and conversation. It is too early to see the impact of both these top-down and bottom-up initiatives, but undoubtedly there is more emphasis on the need for education research to inform practice than ever before.

The debate about how education research can better impact on policy and practice is also linked to debates about research methodologies. In the UK, unlike in most of the rest of Europe, critics have argued that an over-reliance by education researchers on qualitative research methods is a key reason why education research has not had as much impact as might be hoped and why other disciplines, such as economics, have gained traction (Vignoles, 2011; Dearden et al., 2010). It is undoubtedly true that until recently most education research in the UK relied on qualitative methods, though of course academics from other disciplines, particularly economics, have been using quantitative methods to research a range of problems in education for a number of years. Many commentators have argued that, since policy-makers require generalisable evidence and specifically impact upon evaluation research, in order to have more traction, UK research required a shift in the balance of methods used towards more quantitative and mixed-method approaches. Our education research colleagues in Europe, who take mixed methods approaches for granted, look on perplexed at the so-called paradigm wars between quantitative and qualitative methods that have played out in the UK education research field. Happily, the false dichotomy of quantitative versus qualitative in education research is being replaced by an acceptance that what is needed is rigorous evaluation in which researchers apply the most appropriate methods to produce the most robust answers to the right questions. This shift in thinking is likely to increase the impact of education research in years to come.

This point raises another important issue about methods. Goldacre focused particularly on the important issue of establishing causality in education research and recommended extensive use of randomised controlled trials (RCTs). RCTs are undoubtedly a very effective way of establishing causal relationships. We must not forget, however, the importance of generalisability. A limitation of RCTs is that they often take place in very specific contexts, such as particular geographic areas, and this may limit their generalisability. Hence, there is also space for quasi-experimental and indeed non-experimental methods. It should also be said that qualitative research can uncover causal relationships even if it is harder to generalise from such approaches. So again what is needed here is a range of different types of evidence, relevant to the problems facing schools, practitioners and policy-makers, and relying on different methodological approaches.

Evidence for policy and practice is of course also produced outside the research community, and indeed increasingly so. A growing number of third-sector organisations and think tanks, as well as government departments, now undertake a considerable amount of education research. Much of this might be described quite crudely as motivated by the need to know what works, but, even though we might reject that simplistic view of evaluation and indeed research, it is clear that we need studies that can determine causal relationships between policies and practices and pupil outcomes, and that are conducted in such a way that we can generalise from our findings to some wider population.

Although there has been an increasing amount of research into education policy and practice from researchers in universities and other organisations, what is striking is the extent to which policies introduced both by central and local governments, as well as schools, are still not evaluated properly, if indeed they are evaluated at all. This, of course, is the antithesis of evidence-based policy-making. The government and school leaders, therefore, need to have the courage to insist that programmes are properly evaluated, and here we should be very careful to define what we mean by 'properly evaluated'. Almost every government programme in the UK in the last 20 years has been evaluated in some way or other. Millions of pounds have been spent on this activity. However, all too often such evaluations cannot answer the basic question about whether something had a positive causal impact on some measurable outcome or not, and whether any observed impact is generalisable – that is, likely to occur if the policy was implemented in different contexts. In many cases the implementation of programmes was simply not done in a way that would have allowed full evaluation to take place, irrespective of whether resources were actually made available to undertake the evaluation. With no thought given to research design prior to implementation, undertaking a robust evaluation is almost impossible. Clearly education researchers have an important role to play here, in helping to design good evaluation of both government policy and school programmes.

Taking the need for more research evidence on policy and practice in education as given, specifically what might we want to evaluate? In England, there is a range of large policy changes affecting teachers and teaching that urgently need to be evaluated. With more Initial Teacher Education (ITE) being organised by schools, the research community needs robust evaluation of this as a route into teaching. Researchers need to have evidence of the impact of various models of teacher training on the behaviour of teachers in the classroom, their knowledge, their effectiveness and their attrition rate from the profession. There is also a need to know about the impact, negative or otherwise, of becoming a Teaching School on the pupils in those schools – that is, whether they gain from better teacher practice or suffer if there are insufficient additional resources provided to schools that take on teacher training. Another issue on which evidence is needed is teacher pay. The government has given schools more flexibility with regard to teacher pay and has empowered schools to link teacher pay more directly with teacher performance. Researchers need to understand what this will mean for the management of teachers, for teacher recruitment, for the supply of teachers in shortage subjects and of course for teacher performance, however this is measured.

These big policy interventions suggest that national evaluation is required. However, there are also smaller-scale questions about effective practices in schools, and the UCPS research programme is likely to be addressing these latter issues. The evidence tells us that teachers matter a great deal in terms of their influence on pupil achievement and that being taught by one of the most effective teachers is likely to result in substantially more academic progress than being taught by one of the least effective teachers. The impact that teachers have also appears to be greater for students who are more disadvantaged both academically and socio-economically. But knowing this is not enough; it only takes us part of the way there. Our first priority should be to improve our understanding of *how* researchers can help the lowest performing teachers improve their practice. More positively, the research community needs to continue to seek robust evidence on the specific practices and pedagogies that impact positively on pupils' achievement and wider well-being. This is an illustration of what the Faculty of Education–UCPS collaborative research programme might try to do. There is also a need to understand how to design CPD and materials that genuinely enable teachers to teach more effectively. There is huge scope to do more to really determine what particular interventions, materials and policies can help teachers improve their practice. The examples of research that follow are intended to be illustrative of the kinds of opportunities in which the UCPS might be involved. Indeed, all research conducted in the school is to be undertaken within a policy framework determined by the school governors, and subject to the authority and agreement of the headteacher.

The collaborative research approach may be best illustrated by two examples from our own Faculty: the *epiSTEMe* project led by Professor Kenneth Ruthven with Professors Christine Howe, Neil Mercer and Keith Taber (Howe et al., 2015; Ruthven et al., 2016); and the *Learning How to Learn* (LHTL) project led by Professor Mary James (James et al., 2006). Both these examples illustrate what is possible in terms of developing interventions and projects aimed at improving students' experiences and learning in a manner that explicitly explores a causal chain, using both quantitative and qualitative methodologies, and that build on existing research evidence.

epiSTEMe developed a research-informed intervention that was designed to incorporate teaching features known to improve student experience and outcomes, and was targeted at an important transition period in children's lives as they enter secondary school. This intervention organised lessons around problem situations, and tasks were framed and approached in ways that built students' ability to think as mathematicians and scientists. *epiSTEMe* also built on another field of research developed in the Faculty of Education, namely the use of dialogue in the classroom in both small groups and the whole class. The results from this project showed real promise in terms of improving students' scientific understanding, and further research like this is needed that is then trialled and evaluated at scale in primary and secondary school settings. This example, as we set out later in this chapter, highlights a fruitful and attractive possibility for the UCPS.

Learning How to Learn is a prime example of a collaborative research and development project set up with the specific aim of harnessing the strength of both local and more dispersed networks (Hargreaves, 2003) to create and disseminate research evidence. The project extended existing work on assessment for learning (a framework of formative assessment) in combination with a focus on teachers' professional development and schools' improvement in the context of broader educational change. The overriding aim was to explore learning at three levels: in classrooms by pupils and teachers; at the school level by teachers and school leaders; and within both wider physical and virtual school networks. Schools local to the collaborating universities were therefore co-opted into the project and engaged in multi-faceted interventions that would fit with each school's development plan (for instance, training days, and continued support by critical friends). The results of the combination of these interventions (James et al., 2006) highlight both the difficulties inherent in creating knowledge in an inclusive collaborative manner, but also the wide range of opportunities to then disseminate policy-relevant research in which schools have been key stakeholders. It is our hope that the UCPS may play such a role in the future.

EVIDENCE FOR PRACTICE

So how can education research achieve greater impact and influence? Here we discuss how evidence can be produced that can be used in classrooms and schools, focusing specifically on the chain of evidence and how researchers might introduce evidence into schools in particular.

The chain of evidence shown in Figure 1 focuses on teachers and students and represents the journey from teacher education and professional development programmes to student attainment (Timperley et al., 2007; Vermunt, 2014). New knowledge, based on recent research findings and/or other sources, is incorporated in *teacher education* or *teacher professional development programmes*. This knowledge, for example, may pertain to evidence about new pedagogical practices, new neuropsychological findings, a new mathematics curriculum, advances in assessment methods and new

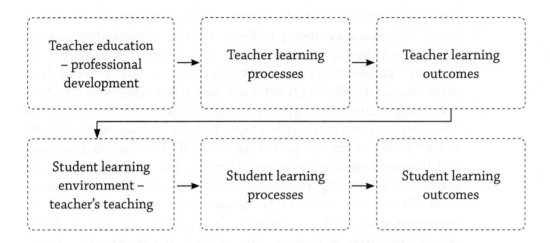

Figure 1: A chain of evidence from teacher education and professional development to student learning outcomes (adapted from Vermunt, 2014).

technological tools, and so on. Teachers may learn about this new knowledge in a variety of ways; for example, through workplace learning (innovations are introduced in practice and teachers learn by working with them), through a professional development programme (e.g. a lesson study in which teachers collaborate in small groups preparing, conducting and reflecting on new practices – see below), or through participating in research projects in collaboration with professional researchers. All these different learning environments may give rise to *teachers' learning processes*. Teachers read and think about the new knowledge, discuss it with colleagues, try it out in their classroom practice, reflect on how and why it worked or didn't work, adapt the new practices based on these reflections, or abandon them due to lack of effects, time or resources. These teacher learning processes lead to teacher learning outcomes: increases in knowledge, development or improvement of pedagogical or diagnostic skills, changes in attitudes towards innovations. In other words, teacher quality improves through gains in professional competence or expertise. All elements of the chain discussed so far are on the level of teachers' professional learning.

When teachers are able and willing to use their new professional expertise in their classroom teaching, we enter the level of impact on students' learning. A change in teachers' teaching reshapes the *learning environment for the students*. Teachers may use the new pedagogy, technological tool, mathematics curriculum or interpersonal skills that have become part of their expertise in their classroom teaching. This is not an automatic process:

evidence about teachers *not* using new expertise in their classroom teaching is abundant in the literature, and may be accounted for by a variety of reasons. The students' learning environment is, of course, broader than teachers' teaching and also includes learning resources, fellow students, the physical environment, and so on. The learning environment as a whole initiates *students' learning processes*. Students read learning materials, try to understand their meaning, discuss them critically, practice applications, complete assignments, memorise certain contents, regulate their learning, evaluate their progress, and so on. These learning activities lead to *student learning outcomes* in terms of increased knowledge, improved skills, changed attitudes, feelings of self-confidence, heightened interest or motivation. Some of these outcomes may be reflected in student attainment scores while some other outcomes are not often measured.

The flow in this chain of evidence can, of course, also go in the other direction: teachers may learn a lot from systematically studying the learning processes of their students; for example, how different students approach learning tasks differently, what specific understandings or misunderstandings students develop as a result of their teaching strategies and how effective students' learning practices are. A core characteristic of the lesson study approach to teacher professional development, for example, is in fact a focus on observing case pupils' learning and understanding during research lessons (Dudley, 2013; Warwick et al., 2016). Students may learn a lot from observing their teachers' learning as well, particularly when they are confronted with new material that they haven't seen before. After all, teachers are supposed to be experts in learning, and observing experts struggling to understand and solve difficult problems may teach them a lot about effective learning strategies.

To date, research that covers the whole chain of evidence described above is scarce. The LHTL project is a notable exception to this (its causal argument chain below in Figure 2 is adapted from James et al., 2006), by prefacing some of the flow already described above, and also highlighting the potential for a two-directional loop of knowledge and practice transmission from network, to school, to classroom and back.

One reason for the lack of research addressing the entire chain of evidence may be that covering the whole chain transcends the duration of an average research project. Another reason is probably that research on teacher learning and student learning is often conducted by different research communities, with little or no cross-fertilisation across the boundaries of their scientific endeavours (see Vermunt, 2013). In our view, however, traditional

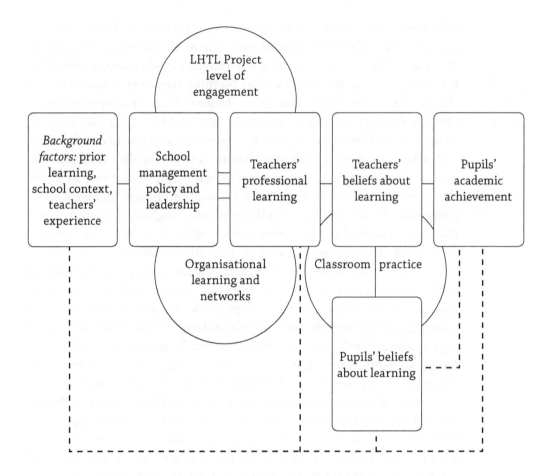

Figure 2: The causal argument chain for the Learning How to Learn project (adapted from James et al., 2006).

boundaries have to be crossed to achieve knowledge advancement about how students' and teachers' learning may benefit each other.

RESEARCH IN THE UNIVERSITY OF CAMBRIDGE PRIMARY SCHOOL

As mentioned earlier, all research at the UCPS will be conducted in accordance with the governors' policy. The Faculty of Education and UCPS intend to work together to produce a relevant, robust research programme that will build on existing theoretical and empirical research, and with practitioner engagement as part of the research from its inception. The research will primarily be designed to augment and advance the pre-primary and primary education evidence base in respect of pedagogy, curriculum and assessment. It will be critical that the research retains its focus on improving the quality of children's learning, both in the UCPS and in other schools, and contributes more generally to our understanding of how we can improve learning and schools. Moreover, wherever possible the focus on children's learning will be supplemented by a focus on teachers' learning to include as many elements of the chain of evidence described above as is feasible.

We anticipate that two broad categories of research might be undertaken. The first would be smaller scale projects, where data-gathering would be conducted exclusively within the UCPS; for example, investigating different teacher practices and school policies within the school itself. As an illustration of this approach, a pilot of a specific dialogic teaching method within a particular topic area might be developed, with the aim then being to scale up the particular approach developed and to go on to trial it in a larger number of schools to judge its impact on pupil outcomes. This second type of research therefore would be collaborative and larger scale, with data-gathering both within UCPS and in a number of Faculty of Education partner schools (including Teaching School alliances), and indeed possibly in schools that are not currently in the Faculty's or UCPS's networks. With this second type of larger scale research, the UCPS would be one of many schools participating in the research but would likely play a key role in leading others.

The research programme would be collaborative and involve consultation with UCPS teachers, parents, partner schools and Faculty of Education colleagues. This consultative approach is essential to ensure that parents are supportive of their children participating in research projects and that all stakeholders understand the purpose of the particular research and the potential gains to be had. We anticipate that staff members from the Faculty will lead on some research projects, colleagues from other disciplines within the university may lead on others (e.g. colleagues from psychology or neuroscience). UCPS staff might also initiate projects since it is critical that the research programme focuses on issues that are of paramount importance to the school, and hence are more likely to be of relevance to practitioners across the English system. Practitioner involvement and practitioner-led projects are likely to be core to the programme and, understandably, are intended to support the teacher education and professional development activities at the UCPS. In this way, knowledge growth about how teachers' and students' learning may benefit each other will be an explicit aim of the programme.

Of course, beyond the impact of the research on the practitioners involved in the research itself, researchers will be striving to achieve a wider impact on the education research community, practitioners and policy-makers. Of paramount importance will be effectively disseminating the research findings, and contributing to the national dividend – an issue that we discuss in more detail below. Genuinely disseminating the research findings across the education system as a whole is, naturally enough, a complex undertaking. Researchers know that achieving real impact is done in a number of different ways, requiring the involvement of a range of stakeholders, and indeed we need to recognise that evidence in and of itself may not be sufficient to achieve genuine impact. At a minimum, however, it is essential that the results from each research project are systematically presented, with key findings summarised in accessible language. It is also vital that key findings are contextualised in relation to the existing evidence base for teaching, to ensure that greater traction is obtained from the results. The expectation is that researchers and practitioners involved in the research will be asked to highlight any potential implications for curriculum, pedagogy and assessment, and wider school improvement, and to identify potential intervention strategies for changing teachers' practice. One possibility is that these summary messages could be made available in a simple form on the websites of the Faculty of Education and the UCPS and, following consultation with other groups, the findings may also be disseminated more widely, as we now discuss.

THE NATIONAL DIVIDEND

It will be recalled from chapter 2 that in the university's submission to the Department for Education (DfE) for the approval and funding of the UCPS there was a commitment to a national educational dividend. This entailed a range of possible local, regional and national collaborative research-related initiatives with a range of agencies. Consistent with the spirit of this dividend, the aim of the Faculty of Education–UCPS collaboration is to produce high quality research, research that is the product of a genuine partnership between two institutions committed to trying to inform and improve practice and policy across the system as a whole. This, of course, will not be easy. Indeed, one challenge will be to ensure that the lessons learned and the research findings produced really do reach right across the education system. Translating research findings and making them accessible to teachers and other practitioners is a crucial part of this task.

In England there have been many attempts to synthesise rigorous education research and bring it to the attention of policy-makers. The National Education Research Forum (NERF),[3] established off the back of the Hargreaves report mentioned earlier, is one such example. Another attempt to create a repository of RCTs in the social sciences (including education), namely the Campbell Collaboration,[4] was established at the turn of this century. More recently, the EEF has also developed web-based resources to spread the message about research findings that might influence policy and practice. Some earlier efforts at dissemination and impact might give cause for concern about whether the research from the Faculty–UCPS partnership really can influence the system as a whole. However, we have two reasons to be hopeful that the partnership really can help build a national dividend from the research programme. First, evidence produced can be incorporated directly into the teacher education and professional development programmes of the Faculty, reaching a large number of new and experienced teachers directly. Second, the recent experience of the EEF and researchED gives us reason to be hopeful that new media can be used effectively to communicate findings. Using web-based repositories of research, building collaborations with key stakeholders and other repositories of research evidence, producing accessible summaries of evidence and making full use of social media and other means to transmit the findings are all ways in which to ensure that the research findings from the Faculty of Education–UCPS partnership really do reach a large number of practitioners and policy-makers. We will be keen to seek partners from across the education system with whom to collaborate to achieve our goals in this regard.

CONCLUSION

Returning to the system-wide issue of how we ensure that education research informs policy and practice, we are, after many decades of trying to influence policy and practice, all too aware that policy is rarely truly evidence-based. (This point is considered further in chapter 10.) Evidence is often used to support policy decisions and less often used to decide what those decisions should be. However, far from giving up completely on the idea of our research informing the world, we need instead to be even more rigorous in our evaluation of what goes on in our education system, and to:

- be critical in our approach to engagement with government policy;

- initiate research in which researchers and practitioners collaborate and both develop ownership of research questions and outcomes;

- undertake research that is long and encompassing enough to cover the whole chain of evidence from teacher knowledge to student outcomes;

- encourage and cajole policy-makers to undertake and fund high quality research and evaluation of policies and, just as importantly, to be relentless in our attempts to better communicate our research to stakeholders, even when faced with resistance to our messages.

We also need to remember that very rapid policy change makes it next to impossible to evaluate the impact of one change before another is upon us. If we discard policies before we even know whether they have worked this will not be optimal. Such rapid change also leaves those working in education with a sense of permanent crisis and failure. Constant change implies that we have a broken system. Indeed some parts of it are broken, but most of it is not. How can we challenge this damaging approach in education? Clearly with great difficulty, but we would argue that practitioners and academics in partnership with one another need to develop our capability as a sector to evaluate rigorously what we do. In the UCPS this is precisely what research should aim to achieve.

Notes

1 See chapter 4, note 7.
2 See chapter 4, note 10.
3 Founded in 1999 by the then Secretary of State for Education (David Blunkett) to create a national strategy for educational research, see http://www.eep.ac.uk/nerf/index.html
4 See http://www.campbellcollaboration.org/.

References

Alexander, R. (2011). Evidence, rhetoric and collateral damage: The problematic pursuit of 'world class' standards, *Cambridge Journal of Education*, 41(3): 265–86.

Alexander, R. (ed.) (2010). *Children, Their World, Their Education: Final Report and Recommendations of the Cambridge Primary Review* (London: Routledge).

Ball, S.J. (2005). *Education Policy and Social Class: The Selected Works of Stephen J. Ball* (Abingdon: Routledge).

Ball, S.J. (1997). Policy sociology and critical social research: A personal review of recent education policy and policy research, *British Educational Research Journal*, 23(3): 257–74.

Dearden, L., Machin, S. & Vignoles, A. (2010). The contribution of the economics of education to education, in J. Furlong & M. Lawn (eds), *Disciplines of Education: Their Role in the Future of Education Research* (London: Routledge).

Dudley, P. (2013). Teacher learning in Lesson Study: What interaction-level discourse analysis revealed about how teachers utilised imagination, tacit knowledge of teaching and fresh evidence of pupils learning, to develop practice knowledge and so enhance their pupils' learning, *Teaching and Teacher Education*, 34: 107–21.

Gale, T. & Densmore, K. (2003). *Engaging Teachers: Towards a Radical Democratic Agenda for Schooling* (Maidenhead: McGraw-Hill Education).

Goldacre, B. (2013). *Building Evidence into Education* (London: Department for Education) http://media.education.gov.uk/assets/files/pdf/b/ben%20goldacre%20paper.pdf.

Hargreaves, D.H. (2003). *Education Epidemic: Transforming Secondary Schools through Innovation Networks* (London: DEMOS).

Hargreaves, D.H. (1999). Revitalising educational research: Lessons from the past and proposals for the future, *Cambridge Journal of Education*, 29(2): 239–49.

Hargreaves, D.H. (1997). In defence of evidence-based teaching, *British Educational Research Journal*, 23(4): 405–19.

Howe, C., Ilie, S., Guardia, P., Hofmann, R., Mercer, N. & Riga, F. (2015). Principled improvement in science: Forces and proportional relations in early secondary-school teaching, *International Journal of Science Education*, 37(1): 162–84.

James, M., Black, P., McCormick, R., Pedder, D. & Wiliam, D. (2006). Learning how to learn, *Research Papers in Education*, 21(2): 101–18.

Oancea, A. (2016). The aims and claims of educational research, in M. Hand & R. Davies (eds), *Education, Ethics and Experience* (Abingdon: Routledge), pp. 109–22.

Rudduck, J. (1998). Educational research: The prospect of change, in J. Rudduck & D. McIntyre (eds), *Educational Research: The Challenge Facing Us* (London: Paul Chapman), pp. 3–13.

Ruthven, K., Mercer, N., Taber, K., Hofmann, R., Ilie, S., Riga, F., Luthman, S. & Guardia, P. (2016). A research-informed dialogic-teaching approach to early secondary-school mathematics and science: The pedagogical design and field trial of the epiSTEMe intervention, *Research Papers in Education*. DOI: 10.1080/02671522.2015.1129642.

Saunders, P. (2010). *Social Mobility Myths* (London: Civitas).

Timperley, H., Wilson, A., Barrar, H. & Fung, I. (2007). *Teacher Professional Learning and Development*, Best Evidence Synthesis Iteration (Wellington: Ministry of Education). Retrieved http://www.oecd.org/edu/school/48727127.pdf.

Tooley, J. & Darby, D. (1998). *Education Research: A Critique (A survey of published educational research)*. London: Office for Standards in Education. Retrieved http://hdl.voced.edu.au/10707/137550.

Vermunt, J.D. (2013). *Teacher Learning and Student Learning: Are they Related?* Inaugural lecture given at the University of Cambridge, Faculty of Education, 22 May.

Vermunt, J.D. (2014). Teacher learning and professional development, in S. Krolak-Schwerdt, S. Glock & M. Böhmer (eds), *Teachers' Professional Development: Assessment, Training, and Learning* (Rotterdam: Sense), pp. 79–95.

Vignoles, A. (2011). Economics of education, in J. Arthur & A. Peterson (eds), *The Routledge Companion to Education* (London: Routledge), pp. 86–94.

Warwick, P., Vrikki, M., Vermunt, J.D., Mercer, N. & Van Halem, N. (2016). Connecting observations of student and teacher learning: An examination of dialogic processes in lesson study discussions in Mathematics, *ZDM Mathematics Education*, (48): 555–69.

Whitty, G. (2006). Education(al) research and education policy making: Is conflict inevitable?, *British Educational Research Journal*, 32(2): 159–76.

10 Research and a standards-based primary teaching profession

Mary James, Andrew Pollard and Peter Gronn

At the same time as there has been a growing focus in English educational circles (and indeed internationally) on research evidence-informed practice in schools (see the previous chapter), there has also emerged the possibility of a college for primary and secondary school teachers (as briefly alluded to in chapter 4). Indeed, after a prolonged period of consultation within the profession, February 2014 saw the launch of a *Blueprint* for a new College of Teaching (Prince's Teaching Institute, 2014). This document makes a number of proposals for raising the status of teaching, its quality and the hoped-for improvement of students' learning. At the heart of the blueprint for the College is the notion of standards of accomplished practice for teachers. While the idea of performance standards *per se* is not new, what is different in the *Blueprint* is, first, the claim that teachers – rather than government ministers and departmental officials – initially as part of a voluntary system of advanced teacher accreditation – should define standards of professional accomplishment, and second, that the legitimacy of such a set of standards is enhanced significantly when these are grounded in research evidence. Given that the generation of research data and the building of professional learning programmes for teachers lie at the heart of the mission of the University of Cambridge Primary School (UCPS), the new school is uniquely placed to contribute nationally to the establishment of a standards-based profession for primary teachers. With this opportunity in mind, the chapter begins by documenting briefly the progress made on the establishment of the College. It then focuses on the idea of professional standards and their justification. That section is followed by a review of problems and possibilities inherent in the use of research evidence as a basis for defining standards of accomplished teaching, including recent English initiatives on the collation and use of evidence. It concludes with some implications for the UCPS.

THE COLLEGE OF TEACHING

A key recent development in the emergence of the idea of a college was the release in April 2012 of the report *Great Teachers: Attracting, Training and Retaining the Best* (House of Commons Education Committee, 2012). Some of the groundwork for what this report recommended had been prepared five years earlier by the Public Services Improvement Policy Group (PSIPG),[1] a body established by the former Prime Minister David Cameron as part of the Conservative Party's policy review at that time. Indeed, that body's report, *Restoring Pride in our Public Services,* was insistent that while the determination of education system outcomes lay with the Secretary of State, 'decisions about how to deliver those outcomes belong with the professionals' (PSIPG, 2007, p. 93). To that end, it recommended the establishment of a royal college of teachers along with a system for commissioning and disseminating 'evidence based practice' to strengthen the pedagogical process (PSIPG, 2007, pp. 94–5). For its part, the House of Commons Education Committee (2012, para. 114) identified support for a college of teaching which as part of its remit might accredit CPD and teacher standards. The existing College of Teachers[2] had suggested (in its submission to the Committee) the establishment of a chartered teacher model, but this proposal was dismissed, as was the College itself, because it was claimed to lack the requisite 'public profile or capacity to implement such a scheme'. Rather, the Committee recommended that the government 'work with teachers and others' to develop proposals for a new College of Teaching, 'along the lines of the Royal Colleges and Chartered Institutions in other professions' (House of Commons Education Committee, 2012, rec. 20).

In September 2012, a workshop of 30 or so educationalists (although without civil servants or politicians present) was convened by the Prince's Teaching Institute (PTI) at the Lansdowne Club in London (at the suggestion of six headteacher participants in a recent PTI headteacher residential programme) to test the appetite for such a college. This meeting was moderated by Sir Richard Lambert (Chancellor of the University of Warwick and previously Director-General of the Confederation of British Industry) and addressed by Professor Jonathan Shepherd (a council member of the

Royal College of Surgeons). After about two hours of small group discussion and a plenary session it was agreed unanimously that the PTI should continue to play an honest broker role by taking forward the process by convening a commission to build on the workshop outcomes, and then disseminating a report to the wider education community (Prince's Teaching Institute, 2012, p. 8). Following a subsequent scoping study by the consultants McKinsey & Coy, the circulation of a discussion document and completion of surveys as part of a public consultation, the establishment of the foreshadowed commission and a committee of teachers (the group which authored and launched the *Blueprint*), *A new member-driven College of Teaching* was ready for release. Such was the momentum sustained during 2014–15 that a groundswell of support from 450 organisations and individuals formed a 'Claim your College' coalition. In October 2015, 14 new College trustees were appointed (with the trust chaired by a teacher, and with the majority of the membership comprising teachers and headteachers). As an 'independent, member-driven and voluntary professional body run by teachers for the benefit of learners', the aim of the new College of Teaching is to give teachers 'equality of status with other professions by advancing high standards, recognising excellence and promoting evidence-based practice and policy'. The college will not have 'a regulatory role' and it will be 'independent of government' (College of Teachers, 2016).

STANDARDS AS MEASURES OF ACCOMPLISHED TEACHING

Standards and standard-setting are central to the new college's work. The *Blueprint* itemised setting standards, enhancing professionals' development, and informing professional practice, standards and policy with evidence, with standards being the means by which the profession would articulate its vision of 'high quality professional practice' (Prince's Teaching Institute, 2014, p. 6). In human activity generally, standards are significant because they provide measures for the making of judgments of quality about a range of products and practices. In schooling, specifically, standards offer a means of articulating what teachers 'should *know*, believe and be able to *do*' (Ingvarson & Rowe, 2008, p. 14, original emphases), and measuring the quality of teaching against standards. The credibility and legitimacy of regimes of standards, however, will vary depending on their authorship and according to the bases on which they rest. The hope for the proponents of standards for teaching is that if these are grounded in forms of knowledge – for example, subject content knowledge (say, of history or science) and pedagogical content knowledge – then their claims to credibility and legitimacy are strengthened significantly. Sadly, however, research-derived knowledge in teaching linked to improved outcomes for learners that might provide a grounding for standards of accomplished practice, has been 'transitory, likely to be named as the work of researchers rather than teachers, inaccessible to other teachers, siloed in academic sub-disciplines, and lost amid a plethora of fads or low priority within academic hierarchies of knowledge and reward systems' (Timperley & Alton-Lee, 2008, p. 334). In light of this rather gloomy prognosis, in the remainder of this chapter we discuss whether recent developments in England provide any grounds for hope, and what these might mean for the UCPS.

'EVIDENCE-BASED' DECISION-MAKING IN EDUCATION

The aspiration that policy and practice in education should be based on research evidence has existed in various forms for a very long time. Data on school provision and performance have been collected in relation to the administrative jurisdictions of the time since the Victorian-era introduction of the elementary school system 150 years ago. A particular expansion of the scope of such analysis followed the post-World War II settlement when patterns of performance began to be more systematically monitored in relation to issues of inequality. In recent decades, following the *Education Reform Act* of 1988 and the establishment of full national systems in England, Northern Ireland and Wales, the collection of administrative and performance data has gone far further – with sophisticated systems for pupil, school and local authority comparison now becoming well established. Where available, formally or informally, comparisons of school performance have been influential on parental decision-making.

Throughout most of the period referred to above, the role of Her Majesty's Inspectors was seen as being to provide independent evidence on the quality of provision, based on professional judgement. The Inspectorate published reports on schools, issues or curricular subjects to provide both the public and the profession with information to promote improvement. Since 1988, inspection (the responsibility, since 1992, of the Office for Standards in Education: Ofsted) has been organised more in relation to school accountability, with inspection frameworks setting criteria for school inspection, and reports on individual schools being published for public consumption.

Taken together, school performance tables and Ofsted reports have a powerful impact on schools.

The use of evidence in the UK, in other words, has its roots in administrative functions, but in recent decades has been reconfigured as a vital component of a new approach to school improvement based on market competition. Robust information on school context and performance, it is believed, can establish the value added by a school, and thus establish standards of performance that can be used to inform decisions on the leadership and future of schools and local authorities. In aggregate, too, such information can also be used to compare whole national systems and to inform policy decisions at the highest levels. Such decisions can thus, in principle, be evidence-based.

However, there are some challenges in the implementation of this goal. In particular, to achieve evidence-based policy and practice assumes the existence of evidence that is scientifically trustworthy and is accepted as such by the stakeholders in education. From 1999 to 2006, the National Education Research Forum (NERF)[3] was established in England to provide strategic coordination of the necessary elements. Attention was paid to funding priorities and foresight on contemporary issues, on research capacity and quality, with particular attention to quantitative research and systematic designs, and on the management of and access to research-based knowledge. Influenced by provision in medicine, the aspiration was to create an evidence centre from which high-quality knowledge on education could be commissioned, validated and disseminated. Although the impetus for NERF faded with changing political leadership, the aspiration very much remains and can be seen in the contemporary commitments of the Education Endowment Foundation (EEF)[4] and the College of Teaching.

'EVIDENCE-INFORMED' DECISION-MAKING IN EDUCATION

It is important to note that alongside the national policy developments described above, there are parallel narratives that are more closely linked to the struggles of researchers and practitioners to describe, analyse and understand school and classroom contexts, and teaching and learning processes – in other words, what economists refer to as the 'black box' that intervenes between inputs and outputs, and which can have profound effects. In the sweep of history, there are great texts on teaching and learning going back, for instance, to Comenius. From such works, as educational provision expanded during the Industrial Revolution, were derived handbooks on teaching used to train and guide new teachers. In parallel, there were descriptive accounts by influential educators of their time, often revealing both their practices and the underlying principles that guided their provision. Some educators, such as Susan Isaacs, based their work on detailed observation, and therefore provided carefully grounded analyses that began to bridge research and practice (Isaacs, 1952). However, historically, social scientific researchers have found it difficult to devise robust designs and methodologies that are capable of capturing the complexity of classroom and school life. In the gathering of research evidence, the tensions between obtaining authentic validity whilst also achieving high reliability and generalisability have, even now, remained considerable.

From the late 1960s, qualitative researchers, working within an interpretative or sociological tradition, often focused on teacher-pupil language, perspectives or interaction. They conducted a large number of detailed case studies in single schools using various forms of ethnographic method to generate grounded theory, and with a particular focus on various dimensions of inequality (e.g., Ball, 1981; Burgess, 1983; Hargreaves, 1967; Lacey, 1970; Willis 1977). Although this work was often insightful and authentic, it was always necessary to be cautious about the representativeness of cases and to understand the framework of analysis.

In recent decades, professional educators have repeatedly attempted to develop expertise in various forms of enquiry, which would enable more systematic evidence on policy and practice to be gathered in school and classroom contexts. The aspiration has been to find ways to combine the best of both quantitative and qualitative approaches, and to draw on concepts and insights from a whole range of disciplinary frameworks that seem relevant to such a multifaceted undertaking. In this respect, the work of Lawrence Stenhouse, who led the Humanities Curriculum Project (HCP), is worth a special mention. A historian by inclination and training, he valued case study especially but was not opposed to quantitative approaches when they were appropriate. His biggest contribution, however, was to promote the notion of teachers as researchers of their classroom practice. Inscribed on his memorial plaque, in the grounds of the University of East Anglia, are his words: 'It is teachers who in the end will change the world of school by understanding it' (Stenhouse, 1975, p. 208). Teachers as researchers have produced sophisticated analyses of classroom activity, including, for instance, Michael Armstrong in his classic study, *Closely Observed Children* (1981), but there are many other activities of this nature that are not publicly documented.

Stenhouse's notion of the teacher as researcher later became associated with Kurt Lewin's (1946) concept of action research through the work of Stenhouse's HCP colleague John Elliott (1991) and another colleague Clem Adelman (1983). In parallel, in the United States, the concept of the reflective practitioner emerged in the work of Donald Schön (1983). All of these ideas became linked to the development of professional expertise and were thus endorsed in teacher education programmes and by teacher associations. There is, however, a crucial difference. In Lewin's and Elliott's conceptions there is an emphasis on collaborative, group activity, on the assumption that collective action is needed to bring about change in constraining contexts, whilst Stenhouse and Schön were focused more on individual teachers' improvement of their own practice.

Most recently, the practice of lesson study has been developing from its roots in the Far East to provide more codified protocols for classroom enquiry (Dudley, 2012, 2015). Elliott (2012) is a key advocate of this approach because, at its core, lesson study is a commitment to *collaborative* inquiry. Moreover, he sees the potential for the development of an experimental science of teaching cast in the form of John Dewey's Laboratory School model (mentioned earlier in the introduction to this book) whereby pedagogical theories are tested and further developed as a source of pedagogical principles (or standards). These ideas are important for the UCPS and the way it formulates its role and contribution. The challenges, however, should not be underestimated.

The technical difficulty of drawing valid, generalisable inferences from work within a single school, or even a cluster of schools, illustrates the rationale for use of the term 'evidence-informed', rather than 'evidence-based', in relation to policy and practice. The weakened truth claim is more realistic, but it also acknowledges that political and professional judgement will necessarily be used when reaching conclusions. Although 'evidence-based' was the term used in the early sections of this chapter in respect of the anticipated role of the new College of Teaching, the term 'evidence-informed', of course, remains consistent with the aspirations of its proponents in respect of teaching standards.

This argument has a more general applicability, for despite the contemporary commitment of some policy-makers and researchers to RCTs and other structured designs, in the belief that what works can be established with a high degree of confidence, many other researchers and practitioners continue to believe that the phenomena involved in education are too complex to be fully analysed by the social and natural sciences alone.

Philosophy, ethics, hermeneutics and historical analysis also have a role to play. Indeed, a balanced position may be to acknowledge that specific research approaches provide particular insights and that a diversity of approaches is valuable. Each may be significant, but no single approach is likely to represent the whole picture. In addition, educational aims and priorities require value judgements that are often contested in contemporary societies, so that the interpretation of research evidence is often challenged. For all these reasons, due modesty in the claims made for the potential use of evidence in education is appropriate.

In summary, we might say that without a systematic quest for, and application of, evidence, the profession and the system are blind, and therefore that a commitment to enquiry and research is essential for contemporary education. But this commitment has to be matched by a realistic appreciation of the limits of research. In particular, only the practitioner or policy-maker can be fully aware of the dilemmas they face and the diverse influences that inform their decision-making.

TOWARDS AN INFRASTRUCTURE FOR EVIDENCE-INFORMED PRACTICE

In the late 1990s, educational research in the UK was subject to stringent criticism (Hargreaves 1996; Hillage et al., 1998; Tooley & Darby 1998), for, as Whitty (2006) summarised, lack of rigour and cumulation, theoretical incoherence, ideological bias, irrelevance, lack of user engagement, poor dissemination, inaccessibility and low value for money. Similar criticisms were made in Europe, the US, Australia and elsewhere across the world.

Some commentators argued that the reasons for this state of affairs, if true, could be that insufficient investment had been made and that the funding available tended to be small, piecemeal, uncoordinated and lacking in strategic direction. As a response, sometimes characterised as 'last chance saloon', different UK governments and agencies set up three initiatives: NERF, mentioned above, to attend to finding priorities and provide strategic direction; the Evidence for Policy and Practice Information and Co-ordinating Centre (EPPI)[5] to provide systematic reviews and syntheses of research evidence along the lines of the Cochrane and Campbell Collaborations in, respectively, health[6] and social policy;[7] and the Teaching and Learning Research Programme (TLRP) of the Economic and Social Research Council (ESRC) to co-ordinate new research focused specifically on teaching and learning in all sectors of education across the life course – that is, from early years education to adult and professional learning. All of these initiatives were committed to evidence-informed policy and practice.

The EPPI Centre continues its work although its remit now includes many areas of social policy including, in addition to education, health, social care, developing economies, sport and crime. The TLRP, including an extension on Technology Enhanced Learning (TEL) concluded its work in 2012. Government support for NERF ceased in 2005 as political priorities changed.

In recognition that the need for strategic vision was still required if the commitment to evidence-informed policy and practice was to be fulfilled, the demise of NERF was followed by the creation of the Strategic Forum for Research in Education (SFRE)[8] to take forward discussion on how to improve the generation and use of evidence in education. However, the initial conception for SFRE was promoted by the TLRP with the particular support of its Steering Committee.[9] In other words, researchers and practitioners seized the initiative as the support of the government fell away, although stakeholders from governments in all four countries of the UK continued to be drawn in. On this basis, SFRE attempted to map the necessary characteristics of an effective knowledge management system for a modern society. The contributions of different forms of research and enquiry, each fit for their purpose, were endorsed, but were also related to the efficacy of the system as a whole. As with NERF, the importance of an infrastructure to make trustworthy research findings publically available was promoted, but the necessary cautions about the application of such knowledge were also emphasised.

In its final report (Pollard & Oancea, 2010, pp. 2–25), SFRE proposed six interacting elements of knowledge development and mobilisation:

Origination and planning – including the conditions and provision for the facilitation and prioritisation of research activity;

Creation and production – focusing on both innovation and the completion of projects in respect of each major type of research;

Assessment and validation – including peer judgement, user and beneficiary validation and the processes, criteria and indicators specific to each assessment context and type of research;

Accumulation and interpretation – concerning issues such as the processing of new knowledge in databases, empirical review and theoretical synthesis;

Mediation and brokerage – addressing the multi-faceted promotional and communication strategies that enable the supply of and demand for evidence to be bridged;

Application and impact – considering the ways in which knowledge is used, scaled up and takes effect within policy and practice.

These elements can be represented in a progressive cycle which, in rational system terms, might provide an idealised template for provision (Figure 1).

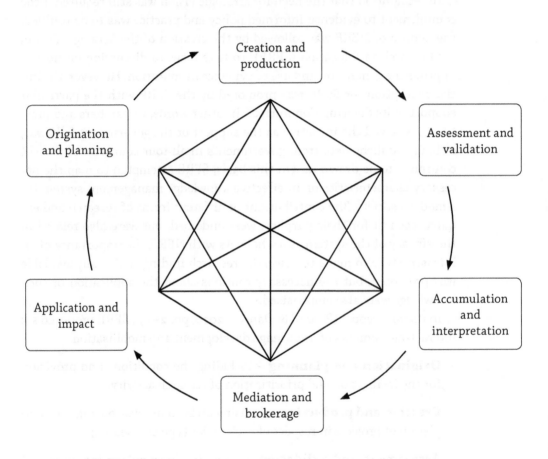

Figure 1: Elements in knowledge development and mobilisation

SFRE identified four main types of research with legitimate calls for funding: disciplinary research designed to contribute to funds of knowledge; applied research; development and evaluation; and practitioner enquiry. The major challenge for the government and other stakeholders was thought to relate to the prioritisation of applied research, both in response to immediate needs but also in the long-term for sustainability. This challenge requires the reviewing of existing provision, horizon scanning of future needs, and negotiation among stakeholders – funders, generators and users of research evidence – of priorities. The experiences of NERF and SFRE suggest that this is perhaps not best co-ordinated by central governments, the political agendas of which change with such rapidity. However, a national strategic overview is needed to inform decisions about the apportionment of scarce resources. The best course might be to recreate a funders' forum, which has existed in the past, working with the new College of Teaching to represent practitioners and the British Educational Research Association (BERA) to represent researchers.

In the present decade much debate has surrounded the best way to generate, assess and validate research findings in education. In 2013, the then Secretary of State, Michael Gove, launched 'a new vision for evidence-based practice in education and teaching', which allowed Ben Goldacre (a medic, academic and journalist) to share his thinking on *Building Evidence into Education* (Goldacre, 2013). He argued for the use of RCTs as a basis for social policy across the public services. In support of this approach, the Cabinet Office launched a network of six 'What Works' evidence centres. The What Works Centre for education is the responsibility of the EEF. The EEF was set up in 2010, as an early initiative by Michael Gove, who was keen to shed the DfE's role in managing research in education. Thus, £125 million over ten years was granted to the Sutton Trust to support the work of the EEF. The EEF funds projects that are designed to evaluate the impact of interventions that aim to raise attainment for disadvantaged groups. RCTs are the preferred methodology.

In collaboration with Durham University, the EEF has produced a toolkit aimed at school headteachers, teachers and parents. This toolkit summarises the results of more than 11 000 studies on the effectiveness of education interventions, as well as the EEF's own studies.[10] For each educational intervention, such as peer-to-peer learning or repeating a year, the toolkit summarises how much difference the intervention makes (measured in months of additional progress); how much it costs (assuming a class size of 25); and how confident researchers are of the effect on the basis of the evidence so far. The idea is that headteachers can base their spending decisions on robust evidence about the impact of interventions on pupils' attainment as measured by national tests. For example, the EEF concludes that the employment of extra teaching assistants is relatively expensive and not a very effective way of boosting pupil performance, whereas small-group teaching and peer-to-peer learning are much more cost effective.

Goldacre's advocacy of RCTs was not without nuance. He acknowledged, for example, that ethical issues associated with random allocation to interventions need to be worked through; that dealing with multiple variables requires statistical sophistication; that RCTs are good at showing that something works but not why, which often requires qualitative research to answer; that choosing the right outcome measure is not always straightforward; and that replication is needed to test the effectiveness of interventions in different settings. He recognised the importance of systems to disseminate and communicate results, and for professional development to enable teachers to understand and appraise the quality of the research that is done. His response to this last challenge was to propose a kind of 'dating service' whereby practitioners and researchers might work together: 'This kind of two-way exchange helps the teacher-researchers of the future to learn more about the nuts and bolts of running a trial; and it helps to keep researchers out of their ivory towers, focusing more on what matters most to teachers' (Goldacre, 2013, pp. 14–15). In reflecting on what should happen next, Goldacre said that it would be bizarre of the DfE to tell teachers what methods of teaching to use. If there is genuine commitment to more autonomy, then teachers need the freedom to judge what is best for their students, albeit informed by high-quality evidence.

However, there are other substantial difficulties in moving from trial results to evidence-based practice and the embodiment of best practice in standards. Decades of research on educational change (e.g., Fullan, 2001) has shown that impact will not simply follow from the dissemination and clear communication of results to discerning end-users. First, the profession requires an ongoing process and infrastructure for evaluating, synthesising and communicating existing and new knowledge, accumulated over decades of research. The What Works Centre in education only addresses this issue in part because it restricts its remit, however worthwhile, to the evaluation of current interventions that are intended to close the gap in student achievement using RCTs and limited measures of performance. Second, educational professionals need to create the organisational cultures and conditions that are required to roll out and scale up innovations in natural settings. This strategy will need as much research effort as the development of formal trials.

In relation to the first point, it is unlikely that a single body would ever be equipped to do all the collection, evaluation, synthesising and communication that would be needed. The EEF, EPPI, the Educational Evidence Portal (EEP),[11] the Centre for the Use of Research and Evidence in Education (CUREE),[12] the Education Resources Information Centre (ERIC),[13] the Education Media Centre (EMC),[14] the Institute for Effective Education (IEE),[15] The Coalition for Evidence-Based Education (CEBE),[16] MESH[17] and others past, present and future, all have their place. There is a case for letting a thousand flowers bloom because each has been fertilised by a committed group of people with a particular purpose in mind. On the other hand, this plethora creates confusion for teachers who do not have the time to scan and appraise all of these potential resources. The SFRE recommended the creation of a comprehensive map of the UK information landscape to increase the accessibility of brokerage organisations and mediated research resources. This is a valuable role that the new College of Teaching could take on for its members.

In relation to the second point, the creation of conditions for the uptake, adaptation, implementation, embedding, spreading and sustaining of evidence-informed innovations in schools will require further research (as academics so often opine!). Here is an important role for the UCPS because it is the particular circumstances of knowledge use that often have a profound impact on outcomes. Fortunately, perhaps, the incentive structures in higher education are changing and the inclusion of impact case studies in the Research Excellence Framework (REF) now encourage researchers to plan 'pathways to impact'. From this perspective, the creation of a University Training School (UTS) in Cambridge that has collaborative research forming part of its core mission provides a unique opportunity for practitioners and researchers to work closely together on investigating the ways in which innovations, developed onsite or elsewhere, can be engineered into practice with positive results, and holds open the possibility of their subsequent incorporation into national standards for the profession.

RESEARCH AND TEACHER EDUCATION

In 2014, BERA and the Royal Society of Arts (RSA) published the final report of their inquiry into the *Research and the Teaching Profession* (BERA-RSA, 2014). The report made the case for the development, across the UK, of self-improving education systems in which teachers are research-literate and have opportunities for engagement in research and enquiry. In other words, they need to be enabled to engage *with* research and to engage *in* enquiry-oriented practice. On the one hand, this suggestion would entail a clear obligation on the part of teachers, perhaps embedded in the terms and conditions of their employment. On the other hand, commissioners of research should have an obligation to build teacher engagement into the commissioning process so that they are active agents rather than passive participants. Similarly, producers of new knowledge, including universities, Teaching School alliances, academy chains, local authorities and individual schools, should endeavour to make their research findings as freely available, accessible and useable as possible. The report concluded that:

> [A]mongst policymakers and practitioners there is considerable potential for greater dialogue than currently takes place, as there is between teachers, teacher-researchers and the wider research community.

And:

> It also concludes that everybody in a leadership position – in the policy community, in university departments of education, at school or college level or in key agencies within the education infrastructure – has responsibility to support the creation of the sort of organizational cultures in which these outcomes, for both learners *and* teachers, can be achieved. (BERA-RSA, 2014, p. 8, original emphasis)

IMPLICATIONS FOR THE UCPS

The discussion above illustrates the scale and scope of the task facing the educational research community if it is to contribute credibly to the future development of a standards-based profession grounded in sound research evidence. The whole infrastructure needs to be considered in terms of its separate elements, how these interrelate, how they are best developed and by whom. There is no need to dismantle what exists already, nor to co-ordinate activity centrally, but there is an urgent need to better map, appraise and communicate information so that policy and practice can be built on best evidence. Only then can standards be distilled from all the available sources.

There is scope here for the UCPS to make an important contribution at several levels, because it will have the advantage of a very close, built-in relationship between practitioners in a school and colleagues in one of the foremost university faculties in the country. Each group will also have access to supporting networks and communities, for example, the College of Teaching and other professional associations in the case of teachers, and BERA and other subject and disciplinary associations in the case of the university researchers. In partnership, they will be able to contribute to discussion about the commissioning of research by identifying gaps in knowledge; work collaboratively on new research; contribute to the collection and evaluation of existing research and, especially, test the validity of research findings in particular classroom contexts; translate, communicate and mediate valued research to other user communities.

THE DISTILLATION OF STANDARDS

As has been indicated, a major ambition of the College of Teaching is to develop research-informed standards for teaching and teachers which could be the basis for professional recognition. One way of facilitating this might be to adopt a framework of effective practices identified in the EEF Toolkit. However, this would narrow the field to only those themes and methodologies supported by the EEF. Another option would be to use a more inclusive and iterative approach, akin to that used by the TLRP to generate principles for effective pedagogy (James & Pollard, 2011, 2012).

A major ambition of TLRP, for both analytic and impact purposes, was to try to produce an evidence-informed statement of general principles of teaching and learning. The basic view was that a great deal is actually known about pedagogy, both in the UK and internationally, but that the synthesis, communication and implementation of such knowledge were far weaker than they should be.

The diverse nature of TLRP's (100+) project and thematic investments, which focused on different research questions in different contexts, sometimes using different methods and theoretical perspectives, did not permit formal quantitative meta-analysis rendering aggregated effect sizes of interventions as indicators of what works. However, each project engaged with existing research in its own particular field or sub-field and built on this to take knowledge forward cumulatively. Through the mechanisms for knowledge exchange set up by TLRP, and drawing on their own particular networks and resources, research teams also developed thinking in dialogue with other researchers and users, nationally and internationally. In this way new insights were located in intellectual and political contexts through social processes.

The expectation of the TLRP that all the research would be carried out in authentic settings of practice made it impossible to control all the variables operating at any one time, although it enabled researchers, working with practitioners, to grapple with the issues of implementation that so often confound best efforts to scale up promising innovations. Furthermore, it enabled practitioners to use their knowledge of the features of particular settings and characteristics of learners to develop and refine generalisations from the original research.

For all these reasons, when TLRP was asked what it (as a programme) had found out about effective teaching and learning, generally, it was not justifiable to make unequivocal claims about findings in terms of categorical knowledge or cause-effect relationships. However, it was possible to offer evidence-informed principles which could engage with diverse forms of evidence whilst calling for the necessary application of contextualised judgement by teachers, practitioners and/or policy-makers. Such principles can enable the accumulation and organisation of knowledge in resilient, realistic and practically useful ways, and have the potential, progressively, to generate understanding and language for use within public debates.

The analytical and synthetic approach to reviewing the TLRP evidence involved an iterative process of working between a conceptual map that TLRP had developed to represent the scope of its interests, with reference to teaching and learning, and the outputs that were beginning to emerge from individual TLRP projects and cross-programme thematic work.

The way in which the TLRP Directors' Team tackled the analytical and synthetic task is best described as narrative review. One piece of thematic work, led by Harry Torrance and Judy Sebba, was explicitly directed towards promoting a better understanding of the nature and roles of reviews of research. A typology of reviews was developed, which distinguished between reviews for academic and scholarly purposes, and those for practice and policy purposes. The iterative review that the TLRP carried out was intended to serve both sets of purposes and attempted to address multiple audiences, albeit in rather different forms of presentation – an example of 'commitment to "multi-vocalism" in review processes' (Torrance & Sebba, 2007, p. 3).

Educational innovation, even that which is primarily classroom-focused, almost always involves changes at several levels, which makes researching it similarly multi-layered. However, by examining the evidence against the categories, and the categories against the evidence, the themes of interest to TLRP were eventually reduced to ten principles in four main clusters: educational values and purposes; curriculum, pedagogy and assessment; personal and social processes and relationships; teachers and policies. These ten principles are (James & Pollard, 2011, pp. 283–312; 2012, pp. 14–43):

Effective pedagogy equips learners for life in its broadest sense. Learning should aim to help individuals and groups to develop the intellectual, personal and social resources that will enable them to participate as active citizens, contribute to economic development and flourish as individuals in a diverse and changing society. This means adopting a broad conception of worthwhile learning outcomes and taking seriously issues of equity and social justice for all.

Effective pedagogy engages with valued forms of knowledge. Pedagogy should engage learners with the big ideas, key skills and processes, modes of discourse, ways of thinking and practising, attitudes and relationships, which are the most valued learning processes and outcomes in particular contexts. They need to understand what constitutes quality, standards and expertise in different settings.

Effective pedagogy recognises the importance of prior experience and learning. Pedagogy should take account of what the learner knows already in order for them, and those who support their learning, to plan their next steps. This includes building on prior learning but also taking account of the personal and cultural experiences of different groups of learners.

Effective pedagogy requires learning to be scaffolded. Teachers, trainers and all those, including peers, who support the learning of others, should provide activities, cultures and structures of intellectual, social and emotional support to help learners to move forward in their learning. When these supports are removed the learning needs to be secure.

Effective pedagogy needs assessment to be congruent with learning. Assessment should be designed and implemented with the goal of achieving maximum validity both in terms of learning outcomes and learning processes. It should help to advance learning as well as determine whether learning has occurred.

Effective pedagogy promotes the active engagement of the learner. A chief goal of learning should be the promotion of learners' independence and autonomy. This involves acquiring a repertoire of learning strategies and practices, developing positive learning dispositions, and having the will and confidence to become agents in their own learning.

Effective pedagogy fosters both individual and social processes and outcomes. Learners should be encouraged and helped to build relationships and communication with others for learning purposes, in order to assist the mutual construction of knowledge and enhance the achievements of individuals and groups. Consulting learners about their learning and giving them a voice is both an expectation and a right.

Effective pedagogy recognises the significance of informal learning. Informal learning, such as learning out of school or away from the workplace, should be recognised as at least as significant as formal learning and should therefore be valued and appropriately utilised in formal processes.

Effective pedagogy depends on the learning of all those who support the learning of others. The need for lecturers, teachers, trainers and co-workers to learn continuously in order to develop their knowledge and skill, and adapt and develop their roles, especially through practice-based inquiry, should be recognised and supported.

Effective pedagogy demands consistent policy frameworks with support for learning as their primary focus. Organisational and system level policies need to recognise the fundamental importance of continual learning – for individual, team, organisational and system success – and be designed to create effective learning environments for all learners.

From 2005 onwards, discussions between researchers, practitioners, policy-makers and other user groups were the principal means of developing, refining and validating both the synthesis of research and the principles that arose from it. Publications based on the principles were distributed to all UK schools and were promoted by the general teaching councils in England, Northern Ireland, Scotland and Wales. The principles chimed with the report of the *Cambridge Primary Review* (Alexander, 2010).

The potential of TLRP's principles to promote educational understanding was taken up by the Cambridge team that worked on the latest edition of *Reflective Teaching in Schools* – an established UK text for both Initial Teacher Education (ITE) and Continuing Professional Development (CPD)

(Pollard, 2014). As with all such publications, evidence and guidance is offered on a comprehensive range of educational topics – learning, relationships, behaviour, curriculum, pedagogy, assessment, inclusion, and so on. The particular feature of this edition, however, is that discussion of these issues is framed by consideration of TLRP principles to support deeper insights. Additionally, the architecture of teacher expertise is represented by a framework of powerful concepts that are embedded throughout the text. *Reflective Teaching in Schools*, together with its associated collection of readings and website,[18] thus directly supports Stenhouse's (1975, p. 208) aspiration that: 'It is teachers who in the end will change the world of school by understanding it.' Versions of this text also now exist for early education (Colwell, 2015), further education (Gregson & Hillier, 2015), and higher education (Ashwin, 2015).

If the TLRP principles continue to be valued as a way to accumulate and organise knowledge, with the potential for further progressive development and use within public debates, then discussion and development will need to continue. Potentially they might be the basis for profession-driven standards.

CONCLUSION

The landscape of recent efforts to try to synthesise research evidence for the purposes of learning improvement in schools that has been reviewed in this chapter has highlighted the possibilities and pitfalls entailed in moving an entire profession forward and shifting its culture. The growth since 2012 of the College of Teaching and the degree of mobilisation that this has triggered among teachers is, as yet, small in scale. Nonetheless, with the awareness that, given the right conditions for their careful nurturance and support, acorns one day are likely to become oak trees, such evidence of momentum as there is, however seemingly small and incipient, has to be taken as an encouraging sign. The existence of the College and educationalists' commitment to it are signs that teachers may be embracing the need to come together to control their own professional destinies. As they do so, one of the things that the emphasis on evidence-based or evidence-informed standards, with these linked to better outcomes for students, will hopefully provide is a guarantee that this thrust is not being undertaken for reasons of naked self-interest. Professional mobilisation, then, is one challenge. The other, as we have shown, hopefully, is the scale of the effort required and the nature of the obstacles to be surmounted in the harnessing and validating of knowledge in the interests of legitimating that professional mobilisation. In this regard, we have suggested that, through its research facility and commitment to research, the UCPS is strongly positioned to play an influential role at a number of points along the knowledge chain, between discovery at one end of the spectrum and implementation at the other. Without us having been in any way prescriptive about the priorities for such UCPS-based or UCPS-partnership school-based research, the close-knit relationship between the University of Cambridge, the Faculty of Education and the school offers, in our view, a unique platform for the determination of such priorities, and for engagement with the initiatives and agencies cited in the discussion.

Notes

1   In her capacity as Deputy Director of the ESRC Teaching and Learning Research Programme, Mary James was a member of the PSIPG steering group and chair of the education advisors to the PSIPG.
2   Incorporated by royal charter in 1849 as the College of Preceptors and which in 1998 became the College of Teachers, see https://en.wikipedia.org/wiki/College_of_Teachers.
3   See chapter 9, note 3.
4   See chapter 4, note 7.
5   See http://eppi.ioe.ac.uk/cms/. Retrieved 19 April 2016.
6   See http://www.cochrane.org/. Retrieved 19 April 2016.
7   See chapter 9, note 4.
8   No web link available, although the final report of SRFE can be found at: https://www.bera.ac.uk/wp-content/uploads/2014/10/SFRE-final-report.pdf?noredirect=1. Retrieved 19 April 2016.
9   Professor Hannele Niemi, co-author of chapter 7, was a member of the TLRP Steering Committee.
10 See http://educationendowmentfoundation.org.uk/toolkit/.
11 See http://www.eep.ac.uk/DNN2/. Retrieved 19 April 2016.
12 See http://www.curee.co.uk/. Retrieved 19 April 2016.
13 See https://eric.ed.gov/. Retrieved 19 April 2016.
14 See http://educationmediacentre.org/. Retrieved 19 April 2016.
15 See https://www.york.ac.uk/iee/. Retrieved 19 April 2016.
16 See http://www.cebenetwork.org/. Retrieved 19 April 2016.
17 See http://www.meshguides.org/about-mesh/. Retrieved 19 April 2016.
18 See http://reflectiveteaching.co.uk/. Retrieved 19 April 2016.

References

Adelman, C. (1993). Kurt Lewin and the origins of action research, *Educational Action Research*, 1(1): 7–24.

Alexander, R. (ed.) (2010). *Children, their World, their Education: Final Report and Recommendations of the Cambridge Primary Review* (London: Routledge).

Armstrong, M. (1981). *Closely Observed Children: Diary of a Primary Classroom* (Littlehampton: Littlehampton Book Services Ltd).

Ashwin, P. (2015). *Reflective Teaching in Higher Education* (London: Bloomsbury).

Ball, S.J. (1981). *Beachside Comprehensive: A Case-Study of Secondary Schooling* (Cambridge: Cambridge University Press).

BERA-RSA (2014). *Research and the Teaching Profession: Building the capacity for a self-improving system*. Final Report of the BERA-RSA Inquiry into the role of research in teacher education (London: British Educational Research Association).

Burgess, R.G. (1983). *Experiencing Comprehensive Education: A Study of Bishop McGregor School* (London: Methuen).

College of Teachers (2016). http://www.collegeofteachers.ac.uk/, retrieved 23 February 2016

Colwell, J. (2015). *Reflective Teaching in Early Education* (London: Bloomsbury).

Dudley, P. (ed.) (2015). *Lesson Study: Professional Learning for Our Time* (London: Routledge).

Dudley, P. (2012). Lesson study in England: From school networks to national policy, *International Journal for Lesson and Learning Studies*, 1(1): 85–100.

Elliott, J. (1991). *Action Research for Educational Change* (Buckingham: Open University Press).

Elliott, J. (2012). Developing a science of teaching through lesson study, *International Journal for Lesson and Learning Studies*, 1(2): 108–25.

Fullan, M. (2001). *The New Meaning of Educational Change*, third edition (New York: Teachers College Press).

Goldacre, B. (2013). *Building Evidence into Education* (London: Department for Education).

Gregson, M. & Hillier, Y. (2015). *Reflective Teaching in Further, Adult and Vocational Education* (London: Bloomsbury).

Hargreaves, D.H. (1967). *Social Relations in a Secondary School* (London: Routledge and Kegan Paul).

Hargreaves, D.H. (1996). *Teaching as a Research Based Profession: Possibilities and Prospects* (London: Teacher Training Agency).

Hillage, J., Pearson, R., Anderson, A. & Tamkin, P. (1998). *Excellence in Research on Schools* (London: Department for Education and Employment).

House of Commons Education Committee (2012). *Great Teachers: Attracting, Training and Retaining the Best*, 1 (London: The Stationary Office).

Ingvarson, L. & Rowe, K. (2008). Conceptualising and evaluating teacher quality: Substantive and methodological issues, *Australian Journal of Education*, 52(1): 5–35.

Isaacs, S. (1952). *The Educational Value of the Nursery School* (London: Headly Brothers Ltd).

James, M. & Pollard, A. (2011). TLRP's ten principles for effective pedagogy: Rationale, development, evidence, argument and impact, *Research Papers in Education*, 26(3): 275–328.

James, M. & Pollard, A. (2012). TLRP's ten principles for effective pedagogy: Rationale, development, evidence, argument and impact, in M. James & A. Pollard (eds), *Principles for Effective Pedagogy: International Responses to Evidence from the UK Teaching & Learning Research Programme* (London: Routledge).

Lacey, C. (1970). *Hightown Grammar: The School as a Social System* (Manchester: Manchester University Press).

Lewin, K. (1946). Action research and minority problems, *Journal of Social Issues*, 2(4): 34–46.

Pollard, A. (2014). *Reflective Teaching in Schools*, fourth edition (London: Bloomsbury).

Pollard, A. & Oancea, A. (2010). *Unlocking Learning? Towards Evidence-Informed Policy and Practice in Education*. Final report of the UK Strategic Forum for Research in Education, 2008–2010 (London: Strategic Forum for Research in Education).

Prince's Teaching Institute (2012). *Investigating the Appetite for and Remit of a new member-driven College of Teaching: An Exploratory Workshop*. Report (London: Prince's Teaching Institute).

Prince's Teaching Institute (2014). *A New Member-Driven College of Teaching, A Blueprint* (London: Prince's Teaching Institute).

Public Services Improvement Policy Group (2007). *Restoring Pride in our Public Services: Submission to the Shadow Cabinet* (London: PSIPG).

Schön, D.A. (1983). *The Reflective Practitioner: How Professionals Think in Action* (New York: Basic Books).

Stenhouse, L. (1975). An Introduction to Curriculum Research and Development (London: Heinemann).

Timperley, H. & Alton-Lee, A. (2008). Reframing teacher professional learning: An alternative policy approach to strengthening valued outcomes for diverse learners, *Review of Education*, 32: 328–69.

Tooley, J. & Darby, D. (1998). *Educational Research – A Critique* (London: Office for Standards in Education).

Torrance, H. & Sebba, J. (2007). Reviewing reviews: Towards a better understanding of the role of research reviews, *TLRP Research Briefing no. 30*, (London: TLRP, Institute of Education, University of London).

Whitty, G. (2006). Education(al) research and educational policy making: Is conflict inevitable?, *British Educational Research Journal*, 32: 159–76.

Willis, P. (1977). *Learning to Labour How Working Class Kids Get Working Class Jobs* (New York: Columbia University Press).

11   The view from Birmingham

Peter Gronn interviews Mike Roden, 21 April 2016

Mike Roden is Principal of the University of Birmingham School, a secondary University Training School (UTS). The school is located on a campus of the University of Birmingham at 12 Weoley Park Road, Selly Oak, B29 6QU.[1]

GRONN: Mike, you are no doubt aware from James Biddulph of Cambridge's primary school UTS model? Could you describe for me the model that Birmingham adopted?

RODEN: The Birmingham School is an 11–18 comprehensive school. In September 2015 we admitted six Year 7 classes, each consisting of 25 students, and recruited 182 students into the Lower Sixth.

GRONN: What makes the school distinctive as a UTS?

RODEN: As a secondary University Training School we are working with the School of Education at the University of Birmingham to develop a new Initial Teacher Education model which will attempt to improve the number and quality of teachers entering into the profession. A second distinctive feature of the school is our multi-nodal admissions system, which is designed to recruit a cohort of pupils that reflects the diversity of the city. Half of the students come from the area immediately around the school building, here in Selly Oak, and the other half of the students come from three areas of the inner-city of Birmingham. These were chosen in liaison with the local authority as they were predicted to have a shortage of school places in the future. We call these four locations 'admission nodes'. I think that in our first year we have been successful as the Year 7 cohort is composed of pupils from 30 different ethnic groups.

The third distinctive feature of the school is that through our links with the Jubilee Centre for Character and Virtue that works here in Birmingham the School ethos is geared to developing the character virtues of our students.[2] Professor James Arthur is the Director of that centre and he was, until September 2015, the Head of the School of Education. He had the idea for a University Training School when the UTS model was included in *The Importance of Teaching* document produced by the former Secretary of State for Education, Michael Gove. We have designed our curriculum and our school day around the idea of delivering a 'taught and caught' programme of character education. The Jubilee Centre is recognised around the world as a leading research centre in the field of character and virtues. The university itself invested a significant amount of money in addition to what the Department for Education gave to help set up the school. I worked closely with James and his colleagues for 16 months before the school opened to develop our education programme.

And so what we have is a bespoke character education course that is taught before the main lessons in the morning between 8.30 and 9 o'clock. This pervades all aspects of the school's provision, including our weekly assemblies. We have opportunities for the students to reflect on their own learning and for the Year 7s to work with the Year 12s on shared reading. The opportunity to develop character virtues is included in all of our schemes of learning. All the subject leaders, for example, as part of the selection procedures, were asked to deliver a presentation on the topic 'How would you integrate character education into the teaching of . . . [geography, etc]'?

The other distinctive part of what we have done is the taught programme of character development. Here we recognise that to actually try to develop character we have to give these students opportunities to learn to be part of a team, to lead a team, to be successful, and to fail, and so we have an extended school day of six hours in addition to the personal learning and development programme at the start of the morning. For five hours each week – that's all Wednesday afternoon for three hours, one hour on Monday and a Friday afternoon, immediately after lunch – we have an integrated enrichment programme of activities which is delivered by all staff together with staff from the university. As a result the students have an unbelievable array of enrichment opportunities which we believe will help develop their character over the course of their time at the University of Birmingham School.

GRONN: When you say staff from the university, do you mean those from the School of Education?

RODEN: No, not really. So, for example, on the Monday and Friday we have a running club with a member of our teaching staff and an alumnus of the university who is an Olympic athlete. We have specialist coaches from the university delivering Taekwondo, pilates, netball and badminton clubs. The very popular Year 12 Philosophy Club is led by a professor of philosophy. We have people at the university who lead activities such as Japanese. This extensive provision is above what the staff at the school provide so that we have, for example provided the opportunity for all the children to get a chance to take part in cricket, rugby, football and lacrosse. We have a knitting club, a school newspaper, a games club, and so on – a real plethora of amazing activities that is significantly enhanced by the additional resources from the university.

GRONN: It sounds like an incredibly rich programme.

RODEN: It is indeed. It has helped to make the school unbelievably popular. In the UK, parents have to opt for which schools they want their children to go to in the October before the following September in which they would be admitted. So, in our first year, I did lots of talks at the university and various locations and primary schools in Birmingham. We didn't have a school and hadn't employed any teachers when the recruitment process was taking place, and yet, in our first year, we were the most popular comprehensive school in the city. We had 1231 applications for 150 places. And in the Sixth Form we had 820 applications for 200 places.

GRONN: There's going to be a fairly heavy emphasis on research at Cambridge's primary school. Where is the research going to fit into the Birmingham model?

RODEN: One of our governors, who is Pro-Vice Chancellor of the College of Social Sciences (in which the School of Education sits), chairs what we call the School–University Advisory Group, and on it sit all the Heads of Education of the six colleges of the university, along with other colleagues, and their task is to make sure that the relationship, the needs of the university and the needs of the school are complementary and that they work. And it's through that group that requests for research to be undertaken with the school come. Following ethical approval we are fortunate to have such a body of experts in terms of research to look at requests and they say:

'We're happy with this'. Then it's up to the school to say: 'Well, actually, can we accommodate it'? Because you can imagine, I'm sure, that we will continue to get lots and lots of requests for research. Currently we have four pieces of research that have been approved and have already started or are in the process of starting.

Helping to facilitate the use of research are the relationships that each subject leader has developed this year with relevant colleagues in the School of Education and the academic departments of the university – all 'linked' colleagues made a visit to the school in our first term.

GRONN: We might pick up those in a moment. Was this the particular reason that this model was adopted?

RODEN: The University of Birmingham was the first civic university set up in the UK, 100 years or so ago by Joseph Chamberlain. The original mission of the university was to advance education in the City of Birmingham. So what the university authorities saw, when this opportunity to open a school came about, was the chance to take that next leap and try to influence the quality of education at pre-university level. So there's a civic mission to establish a truly inclusive and comprehensive school. That is why we use the multi-nodal admissions system to make sure that pupils from all types of background can gain access to the school. And, of course, the other part is that the School of Education has some outstanding areas of research recognised in the recent Research Excellence Framework (REF). The School of Education has recently been ranked 28th in the world, and therefore areas like inclusion, race and equality, and character education are opportunities to link with the school and to be able to undertake research for its own sake and which also advances practice in schools.

GRONN: Thinking back to when the model evolved and when government approval had to be obtained, what was the level of support coming from the University of Birmingham and the School of Education? It was obviously fairly strong from what you are saying.

RODEN: 'Phenomenal' would be my reflection on it. Obviously James Arthur as Head of the School of Education had made the original proposal for the school, and so the School of Education had colleagues working alongside him who did a lot of the work in terms of designing the original application. We also had the Assistant Registrar from the Vice Chancellor's Office, who led on putting the application together. The Vice Chancellor and the senior leadership of the university have taken a personal interest in this project, and indeed the Registrar chaired the strategy group, which was tasked with ensuring a successful opening. Only recently we hosted the University Council at the school and it was clear there that the support for the school continues to be fantastic.

GRONN: So are you able to talk about the bid process itself? Was the process a smooth one?

RODEN: From my experience of it I think the university was really under pressure in terms of putting an application together for such a distinctive type of school in a very tight timescale. I know that there were a number of conversations and debate with the Department for Education about how much they would fund the school. And so there were several conversations which took place between the university and the Department for Education to agree on a capital budget that would reflect the aspirations of the university for this high-profile and distinctive school as the first and currently only secondary. This sum was supplemented by the university itself. I am not sure about how long this process took place but it led to a delay, as the original idea was that the school would open in September 2014, but in the end it didn't. I was actually appointed in December 2013 and took up my post at the university in April 2014, with the school opening some 16 months later in September 2015.

GRONN: What about the local community, given the civic engagement ethic of Birmingham? Was there a period and process of consultation to gauge community support?

RODEN: Yes, there was. The university employed, I think, a professional company to undertake consultation across the city and in the local area around the school. You can imagine that placing a 1150-pupil school (when we're fully open) in a residential environment, even though it was a former university site, led to objections concerning the impact on such things as traffic. But they undertook the consultation around Birmingham and the response was that there was strong support overall for a school. Birmingham is one of the fastest growing and youngest cities of Western Europe, and the local authority produced a report a few years ago that said that the city would need some 14 800 additional secondary school places by 2020. So, to some extent, our opening is also in response to the needs of the city.

GRONN: Let's turn now to your appointment. How was it that you became the headteacher of the school? Were you approached or did you apply? And what particularly interested you about the role?

RODEN: Well, part of the original consultation, apparently in terms of the local community, was also consultation with schools. And as you can imagine, by placing a big new school like this, a lot of schools felt threatened by it in terms of competition – and they still do. I went to one of the original consultations with schools at the university. That's when I first met James Arthur. It obviously sounded very interesting. I previously was headmaster of one of the highly selective grammar schools in Birmingham and so I was aware of the proposal by the university to open a school. But then in September 2013 the recruitment firm tasked with the appointment of the new principal by the university did get in contact with me, and I'm sure a number of other people around the city, and around the country. After a conversation with Professor Arthur I began to realise the attraction of working with a world-class university and of having the freedom to use my experience of working in outstanding schools to design a new model of secondary schools for the city and country. I'd been a headteacher previously for six years and a senior leader for 20 years. I decided to apply for the position, viewing it as a really unique and distinctive, let's say final, challenge in my career.

GRONN: The next question is about the enrolment profile of the school, its social composition and projected growth. You've touched on that already. Is there anything you want to add on that point?

RODEN: I suppose that we, in our first year, have not only been very successful in terms of numbers – priority access to the school, above distance, is for pupils with educational and healthcare plans, and for pupils who are looked after or were previously looked after. And so, in addition to the wide socio-economic and ethnic diversity in the school, it is also great to have diversity in terms of special educational and other needs. We are just about finishing our recruitment process for the following year, and in fact the numbers who have applied for the school for September 2016 have increased even more; they've gone up to 1571, and we are almost three times over-subscribed for first choices for the school. So it could be that we may even be the most popular school of any type in the city for September 2016.

GRONN: You've also described many of the features of the curriculum, with the emphasis on the character education and where that fits. Is there anything else you want to comment on there?

RODEN: Yes, we are delivering an academic curriculum for all students which is designed to support their transition to higher education, vocational training or employment. We teach chemistry, physics and biology as separate distinct disciplines from Year 7. We have computer science and provide the full range of the National Curriculum subjects. We advise our students that, when they apply to Sixth Form, they should try to take at least two of what are known as the Russell Group-facilitating subjects. These are the ones that the Russell Group of selective universities recommend: 'If you do these subjects, you've got the best chance of getting into competitive universities'. So in response to that, in the Sixth Form, for example, we've had a huge demand for STeM. And in our Lower Sixth alone, we have six teaching groups of biology and chemistry along with three of physics. We have six teaching groups of mathematics, a further mathematics group, and two groups of computer science. We've been fortunate that, quite obviously because of the name of the school, and our ethos and vision to transform people's lives, we've been successful in being able to recruit some fantastic subject leaders and teachers. In fact, last year, for 35 posts in the school, including our professional services, we had around 1000 applications.

GRONN: Just in relation to research – we've had a bit of a word about that already – are the projects that you are going to be opening up soon, or getting under way, going to be related to the teacher training side of things? Is that the emphasis?

RODEN: Not at the moment, because we are still liaising with the university and the National College for Teaching and Leadership to develop a new partnership model of delivering ITE. This is intended to model the specialist subject and academic input from the university together with teaching practice in its partner schools.

The research that we're undertaking at the moment is probably more linked to the research centres of the School of Education referred to previously. We're starting a piece with the colleagues at the university about how you set up a truly inclusive school, a piece of research with sport and exercise science about looking at healthy lifestyles for the pupils and a research project that is linked colleagues from the geography department of the University of Birmingham looking at transfer into Year 7.

We've had a number of other requests of course. I think the idea is that we will probably do an annual call for research, but the main issue we face with having only two year groups is one of capacity, whilst ensuring that the activity does not disrupt teaching and learning or interfere with the smooth running of the school.

GRONN: Can we turn now to the school's governance: how does that work?

RODEN: Well, the University of Birmingham School is a subsidiary charitable company of the university. The university appoints the members of the charity and then the members appoint the governors. A former Vice-Principal of the university was the nominated Chair of Governors for the school by the university from the very start and he led the project through until December after we opened. He has been replaced by a former member of the Council of the University who has been involved in the project from the outset. In our first term we then recruited staff governors and parent governors.

GRONN: Has progress with the school gone according to plan or have there been any unanticipated issues?

RODEN: Well I think probably the level of interest from prospective parents and pupils has been, as I said, phenomenal, as has the level of interest, because it is a new school of its type, from the local and national media. I suppose the final unanticipated issues have been the number of students who came through our doors in September who have significant personal needs, and we perhaps found those a challenge as a small staff in a new school, to be able to deal with that, but we're working hard with that.

GRONN: How have you gone about establishing or cementing the vision with the staff? Have there been any challenges there?

RODEN: Our first appointment was a colleague seconded from the university to be the Director of Operations who has worked closely with me for the past two years. She has done a truly wonderful job across a wide range of responsibilities. These have included the use of social media and our website to ensure we have been able to effectively communicate our vision to the outside world.

When we went through our recruitment procedures, particularly in the first year, I spent a lot of time, prior to the final shortlist interviews, with those people who were going to be there on the interview day – meeting with them, and giving them an opportunity to ask about the vision and the ethos of the school. That also provided an opportunity for me to make sure that they understood the distinctive nature of the school and our expectations of them. In the UK there's a lot of pressure for the accountability measures, in terms of Ofsted, and a lot of schools are focused on trying to secure at least a 'Good' Ofsted grade. We were very clear from the outset that while examination results are important, our main focus is on the personal development of the pupils through the character education programme.

GRONN: You've touched on this already, but you might want to elaborate further: how have the local schools responded to UTS? Have they seen you as a threat or as a partner?

RODEN: I think it would be fair to say that, obviously in the areas around the school where we recruit half our pupils from, we are seen as a threat to their admissions. As we've only been open seven or eight months now, we're beginning to work to try to get involved with the local headteacher networks. We have hosted a headteacher conference. We're hoping to try to demonstrate the benefits of having a University of Birmingham School, such as making the lunchtime talks on admissions to medical school open to students from other schools. We've delivered master classes for Year 11 mathematicians and science classes for primary schools. So over the longer term we would like to play our part in improving the educational opportunities for all of the children in the city.

GRONN: In light of the latest government white paper (*Educational Excellence Everywhere*, March 2016),[3] how do you envisage the school being part of wider academy system?

RODEN: Currently the government has announced its intention to give all schools academy status and to encourage them to form into multi-academy trusts (MATs). We already benefit from the cost effectiveness of the MAT structure through the university's buying power, for example, for things like energy. We have service-level agreements with security, grounds and cleaning. We know that the government is interested in trying to encourage universities to think about opening up university schools, so in time there may be some interest and encouragement to establish our own MAT. In my latest conversation with the Vice Chancellor, I think our view at the moment is: 'We're a young organisation. We want to make sure this works first before we consider expanding the brand'.

GRONN: Thinking personally, Mike, what's it been like for you opening a school?

RODEN: In preparation for this interview I wrote down three words: *groundbreaking*, *challenging* and *fulfilling*. Who gets the chance to establish your own school and develop an ethos based around your own educational philosophy? Every day is different. We have described the project as a ship that has been launched into the educational ocean but it is one that we continue to build on our journey. Every day is different in your first year, which is the hardest aspect, but we are united by our belief in our vision to utilise the physical and intellectual resources at our disposal in order to provide a transformational education experience.

Notes

1 See http://www.universityschool.bham.ac.uk/.
2 See http://www.birmingham.ac.uk/research/activity/education/jubilee-centre/index.aspx.
3 See https://www.gov.uk/government/uploads/system/uploads/attachment_data/file/508447 /Educational_Excellence_Everywhere.pdf.

Conclusion

James Biddulph

Those readers who are familiar with the iconic 1980s film, *Back to the Future*, will remember that, for Marty McFly (the main character), 'the future' where the time-travelling car was going, was a mythical date, 21 October 2015 (back in the 1980s this was a distant eternity). In the comedy time-travelling film, Doc (the mad but visionary scientist) explains to Marty that there are 'a few problems with the kids in 2015' and that they need to return to the future to 'sort it out'.

We do not think there are problems with the kids, despite childhood now being a politicised concept with much at stake. Instead, what this book hopes to have illustrated is that educators (academics and teachers in partnership) look to be inspired by children, to be surprised by them and stimulated by the potential of theorising practice and practising theory in improving the quality of the educational experience for them. They remain hopeful even considering the politicisation of education that hurls teachers, headteachers and the schools that they love into a vortex, the black holes where time travel normally looks backwards to a perceived 'golden age' of education, normally around the time when our politicians went to school.

Back to reality: on 21 October 2015, the UCPS welcomed about 40 visiting teachers and academics to its 100-seater seminar room. This gathering was in name of the newly opened academic research centre, the Centre for Play in Education, Development and Learning (PEDAL). This new Centre, funded by the Lego Foundation, marked a new and exciting venture to explore how children play and how this could be developed within schools. I told the children that the Lego family was visiting our school to help launch the Centre. Having overcome their disappointment that life-size plastic Lego characters did not arrive at our school, the children rather enjoyed meeting one of the family members of the Lego family business and talked about how they had used Lego toys to develop ideas that in turn improved their ideas for writing. The gathering also provided an example of how we hope to work in the future: bringing together academics, teachers, school leaders, business leaders and children (yes, they were the real experts on the day) to advance thinking about education, teaching and learning. It is the kind of opportunity that the UCPS presents because of the relationship with the University and Faculty of Education.

As well as this, even in our first two terms, our staff have embraced the challenges and opportunities: one of our teachers has been selected to be one of the 140 Maths Mastery hub teachers in the country connected with other schools, building a collective and shared resource that looks outward to create new professional research-informed practices. Our assistant headteacher regularly works with Dr David Whitebread and Penny Coltman (the authors of chapter 6) to find ways to invigorate early years pedagogy, by building upon our already established close relationships with an outstanding university. Our teaching assistants engage in their own reading about education so that they can expand their thinking and practice. Another teacher has been so inspired by working with Pie Corbett (children's poet) that she has started organising a professional development event to share her inspired experiences with schools in our area. As well as being headteacher of the school, my doctoral studies inspire me to rethink the assumptions that I make about many aspects of school and consider new imaginative possibilities. Working closely with Professor Pamela Burnard and Dr Mandy Swann, my PhD supervisors, continues to challenge, inspire and motivate my thinking, which translates into new thinking in my role as headteacher. It is the necessary practising of theory and theorising practice that is also a key feature of our vision. Interestingly, and not planned, the University of Birmingham School has developed a vision and desire to partner with variety of organisations that is not dissimilar to UCPS's plans. Mike Roden's discussion with Peter Gronn (that immediately precedes this conclusion) illustrates many themes that can be seen in the UCPS, as described and discussed by the authors herein: essentially, how do we gather evidence to demonstrate ways to make learning better for children?

Whilst we remain serious about ensuring the best for children, we also recognise that childhood and learning is playful, and that it should be playful in school (a view not often recognised by those who set policy, despite the wealth of research, as described by David Whitebread and Penny Coltman in chapter 6). At the UCPS we are serious about playful learning (for children and teachers) because of the potential to develop the creative possibility thinkers of the future. Embedding our values, we use stories, songs and other media to create imaginative possibilities and sustain playfulness. During one assembly a fable was relayed to the children:

> Once there were three frogs that had fallen down a hole. One frog wore a hat – no child ever seems to question this which is delightful and reminds us of the vital need to capture and maintain an imaginative childhood for all children. There were other frogs at ground level who shouted down to the unfortunate amphibians in the hole: 'You will never make it. The hole is too deep. There is no point in trying to jump out of the hole'. The frogs in the hole did not move: 'Why bother, we will never jump free', they said. After a while of listening to the negative diatribe from the frogs at ground level, the frog in the hat bent down low and with a mighty jump, she leapt out of the hole. She had not heard what the others were saying because of her hat. She hopped to the nearest pond in full belief that with effort she could achieve the impossible.

The Vice Chancellor and his wife were visiting during this assembly, and saw how children were developing their thinking about learning and about their school. The children laughed, they talked and they played. As Mike Roden has explained, without explicit and implicit teaching of values and discussing the features of 'good learners', our children will not really understand how to contribute fully in a school with democratic notions at its core.

Back to the future: what is the purpose of education? The university, an outstanding seat of learning, demands high expectations of itself and the people who work within it. Its vision is to inspire life-long education. Our school has similar demands. Our start has been a positive one. Our future is hopeful but, as has been described by authors in this book, hope is not enough in the complex, challenging and risky business of running schools. As Mary James, Andrew Pollard and Peter Gronn indicate (in chapter 10): 'The challenges, however, should not be underestimated'.

Opening a new school is an exhausting, exhilarating and energising feat of imagination, creativity and organisation. It requires a gritty determination to find ways through. It demands staff to be highly reflective and build internal capacity to manage the multiple realities of the day-to-day tasks, and yet be always looking to the future. Mike Roden, the principal of the University of Birmingham School, and I have been privileged to experience the joys and learnt from the challenges. We know this a marathon. At the UCPS, we feel that we are in parallel time-travelling universes much of the time. We know that there is something special in our vision. We hope that our children, the time travellers of the future, will look back to their primary school experience with a golden hue of fondness because their education with us enabled them to be the future possibility makers. They will be successful because they are kind, considerate, active citizens with the ability to communicate in various ways: passionate enquirers, inspired artists and scientists who can change the world for the better, historians who learn from the past to not repeat our mistakes, linguists who interculturally connect our global community and, perhaps, the future teachers who will seek every opportunity to make a difference to the lives of the children whom they teach.

We wonder what it will be like on 21 October 2085, when our first cohort of children will retire. Will our pedagogy and democratic notion of education have prepared them for a good life? We believe it will. We continue to pursue answers to the question: What is the purpose of education? Our journey is long and this book marks a milestone on our first steps. On our journey in partnership with our university we 'stand on the shoulders of giants', as Isaac Newton said; we will survive in the shifting landscapes because we will be responsive to change, and as Charles Darwin is claimed to have said: 'in the long history of humankind, those who learned to collaborate and improvise most effectively have prevailed' – and so we will strive to build partnerships beyond the university. Another alumnus of the university, Samuel Taylor Coleridge, reminds us that 'nothing is as contagious as enthusiasm'—and so with an epidemic of enthusiasm, hard work, imagination and professionalism we will aim high, reflect deeply, and learn through the many possibilities and challenges that arise in our future. The world has provided an opportunity to create a new school in a new community. What we hope to give back could be something great. As John Rallison states at the beginning of this book, the hard work starts now. We must be like frogs with hats. We must believe in ourselves. We must take a leap of faith. The world gave us an opportunity to open a primary school ... we give back countless possibilities and thousands of leaping frogs.

Afterword

Professor Sir Leszek Borysiewicz

My family emigrated to the UK from Poland after World War II. I grew up on an estate in Cardiff in a small Polish-speaking community. I did not speak English until I was five years old but my parents were passionate about education and they encouraged me to learn. They understood that education is about opening doors, finding possibilities and working hard to make them a reality. Like a whole generation of children from my estate, I was fortunate enough to have that desire to learn fostered by Gerald Owen, a primary teacher as brilliant as he was inspirational. Over the years, various other teachers would help expand my thinking and encourage me to push myself. So, to my good fortune, I have personal experience of the transformative power that a school can have on a young person.

In November 2014 I walked onto the muddy field that was once the University of Cambridge's farm. It was the first groundbreaking ceremony on the North West Cambridge Development. Ten months later, the school, the first primary school in the UK to be granted University Training School status by the Department for Education, opened its doors to 120 children.

Creating a primary school is a new and exciting venture for a university, but we have a history of embracing opportunities and sharing the benefits of our breakthroughs with society. This spirit lies at the heart of our new primary school. The world is changing fast and we must equip our young people for the future, and everything suggests that the earlier we begin that commitment to helping them to realise their potential the better. To overcome these challenges, policy-makers and educators must draw on the best research from across the world.

Our Faculty of Education comprises one of the largest and most respected groups of educational researchers in the UK, and is dedicated to the improvement of educational policy and practice, both at home and internationally. Our teachers strive to ignite the flames of curiosity for all children and James Biddulph, the headteacher, speaks of this in chapter 5. Due to the relationship between the university and the primary school, our researchers are uniquely placed to collaborate with the school to ensure that research insight contributes valuable new ideas to support teaching and learning. The Faculty supports the excellent learning environment enjoyed by our pupils while simultaneously researching better ways of teaching and learning during those formative early years.

I was fortunate to visit the school in its first few weeks. It is a beautiful building, but more importantly every part of its design serves the well-being and educational experience of our students. It was clear then that the children were engaged, questioning, and continuing that desire to challenge themselves and others. In response to hearing a fable about triumph in the face of doubt, a five-year old student told the school assembly: 'You should not listen to others who do not believe in you – you must believe in yourself. You have to just try, give it a go, and who knows, you might make it. But you have to do it'.

At first glance, this is a book about teaching children in one community in the East of England. But the work undertaken in these classrooms will inform our research, and the ideas that emerge from this school will be shared across the world and will, we hope, help to improve educational opportunities in many other communities.

Index